GEOMETRY

Library of Congress Cataloging-in-Publication Data is available.

ISBN 978-1-5235-0437-4

Writer: Christy Needham   Illustrator: Kim Ku
Reviewer: Kristen Drury
Designer: Jessie Gang and Olivia Kane
Concept by Raquel Jaramillo

Workman books are available at special discounts when purchased in bulk for premiums, sales promotions, fundraising, catalogs, subscription boxes, and more. Workman also offers special discounts for schools and educators purchasing books in bulk. For more information, please email specialmarkets@workman.com.

Workman Publishing Co., Inc.
225 Varick Street
New York, NY 10014-4381
workman.com

WORKMAN, BRAIN QUEST, and BIG FAT NOTE-BOOK are registered trademarks of Workman Publishing Co., Inc.

Printed in Thailand

First printing September 2020

10 9 8 7 6 5 4 3

FSC
www.fsc.org
MIX
Paper from
responsible sources
FSC® C005748

EVERYTHING
YOU NEED TO ACE

GEOMETRY

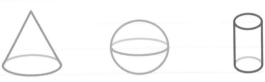

IN ONE BIG FAT
NOTEBOOK

WORKMAN PUBLISHING

NEW YORK

GEOMETRY

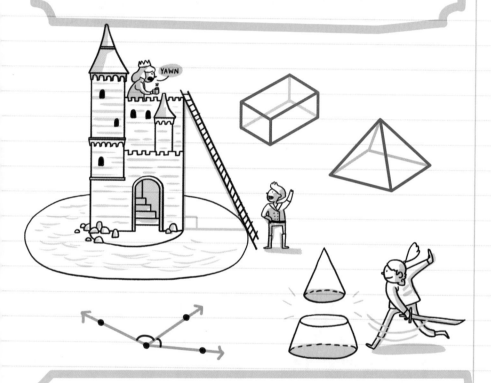

This notebook is designed to support you as you work through the major areas of geometry. Consider these the notes taken by the smartest person in your geometry class. The one who seems to "get" everything and who takes clear, understandable, accurate notes.

Within these chapters you'll find important concepts presented in an accessible, relatable way. Plane and solid geometry, congruence, proofs, transformations, and coordinate geometry are all presented in a language you can easily understand. It's geometry for the regular kid.

Notes are presented in an organized way:

- Important vocabulary words are highlighted in **YELLOW**.
- All vocabulary words are clearly defined.
- Related terms and concepts are written in BLUE PEN.
- Examples and calculations are clearly stepped out and supported by explanations, illustrations, and charts.

If you want a fun, easy-to-understand resource to use as a companion to your textbook, and you're not so great at taking notes in class, this notebook will help. It hits all the major points you'll learn in geometry.

CONTENTS

UNIT 1:
BASICS OF GEOMETRY 1

YOU'RE SO SMART!

YOU'RE SMARTER!

UNIT 2:
PARALLEL LINES 87

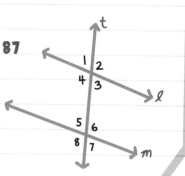

REFLECTION

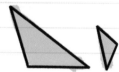

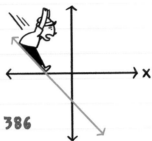

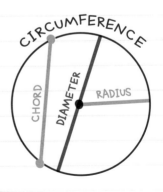

12 FT

PERFECT, LET'S GET STARTED.

Unit

1

Basics of Geometry

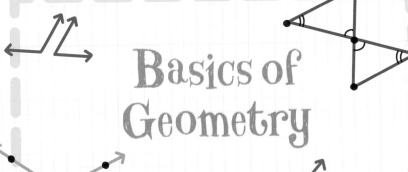

Chapter 1

POINTS, LINES, AND PLANES

Geometry is the branch of mathematics that is the study of shapes, lines, angles, and space and the relationship between them. An example of geometry is the calculation of a quadrilateral's angles.

Here are some key concepts and basic terms used in geometry:

TERM AND DEFINITION	SYMBOL	EXAMPLE
POINT: indicates a location	The name of the point. For example, A	•A
LINE: a straight path extending infinitely in opposite directions	A horizontal arrow above two points on the line. $\overleftrightarrow{BC}$, $\overleftrightarrow{CB}$, or ℓ	

TERM AND DEFINITION	SYMBOL	EXAMPLE
LINE SEGMENT: part of a line with two endpoints	A horizontal bar above two points on the line. $\overline{AB}$ or $\overline{BA}$ length: AB	A ●——————● B ENDPOINT ENDPOINT
RAY: part of a line that starts at a point and extends infinitely in one direction	A horizontal arrow that extends in one direction. $\overrightarrow{GH}$	G ●——————● H → ENDPOINT
VERTEX: the point of intersection of two or more line segments, rays, or lines	The name of the angle that forms the vertex. A	B SIDE A SIDE C VERTEX
ANGLE: formed by two rays with the same endpoint, the vertex	$\angle A$, $\angle BAC$, or $\angle CAB$	A ●

TERM AND DEFINITION	SYMBOL	EXAMPLE
TRIANGLE: shape with three sides and three vertices	△ ABC (or △ symbol followed by any combination of the letters A, B, and C)	VERTEX B SIDE / B \ SIDE A ——— SIDE ——— C VERTEX A VERTEX C
PARALLEL LINES: lines that are always the same distance apart. They NEVER meet.	written as: ℓ ∥ m	ℓ ←————————→ m ←————————→
PERPENDICULAR LINES: lines that intersect to form four right angles	written as: ℓ ⊥ m	ℓ ↑ ←——┐——→ └┘ m

LINES

A **LINE** is straight, has no width, and extends infinitely in opposite directions. It is ONE-DIMENSIONAL, or flat.

Name a line by listing:

1. any two points on the line with a double-sided arrow above them; or

2. using the lowercase italicized letter next to the arrow (if it has one).

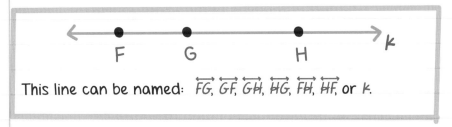

This line can be named: $\overleftrightarrow{FG}$, $\overleftrightarrow{GF}$, $\overleftrightarrow{GH}$, $\overleftrightarrow{HG}$, $\overleftrightarrow{FH}$, $\overleftrightarrow{HF}$, or k.

COLLINEAR points lie on the same line.
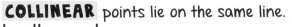
sharing line

Points H, I, and J are collinear .

Points D, E, and F are not collinear . (The points are not on the same line. A line is straight.) These are two rays.

PLANES

Plane geometry deals with "flat" shapes such as squares and triangles. Flat shapes are TWO-DIMENSIONAL, or 2-D.

A **PLANE** is a flat surface (two-dimensional) that extends infinitely in all directions.

To name a plane,

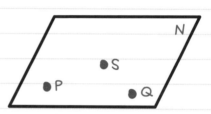

1. use a capital letter on the plane; or

2. any three points on the plane (in any order).

as long as the points do not form a straight line.

This plane can be named PSQ, PQS, SPQ, SQP, QPS, QSP, or plane N (capital letter with no point).

COPLANAR points lie on the same plane.

sharing plane

Points P, Q, and R are **coplanar**. They lie on the horizontal plane.

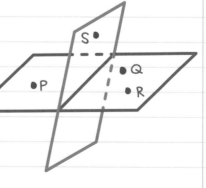

Point S **is not** coplanar to P, Q, and R, because it lies on a different (vertical) plane.

INTERSECTION OF LINES AND PLANES

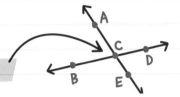

INTERSECT
to pass through or lie across each other.

Two lines **INTERSECT** at a point.

intersection: point C

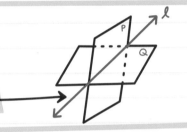

Two planes intersect along a line.

intersection: line ℓ

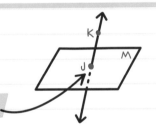

A plane and a line intersect at a point.

intersection: point J

The cube shows six planes. The intersection of plane ABD and plane DHG is $\overleftrightarrow{DC}$.

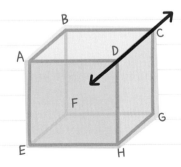

POSTULATES AND THEOREMS

Proofs are used to communicate mathematical ideas. They are logical reasons used to confirm an idea. Postulates and theorems are used to support proofs.

A **POSTULATE** is a statement that is accepted as fact, without proof. A **THEOREM** is a statement that has been proven to be true using other theorems, definitions, or postulates.

LINE SEGMENT POSTULATE

Not all postulates have names.

SEGMENT ADDITION POSTULATE

If B is a point on line segment $\overline{AC}$, then AB + BC = AC.

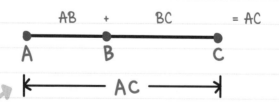

AB   +   BC   = AC

A   B   C

$\longmapsto$———— AC ————$\longmapsto$

Add the lengths of the smaller segments to find the length of the entire segment.

Note:

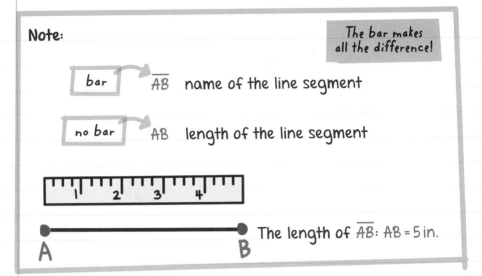

bar → $\overline{AB}$ name of the line segment

no bar → AB length of the line segment

The length of $\overline{AB}$: AB = 5 in.

A   B

EXAMPLE: If R is between Q and S, QR = 14, and RS = 17, find the length of QS.

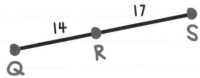

17

14

Q   R   S

QS = QR + RS
QS = 14 + 17 = 31

EXAMPLE: If U is between T and V, TV = 21, TU = 2x, and UV = 15, find the value of x.

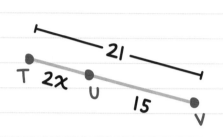

SINCE 2X AND 15 ADD TO 21, I CAN SET UP AN EQUATION.

TU + UV = TV

2x + 15 = 21   Substitute.

2x + $\cancel{15}$ – $\cancel{15}$ = 21 – 15   Subtract 15 from both sides.

2x = 6

$\dfrac{\cancel{2}x6}{\cancel{2}\,2}$ Divide both sides by 2.

x = 3

Congruent Line Segments

Two line segments are **CONGRUENT** if they have the same length.

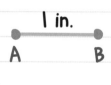

$\overline{AB}$ is congruent to $\overline{CD}$.

Use a CONGRUENCE STATEMENT to show that line segments are congruent:

is the symbol for congruence

$$\overline{AB} \cong \overline{CD}$$

$\overline{AB} \cong \overline{CD}$ is read as "line segment AB is congruent to line segment CD."

TICK MARKS (I) are sometimes used to show that line segments are congruent. The same number of tick marks shows which segments are congruent to each other.

$$\overline{EF} \cong \overline{GH} \qquad \overline{IJ} \cong \overline{KL}$$

EXAMPLE: Which of the line segments are congruent in the figure?

This figure is made of four line segments: $\overline{MN}$, $\overline{NO}$, $\overline{OP}$, and $\overline{PM}$. The tick marks on $\overline{MN}$ and $\overline{NO}$ show that they are congruent.

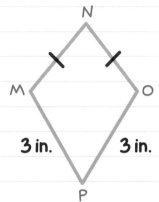

3 in.   3 in.

Length MP is equal to length PO, so $\overline{MP}$ is congruent to $\overline{PO}$. Therefore, $\overline{MN} \cong \overline{NO}$ and $\overline{MP} \cong \overline{PO}$.

SEGMENT BISECTORS

The **MIDPOINT** of a line segment is the halfway point; it divides the line segment into two congruent segments.

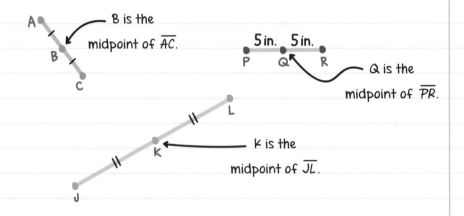

B is the midpoint of $\overline{AC}$.

5 in.   5 in.

Q is the midpoint of $\overline{PR}$.

K is the midpoint of $\overline{JL}$.

A **SEGMENT BISECTOR** is a line, ray, segment, or plane that passes through a segment at its midpoint (bisects it).

Bisect means "to divide into two equal parts." The measure of each congruent segment is one-half the measure of the original segment.

OH NO! I BROKE MY LINE SEGMENT IN HALF!

IT MUST HAVE HAD A WEAK MIDPOINT.

BUT LOOK! NOW YOU HAVE TWO CONGRUENT SEGMENTS!

Examples of segment bisectors of $\overline{FG}$:

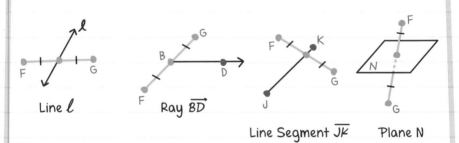

Line ℓ

Ray $\overrightarrow{BD}$

Line Segment $\overline{JK}$

Plane N

Line j is not a segment bisector of $\overline{FG}$ because it **does not** bisect $\overline{FG}$ at its midpoint.

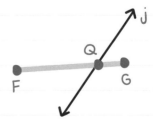

For questions 1-4, use this figure.

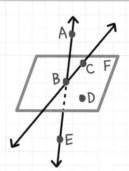

1. Name three collinear points.

2. Name three coplanar points.

3. Name the intersection of line $\overleftrightarrow{AE}$ and plane F.

4. What are the other six names for plane F?

For questions 5 and 6, use this figure.

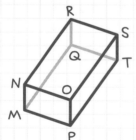

5. How many planes are shown in the figure?

6. What is the intersection of plane MPT and plane MNR?

7. What is the Segment Addition Postulate?

8. Find the length of segment $\overline{GI}$.

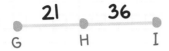

9. Find the value of x.

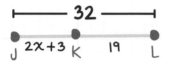

10. Write a congruence statement for the congruent segments in the figure below.

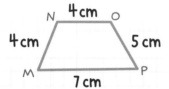

11. Write congruence statements for the congruent segments in the figure below.

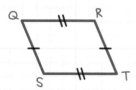

12. What is a segment bisector?

CHECK YOUR ANSWERS

1. A, B, and E

2. B, C, and D

3. Point B

4. Planes BCD, BDC, CDB, CBD, DBC, DCB

5. Six

6. Line $\overleftrightarrow{MQ}$

7. If B is between A and C, then AB + BC = AC.

8. GI = 57

9. JL = JK + KL; 32 = 2x + 3 + 19; 32 = 2x + 22; 2x = 10; x = 5

10. $\overline{MN} \cong \overline{NO}$

11. $\overline{QS} \cong \overline{RT}$ and $\overline{QR} \cong \overline{ST}$

12. A segment bisector is a line, ray, segment, or plane that passes through a segment at its midpoint.

Chapter 2

ANGLES

An **ANGLE** (∠) is formed by two RAYS with a common ENDPOINT.

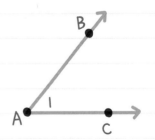

Name an angle in three ways:

1. the vertex: ∠A

2. three points, with the vertex in the middle: ∠BAC or ∠CAB

3. the number inside the angle: ∠1

If two or more angles share the same vertex, you cannot name the angles using only the vertex.

This figure shows **three** angles: ∠HGJ, ∠2, and ∠3. Each angle has G as its vertex. DO NOT use ∠G as a name for any of the angles, since it would not be clear which angle you're referring to.

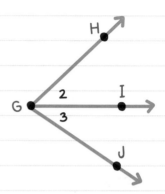

The space around an angle can be classified as interior or exterior.

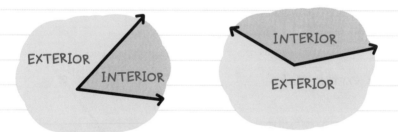

ANGLE MEASURE
The MEASURE of ∠A (the size of the angle) is written as m∠A.

We use DEGREES (°) to measure the size of an angle. There are 360° in a circle.

Basic angles:

A 180° angle is a half rotation in a circle. It forms a straight line.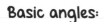

180°

A 90° angle is a quarter of a rotation in a circle. It is also known as a **right angle.**

90°

A 360° angle is a complete rotation in a circle.

360°

TYPES OF ANGLES

ANGLE(S)	DEFINITION AND EXAMPLES
RIGHT ANGLE	Measures exactly 90° m∠A = 90° A
ACUTE ANGLE	Measures greater than 0° but less than 90° 0° < m∠A < 90° 47° A
OBTUSE ANGLE	Measures greater than 90° but less than 180° 133° A 90° < m∠A < 180°

ANGLE(S)	DEFINITION AND EXAMPLES

STRAIGHT ANGLE
(straight line)

Measures exactly 180°

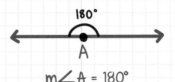

$m\angle A = 180°$

ADJACENT ANGLES

Angles that lie in the same plane, have a common (the same) vertex, share a common side, and have no common interior points.

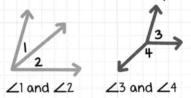

∠1 and ∠2   ∠3 and ∠4

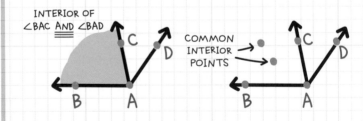

INTERIOR OF ∠BAC AND ∠BAD

COMMON INTERIOR POINTS

NON-ADJACENT ANGLES

Angles that do not have a vertex or a side in common.

∠5 and ∠6 do not share a vertex or a common side.

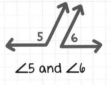

∠5 and ∠6

If point R is in the interior of ∠QPS, then
m∠QPR + m∠RPS = m∠QPS.

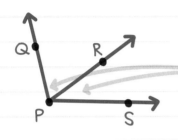

Add the measures of the smaller angles to find the measure of the larger angle.

EXAMPLE: Find m∠ABC.

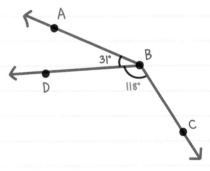

m∠ABD + m∠DBC = m∠ABC

31° + 118° = m∠ABC   Substitute.
m∠ABC = 149°   Add.

EXAMPLE: m∠UTW = 120°. Find the value of *x*.

m∠UTV + m∠VTW = m∠UTW

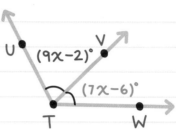

$(9x - 2)° + (7x - 6)° = 120°$ Substitute.

$16x - 8 = 120$ Simplify.

$16x - 8 + 8 = 120 + 8$ Add 8 to both sides.

$16x = 128$

$\dfrac{16x}{16} = \dfrac{128}{16}$ Divide both sides by 16.

$x = 8$

CONGRUENT ANGLES

Two angles are CONGRUENT
if their angle measures
are equal.

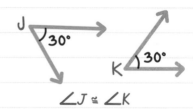

∠J ≅ ∠K

22

Note: We can use matching angle marks to show that angles are congruent.

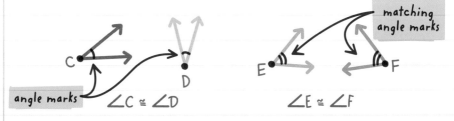

angle marks → ∠C ≅ ∠D

matching angle marks

∠E ≅ ∠F

EXAMPLE: Is ∠HGI ≅ ∠LGJ?

m∠LGJ = 72° + 58°
        = 130°

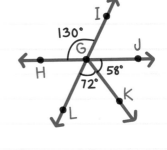

Since ∠HGI and ∠LGJ both measure 130°, they are congruent.

∠HGI ≅ ∠LGJ

DO ∠HGI AND ∠LGJ HAVE THE SAME MEASURE?

CHECK YOUR KNOWLEDGE

1. Give the three names for the shaded angle.

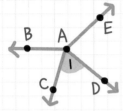

For questions 2–5, classify the angles as *right*, *acute*, *obtuse*, or *straight*.

2.

3.

4.

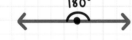

5.

6. Complete the following statement:

m∠BAC + m∠CAD = m _____.

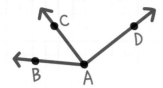

7. Given m∠KJM = 170°, find the value of x.

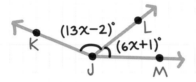

For questions 8 and 9, use the figure below.

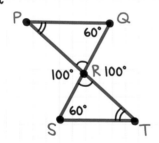

8. ∠RPQ ≅ _____

9. ∠PRS ≅ _____

10. Name the pair of congruent angles in the figure below.

CHECK YOUR ANSWERS

1. $\angle 1$, $\angle CAD$, or $\angle DAC$

2. acute

3. right

4. straight

5. obtuse

6. $\angle BAD$

7. $m\angle KJM = m\angle KJL + m\angle LJM$; $170 = (13x - 2) + (6x + 1)$;
$170 = 19x - 1$; $171 = 19x$; $x = 9$

8. $\angle RTS$ (or $\angle STR$)

9. $\angle QRT$ (or $\angle TRQ$)

10. $\angle I \cong \angle EFG$

Chapter 3

ANGLE PAIRS

Two angles can be related to each other by their measures or orientations. These are called **ANGLE PAIRS**. There are different types of angle pairs.

ADJACENT ANGLES lie in the same plane, have a common vertex, share a common side, and have no common interior points.

∠1 and ∠2 are adjacent

∠3 and ∠4 are adjacent

VERTICAL ANGLES are nonadjacent and opposite each other. They are formed when two lines intersect. They share the same vertex.

∠1 and ∠3 are vertical   ∠2 and ∠4 are vertical

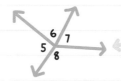

These are not straight lines. There is no intersection.

∠5 and ∠7 and ∠6 and ∠8 are not vertical

Vertical angles are congruent.

$\angle 1 \cong \angle 3$

$\angle 2 \cong \angle 4$

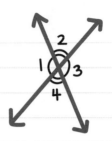

EXAMPLE: Find the value of x.

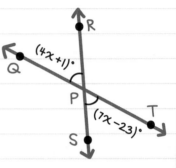

Since $\angle QPR$ and $\angle SPT$ are
vertical angles, they are congruent.

$m\angle QPR = m\angle SPT$	
$4x + 1 = 7x - 23$	Substitute.
$\cancel{4x} + 1 - \cancel{4x} = 7x - 23 - 4x$	Subtract $4x$ from both sides.
$1 = 3x - 23$	
$1 + 23 = 3x - \cancel{23} + \cancel{23}$	Add 23 to both sides.
$24 = 3x$	
$\dfrac{24}{3} = \dfrac{\cancel{3}x}{\cancel{3}}$	Divide both sides by 3.
$x = 8$	

Does m∠QPR = m∠SPT?

m∠QPR = (4x + 1)° = (4 × 8 + 1)° = 33°

m∠SPT = (7x – 23)° = (7 × 8 – 23)° = 33° ✓

More angle pairs:

ANGLE PAIR	DEFINITION	EXAMPLE
COMPLEMENTARY ANGLES	Two angles whose sum is 90°	 ∠A is complementary to ∠B. ∠1 is complementary to ∠2.

ANGLE PAIR	DEFINITION	EXAMPLE
SUPPLEMENTARY ANGLES	Two angles whose sum is 180°	118° A B 62° ∠A is supplementary to ∠B. 1 2 ∠1 is supplementary to ∠2.
LINEAR PAIR next to each other	Two angles that are adjacent and supplementary	the angles form a straight line, 180° 1 2 ∠1 and ∠2 are a linear pair.

complimentary
angles

YOU'RE SO SMART!

YOU'RE SMARTER!

EXAMPLE: If ∠B is supplementary to ∠A and m∠A = 42°, find m∠B.

Since ∠B is **supplementary** to ∠A, their measures add to 180°:

m∠B + m∠A = 180°
m∠B + 42° = 180°
m∠B + 42° – 42° = 180° – 42°
m∠B = 138°

EXAMPLE: Two complementary angles have a difference of 16°. What are the measures of the two angles?

Part 1:
We don't know the measure of the first angle, so assign it the variable $x°$.

Since the angles are **complementary**, the second angle will have a measure of $(90 – x)°$.

Subtract x from 90 to get the measure of the second angle.

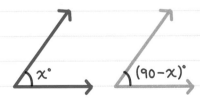

$x°$ $(90-x)°$

The difference of these two angles is 16°, so:

Part 2:

$(90 - x) - (x) = 16$

$90 - 2x = 16$ Simplify.

$90 - 2x - 90 = 16 - 90$ Subtract 90 from both sides.

$-2x = -74$

$$\frac{-2x}{-2} = \frac{-74}{-2}$$ Divide both sides by −2.

$x = 37$

The first angle is 37°.

The second angle is: $(90 - x)° = (90 - 37)° = 53°$

The measures of the two angles are 37° and 53°. ⬅

CHECK YOUR WORK

→ The angles are complementary: 37° + 53° = 90° ✓

→ The angles have a difference of 16°: 53° − 37° = 16° ✓

ANGLE BISECTORS

An **ANGLE BISECTOR** is a ray that divides an angle into two congruent angles.

If $\overrightarrow{AC}$ is the angle bisector of $\angle BAD$, then $\angle BAC \cong \angle CAD$.

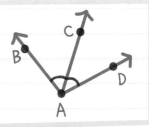

If $\overrightarrow{QS}$ bisects $\angle PQR$ and $m\angle PQR = 42°$, then $m\angle PQS = 21°$ and $m\angle SQR = 21°$.

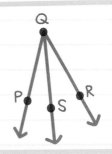

EXAMPLE: $\overrightarrow{EG}$ is the angle bisector of $\angle FEH$, $m\angle FEG = (9x - 5)°$, and $m\angle GEH = (7x + 11)°$. Find $m\angle FEH$.

First, find the value of x.

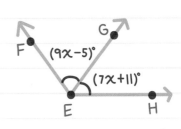

Since $\overrightarrow{EG}$ divides $\angle FEH$ into two congruent angles, their measures are equal:

$m\angle FEG = m\angle GEH$

$9x - 5 = 7x + 11$ Substitute.

$9x - 5 - 7x = 7x + 11 - 7x$ Subtract 7x from both sides.

$2x - 5 = 11$

$2x - 5 + 5 = 11 + 5$ Add 5 to both sides.

$2x = 16$

$$\frac{2x}{2} = \frac{16}{2}$$ Divide both sides by 2.

$x = 8$

So: $m\angle FEG = (9x - 5)° = (9 \times 8 - 5)° = 67°$

$m\angle GEH = (7x + 11)° = (7 \times 8 + 11)° = 67°$

We now have the information we need to find $m\angle FEH$:

$m\angle FEH = m\angle FEG + m\angle GEH$ **Angle Addition Postulate**

$= 67° + 67°$ Substitute.

$= 134°$

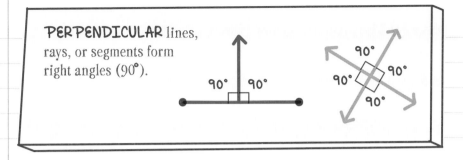

PERPENDICULAR lines, rays, or segments form right angles (90°).

A **PERPENDICULAR BISECTOR** is a line, ray, or line segment that divides a line segment into two congruent segments and forms four right angles with it.

IT'S A SEGMENT BISECTOR, BUT PERPENDICULAR!

EXAMPLES:

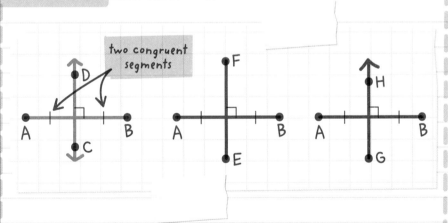

two congruent segments

$\overleftrightarrow{CD}$, $\overline{EF}$, and $\overrightarrow{GH}$ are all perpendicular bisectors of $\overline{AB}$.

EXAMPLE: In the figure below, RS = 2a + 5, ST = 17, and m∠UST =(15b)°. Find the values of a and b so that $\overleftrightarrow{US}$ is a perpendicular bisector of $\overline{RT}$.

In order for $\overleftrightarrow{US}$ to be the perpendicular bisector, $\overline{RS}$ and $\overline{ST}$ must be congruent:

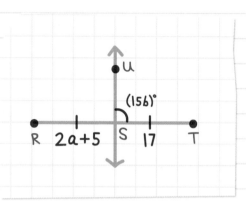

RS = ST	Congruent segments have equal measure.
2a + 5 = 17	Substitute.
2a + ~~5~~ − ~~5~~ = 17 − 5	Subtract 5 from both sides.
2a = 12	
$\dfrac{2a}{2} = \dfrac{12}{2}$	Divide both sides by 2.

$a = 6$

and ∠UST must be a right angle.

$m∠UST = 90°$

$15b = 90$ Substitute.

$\dfrac{15b}{15} = \dfrac{90}{15}$ Divide both sides by 15.

$b = 6$

CHECK YOUR KNOWLEDGE

For questions 1–5, use the figure below to complete the angle pairs.

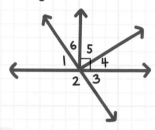

1. Adjacent Angles: ∠4 and _____, ∠4 and _____

2. Vertical Angles: ∠1 and _____

3. Complementary Angles: ∠4 and _____

4. Supplementary Angles: ∠1 and _____

5. Linear Pair: ∠3 and _____

6. Find the value of x in the figure.

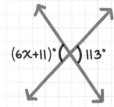

(6x+11)° ( ) 113°

7. If $\angle B$ is supplementary to $\angle A$ and $m\angle A = 107°$, find $m\angle B$.

8. Two complementary angles have a difference of 24°. What are the measures of the two angles?

9. What is an angle bisector?

10. In the figure below, ℓ is a perpendicular bisector of $\overline{PR}$, PQ = 3y + 2, QR = y + 8, and $m\angle$ PQS = (2x – 18). Find the values of x and y.

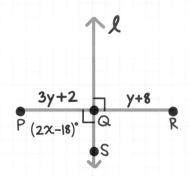

1. $\angle 5$, $\angle 3$

2. $\angle 3$

3. $\angle 5$

4. $\angle 2$

5. $\angle 2$

6. $6x + 11 = 113$; $6x = 102$; $x = 17$

7. $m\angle B = 73°$

8. $57°$ and $33°$

9. An angle bisector is a ray that divides an angle into two congruent angles.

10. $PQ = QR$; $3y + 2 = y + 8$; $2y + 2 = 8$; $2y = 6$; $x = 54$, $y = 3$

Chapter 4

CONSTRUCTIONS

We can use a compass and a straightedge (ruler) to
CONSTRUCT, or draw, accurate shapes, angles, and lines.

COMPASS

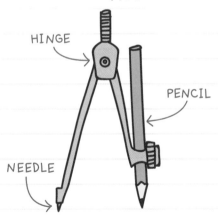

HINGE

PENCIL

NEEDLE

STRAIGHTEDGE

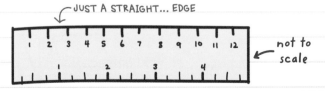

JUST A STRAIGHT... EDGE

1 2 3 4 5 6 7 8 9 10 11 12

1   2   3   4

not to
scale

CONSTRUCTING PERPENDICULAR LINES

To construct a perpendicular bisector to $\overline{AB}$:

A ●————————————● B

One way:

1. **Set compass width.** Keep this width for all 4 steps.

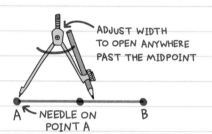

ADJUST WIDTH TO OPEN ANYWHERE PAST THE MIDPOINT

A — NEEDLE ON POINT A — B

2. **Draw a large arc across segment $\overline{AB}$.** With the needle on point A, move the pencil, starting below the line segment to draw a large arc.

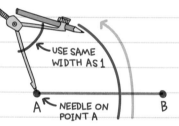

USE SAME WIDTH AS 1

A — NEEDLE ON POINT A — B

3. **Repeat on the right side.** With the needle on point B, move the pencil to create a large arc. Be sure to overlap with the first arc.

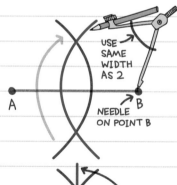

USE SAME WIDTH AS 2

A — NEEDLE ON POINT B — B

4. **Draw a vertical line** to connect the intersections of the two arcs.

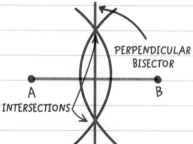

PERPENDICULAR BISECTOR

A — B

INTERSECTIONS

Another way to construct a perpendicular bisector:

1. Draw two small arcs on $\overline{AB}$. Place the needle on point P. Open the compass any width to draw a small arc across $\overline{AB}$. Keeping the needle on point P, lift and move the pencil to the opposite side of the line and draw a second arc.

2. Draw an arc below $\overline{AB}$. Place needle on the left small arc and move the pencil to create an arc below the line segment, under P.

3. Repeat on the right side.

4. Draw a vertical line to connect point P and the intersection of the bottom two arcs.

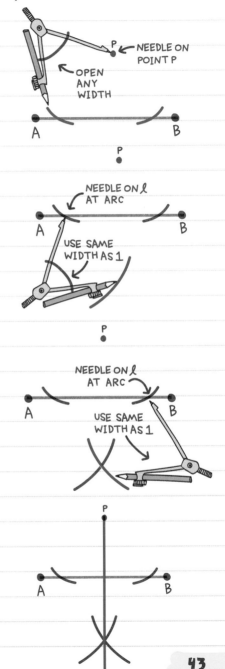

P ← NEEDLE ON POINT P

← OPEN ANY WIDTH

A   B

P

NEEDLE ON ℓ AT ARC

A   B

USE SAME WIDTH AS 1

P

NEEDLE ON ℓ AT ARC

A   B

USE SAME WIDTH AS 1

P

A   B

CONSTRUCTING PARALLEL LINES

To construct a line through point P and parallel to ℓ:

1. Use a straightedge to draw a long line through P and any point on ℓ.

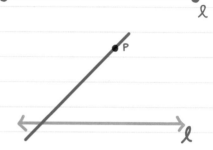

2. Draw an arc through the two lines. The arc can be anywhere below point P.

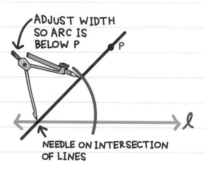

ADJUST WIDTH SO ARC IS BELOW P

NEEDLE ON INTERSECTION OF LINES

3. Move the compass needle to P, and draw a second arc above P.

USE SAME WIDTH AS 2

NEEDLE ON POINT P

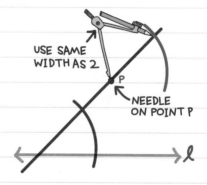

4. Set the compass width to match the two intersecting points of the first arc.

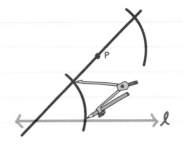

5. Use that width to draw a third small arc on the upper arc. Draw a point at the intersection.

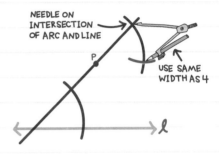

NEEDLE ON INTERSECTION OF ARC AND LINE

USE SAME WIDTH AS 4

6. Draw a line that connects P and the point made in step 5. The new line is parallel to line l.

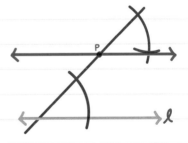

I'VE GOT SOME GOOD MOVES!

CONSTRUCTING ANGLES

To construct an angle congruent to ∠G:

1. Draw a ray.

2. Draw a large arc on ∠G. Draw it again on the ray.

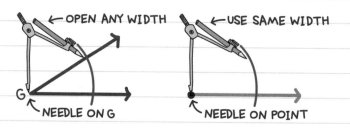

← OPEN ANY WIDTH   ← USE SAME WIDTH

NEEDLE ON G   NEEDLE ON POINT

3. On the ray, draw a small arc across the first arc. Set the width by placing the needle and the pencil on the intersection points of ∠G.

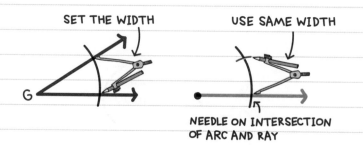

SET THE WIDTH   USE SAME WIDTH

NEEDLE ON INTERSECTION
OF ARC AND RAY

4. Draw a ray from the point through the intersection of the small and large arcs.

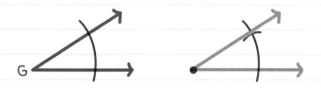

CONSTRUCTING ANGLE BISECTORS

To construct an angle bisector of ∠M:

1. Draw a large arc that intersects both rays.

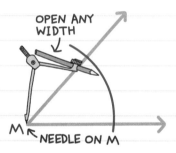

OPEN ANY WIDTH

M ← NEEDLE ON M

2. Draw a small arc across the center of the angle. Place the needle on the upper intersection of the arc. Draw a second arc. The size isn't important— just make sure it passes through the center of the angle.

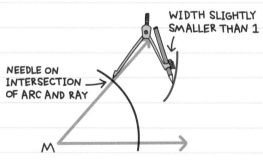

WIDTH SLIGHTLY SMALLER THAN 1

NEEDLE ON INTERSECTION OF ARC AND RAY →

M

3. Repeat on the opposite ray. Draw an arc to intersect with the arc made in step 2.

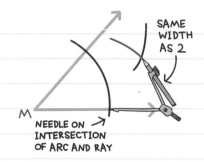

SAME WIDTH AS 2

M

NEEDLE ON INTERSECTION OF ARC AND RAY

4. Draw a ray from the vertex of ∠M through the intersection of the two small arcs.

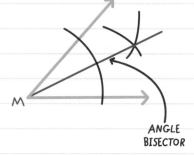

M

ANGLE BISECTOR

DID YOU SEE THAT TWIST? I'M AWESOME!

Copy the figure in each exercise and use a compass and straightedge to construct the following:

1. A perpendicular bisector to $\overline{AB}$.

2. A perpendicular bisector to $\overline{CD}$.

3. A perpendicular line from point A to line *n*.

4. A perpendicular line from point P to line *m*.

5. A line through point R and parallel to line *t*.

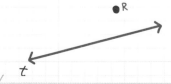

6. An angle that is congruent to ∠D.

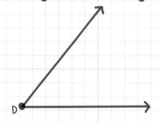

7. An angle that is congruent to ∠K.

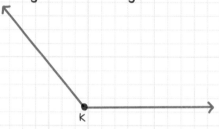

8. The angle bisector of ∠M.

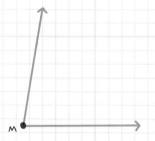

9. The angle bisector of ∠J.

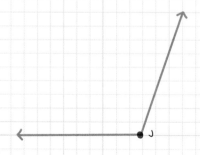

1.

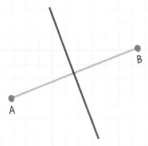

2.

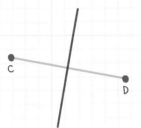

3.

4.

5.

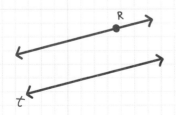

6.

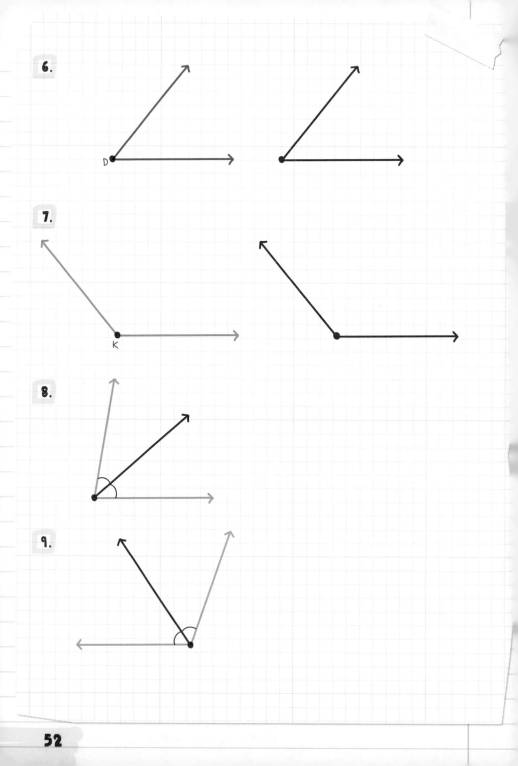

7.

8.

9.

Chapter 5

LOGIC AND REASONING

INDUCTIVE REASONING

INDUCTIVE REASONING is used to form hypotheses (explanations) based on a set of observations. The explanation, or conclusion, is called a **CONJECTURE**.

OBSERVATION $\longrightarrow$ **CONJECTURE**

EXAMPLE:

Every cat Emily meets purrs. Emily then assumes all cats purr.

observation

PURRR

conjecture

Inductive reasoning involves:

1. Examining a few examples

2. Observing a pattern

3. Assuming that the pattern will always hold

To prove that a conjecture is false, we need to find just one counterexample.

A **COUNTEREXAMPLE** is an exception to the observation. It shows that a statement is **false**.

EXAMPLE: If Emily finds one cat that does not purr, her conjecture that all cats purr would be false.

Conjecture: All cats purr.

Counterexample: One cat that does not purr.

The conjecture is false.

EXAMPLE: Prove the following conjecture is false:

Conjecture: All supplementary angles are a **LINEAR PAIR**, meaning adjacent and supplementary.

Show a counterexample.

These angles are supplementary (180°) but not adjacent. They are not a linear pair.

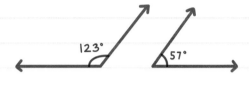

Note: The counterexample is only used to prove the conjecture is false. If you can't find a counterexample, that does not prove that the conjecture is true.

Conditional Statements

CONDITIONAL STATEMENTS are statements that have the form *if-then*. For example, IF a condition is met THEN an action is performed.

Conditional statements are either true or false.

To prove that a conditional statement is true, you must show that the conclusion occurs for all cases.

To show that a conditional statement is false, present a counterexample that shows the statement is not true.

Conditional Statements are written as: If p, then q.

The part of the statement after "If" is called the HYPOTHESIS (p).

The part after "then" is the called the CONCLUSION (q).

If you stay up all night, then you will be tired at school tomorrow.

Hypothesis (p): you stay up all night

Conclusion (q): you will be tired at school tomorrow

If p, then q can be written as

$$p \rightarrow q.$$

Regular statements can be rewritten as conditional statements. For example:

Regular statement:
All fish have gills.

Conditional statement:
If it is a fish, then it has gills.
     (p)   (q)

EXAMPLE: Write the following statement as a conditional statement:

Two congruent line segments have the same length.

Conditional statement:

If two line segments are congruent, then
　　　　　(p)
they have the same length.
　　　　　(q)

The CONVERSE of a conditional statement is formed by switching the hypothesis and the conclusion.

If the original statement is If p, then q, then the converse is:

If q, then p, or q → p.

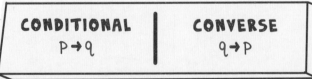

CONDITIONAL	CONVERSE
p → q	q → p

The converse of a true conditional statement **is not** always true.

EXAMPLE:

Conditional: If Lily sees a puppy, then she smiles.
(p)   (q)

Converse: If Lily smiles, then she sees a puppy.
(q)   (p)

The converse is not true in this case.

59

Conditional: If $x = 5$, then $x^2 = 25$.
          (p)   (q)

The converse is:

If $x^2 = 25$, then $x = 5$.
     (q)   (p)

This is not always true. x can also be -5, since $(-5)^2 = 25$.

The counterexample of $x = -5$ shows the converse is false.

Biconditional Statements

In a BICONDITIONAL statement, the conditional is true and its converse is true.

Bi means two.
A **biconditional statement** is a combination of two statements.

True Conditional + True Converse = Biconditional

A biconditional statement is written as:

p if and only if q (written as p iff q)

It is also written as:

$$p \leftrightarrow q$$

stands for
"if and only if"

This means: if p, then q, and if q, then p.

(p → q   and   q → p)

Conditional: If ∠A and ∠B are congruent, then
(p)

they have the same measure.
(q)

$$p \to q$$

Converse: If ∠A and ∠B have the same measure, then
(q)

they are congruent.
(p)

$$q \to p$$

Biconditional: ∠A and ∠B are congruent if and only if
(p)

they have the same measure.
(q)

$$p \leftrightarrow q$$

Conditional: If $\angle A$ is a straight angle, then $m\angle A = 180°$.
$\qquad\qquad\qquad$ (p) $\qquad\qquad\qquad\qquad\qquad$ (q)

Converse: If $m\angle A = 180°$, then $\angle A$ is a straight angle.
$\qquad\qquad$ (q) $\qquad\qquad\qquad\qquad$ (p)

Biconditional: $\angle A$ is a straight angle if and only if
$\qquad\qquad\qquad\qquad$ (p)
$m\angle A = 180°$.
$\qquad$ (q)

DEDUCTIVE REASONING

DEDUCTIVE REASONING uses given facts and statements to reach a conclusion logically.

Laws of Deductive Reasoning

There are two laws of deductive reasoning:

- Law of Detachment
- Law of Syllogism

LAW OF DETACHMENT
If the statements $p \rightarrow q$ and p are true,
then the third statement q is true.

The following two statements are true:

1. If John eats sushi, then he uses chopsticks.
         (p)   (q)

2. John eats sushi.
     (p)

Using the LAW OF DETACHMENT,
we can conclude that the statement:

John uses chopsticks is true.
      (q)

EXAMPLE: What can you
conclude from these statements?

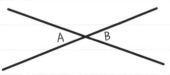

If ∠A and ∠B are vertical angles, then m∠A = m∠B.
          (p)   (q)

∠A and ∠B are vertical angles.
        (p)

m∠A = m∠B
   (q)

The following statements are true.

1. If I watch a scary movie, then I get scared.
                 (p)   (q)

2. If I get scared, then I will hide under my blankets.
            (q)   (r)

Using the LAW OF SYLLOGISM, we can conclude that:

If I watch a scary movie, then I will hide under my blankets.
            (p)   (r)

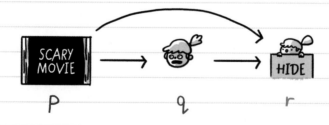

Inductive Reasoning: uses specific examples or past observations to reach a conclusion.

> CONDITIONAL STATEMENT: If p, then q. (p → q)

> BICONDITIONAL STATEMENT: p if and only if q. (p ↔ q)

Deductive Reasoning: uses given facts and statements to reach a conclusion logically.

> LAW OF DETACHMENT: If p → q is true and p is true, then q is true.

> LAW OF SYLLOGISM: If p → q and q → r are true, then p → r is true.

CHECK YOUR KNOWLEDGE

1. What is inductive reasoning?

2. Prove the following conjecture is false using a counterexample.

   All complementary angles are adjacent.

3. Write the following as a conditional statement.

   All penguins are birds.

4. Write the converse of the following conditional statement and determine if it is true.

   If $\overline{AB} \cong \overline{CD}$, then AB = CD.

5. Form a biconditional using the following conditional and its converse.

   Conditional: If $m\angle A = 90°$, then $\angle A$ is a right angle.
   Converse: If $\angle A$ is a right angle, then $m\angle A = 90°$.

6. What is deductive reasoning?

7. Given the following true statements, write a logical conclusion using the Law of Detachment.

Given: If $\overrightarrow{BD}$ bisects $\angle ABC$, then $m\angle ABD = m\angle DBC$. $\overrightarrow{BD}$ bisects $\angle ABC$.

8. Given the following true statements, write a third statement using the Law of Syllogism.

If Abby studies hard, then she will get good grades.
If Abby gets good grades, then she will get into a good university.

ANSWERS

CHECK YOUR ANSWERS

1. Inductive reasoning uses specific examples or past observations to reach a conclusion.

2. One possible example:

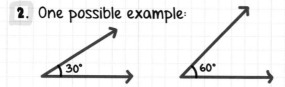

3. If it is a penguin, then it is a bird.

4. If AB = CD, then $\overline{AB} \cong \overline{CD}$. This is true.

5. $m\angle A = 90°$ iff $\angle A$ is a right angle.

6. Deductive reasoning uses given facts and statements to reach a conclusion logically.

7. $m\angle ABD = m\angle DBC$

8. If Abby studies hard, then she will get into a good university.

Chapter 6

GEOMETRIC PROOFS

PROOFS

A proof, or logical argument, can be used to show why a conjecture is true.

We use properties of equality (from algebra) and properties of congruence to show proofs.

A COUNTEREXAMPLE SHOWS THAT A CONJECTURE IS FALSE.

A PROOF SHOWS THAT IT IS TRUE!

EQUALITY PROPERTIES: Whatever you do to one side of an equation should also be done to the other side.

PROPERTIES OF EQUALITY AND CONGRUENCE

PROPERTY	DEFINITION	EXAMPLE
ADDITION-SUBTRACTION PROPERTY OF EQUALITY	The same number can be added to/ subtracted from both sides of an equation.	If $a = b$, then $a + c = b + c$. $a - c = b - c$.
MULTIPLICATION PROPERTY OF EQUALITY	The same number can be multiplied to both sides of an equation.	If $a = b$, then $a \times c = b \times c$.
DIVISION PROPERTY OF EQUALITY	Both sides of an equation can be divided by the same non-zero number.	If $a = b$, then $\dfrac{a}{c} = \dfrac{b}{c}$ $(c \neq 0)$.
REFLEXIVE PROPERTY OF EQUALITY-CONGRUENCE	A number is equal to itself.	$a = a$ $\overline{AB} \cong \overline{AB}$

PROPERTY	DEFINITION	EXAMPLE
SYMMETRIC PROPERTY OF EQUALITY	The order of an equality can be reversed.	If $a = b$, then $b = a$.
SYMMETRIC PROPERTY OF CONGRUENCE		If $\overline{AB} \cong \overline{CD}$, then $\overline{CD} \cong \overline{AB}$.
TRANSITIVE PROPERTY OF EQUALITY	If two numbers are equal to the same number, those numbers are equal.	If $a = b$ and $b = c$, then $a = c$.
TRANSITIVE PROPERTY OF CONGRUENCE		If $\overline{AB} \cong \overline{CD}$ and $\overline{CD} \cong \overline{EF}$, then $\overline{AB} \cong \overline{EF}$.
SUBSTITUTION PROPERTY OF EQUALITY	If two numbers are equal, you can replace one with the other in an expression.	If $a = b$, then b can be substituted for a in any expression.
DISTRIBUTIVE PROPERTY	Multiply the number outside the parentheses with each term inside the parentheses.	$a(b + c)$ $= ab + ac$

There are different types of proofs, but there is no single correct answer when writing a proof, as long as it is logical and supported with evidence.

THROUGH THIS SERIES OF FACTS, I CAN PROVE THIS MAN IS INNOCENT!

Two-Column Proofs

A **TWO-COLUMN PROOF** is a proof that is arranged in a two-column table. It starts with the given statement, and follows steps to reach the statement being proven.

For each statement in the left column, the reason for that step is in the right column. Reasons can be:

- given information
- theorems
- postulates
- definitions
- properties

Two-column proofs are set in the following format:

Given: $\overline{AB} \cong \overline{BC}$, $AB = 2x$, $BC = 16$
Prove: $x = 8$

TWO-COLUMN PROOF TIPS:

- Make a game plan.
- Draw a picture and label it.
- Start with the given information.
- End with the statement being proven.
- Write the statements in order so they follow the process to get from the first to last statement. The number of statements will vary depending on the proof.
- Give every statement a reason.
- Reasons can be: given information, theorems, postulates, definitions, properties.
- If you get stuck, work backward. Try to figure out the second-to-last statement.

STATEMENTS	REASONS
1. $\overline{AB} \cong \overline{BC}$, $AB = 2x$, $BC = 16$	1. Given ← *always start with the given*
2. $AB = BC$	2. Definition of congruence
3. $2x = 16$	3. Substitution Property of Equality
4. $x = 8$	4. Division Property of Equality

each statement needs a reason

logical steps to get from statements 1 to 4

what we're proving

EXAMPLE: Prove that if $\overrightarrow{KM}$ and $\overrightarrow{KN}$ are bisectors of $\overline{LN}$ and $\overline{MO}$, then $\overline{LM} \cong \overline{NO}$.

List all known information.

What I know:
$\overrightarrow{KM}$ is a bisector of $\overline{LN}$,
so: $\overline{LM} \cong \overline{MN}$

$\overrightarrow{KN}$ is a bisector of $\overline{MO}$,
so: $\overline{MN} \cong \overline{NO}$

I'LL USE THE TRANSITIVE PROPERTY OF CONGRUENCE TO PROVE THAT $\overline{LM} \cong \overline{NO}$.

TRANSITIVE PROPERTY OF CONGRUENCE

If $\overline{AB} \cong \overline{CD}$ and $\overline{CD} \cong \overline{EF}$, then $\overline{AB} \cong \overline{EF}$.

The two-column proof is:

Given: $\overrightarrow{KM}$ is a bisector of $\overline{LN}$.
$\overrightarrow{KN}$ is a bisector of $\overline{MO}$.
Prove: $\overline{LM} \cong \overline{NO}$

STATEMENTS	REASONS
1. $\overrightarrow{KM}$ is a bisector of $\overline{LN}$. $\overrightarrow{KN}$ is a bisector of $\overline{MO}$.	1. Given
2. $\overline{LM} \cong \overline{MN}$	2. Definition of segment bisector
3. $\overline{MN} \cong \overline{NO}$	3. Definition of segment bisector
4. $\overline{LM} \cong \overline{NO}$	4. Transitive Property of Congruence

Note: Since statements 2 and 3 have the same reason, they can be combined into one step.

Flowchart Proof

A **FLOWCHART PROOF** is a diagram that uses boxes and arrows to show the logical order of each statement leading to a conclusion.

FLOWCHART PROOF TIPS:

- Set each statement in a box.
- List reason below the box.
- Start with the given.
- If there is more than one given statement, separate each statement into its own box.
- Add more statements and reasons in a logical order.
- End with the statement being proven.

Given: $\overline{BD}$ bisects $\overline{AC}$, BD = BC
Prove: AB = BD

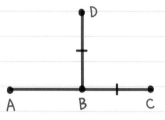

| $\overline{BD}$ bisects $\overline{AC}$ | | BD = BC |
| Given | | Given |

$\overline{AB} \cong \overline{BC}$
Definition of segment bisector

$\overline{BD} \cong \overline{BC}$
Definition of congruence

$\overline{AB} \cong \overline{BD}$
Transitive Property of Congruence

AB = BD
Definition of congruence

Given: $\angle PQR$ is a right angle
Prove: $\angle 1$ and $\angle 2$ are
complementary angles

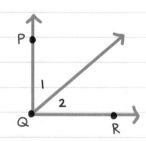

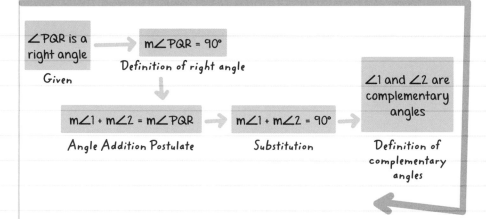

Paragraph Proof

A **PARAGRAPH PROOF** (or **informal proof**) explains why a conjecture is true in paragraph form. It still follows logical steps and gives reasons for them. It's less formal than the two-column proof.

EXAMPLE:

Prove vertical angles ∠1 and ∠2 are congruent.

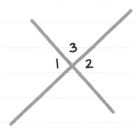

Sample paragraph:

We are given that ∠1 and ∠2 are vertical angles. Since linear pair angles are supplementary, $m\angle 1 + m\angle 3 = 180°$ and $m\angle 2 + m\angle 3 = 180°$. Using substitution, $m\angle 1 + m\angle 3 = m\angle 2 + m\angle 3$. Subtracting $m\angle 3$ from both sides gives $m\angle 1 = m\angle 2$. By the definition of congruence, $\angle 1 \cong \angle 2$.

EXAMPLE:

Given: $\angle 1 \cong \angle 2$, $m\angle 2 = m\angle 3$

Prove: $\angle 1 \cong \angle 3$.

Here is this proof in three different formats.

Two-Column Proof

Given: $\angle 1 \cong \angle 2$, $m\angle 2 = m\angle 3$

Prove: $\angle 1 \cong \angle 3$

STATEMENTS	REASONS
1. $\angle 1 \cong \angle 2$, $m\angle 2 = m\angle 3$	1. Given
2. $\angle 2 \cong \angle 3$	2. Definition of congruence
3. $\angle 1 \cong \angle 3$	3. Transitive Property of Congruence

Flowchart Proof

$m\angle 2 = m\angle 3$

Given

$\angle 1 \cong \angle 2$

Given

$\angle 2 \cong \angle 3$

Definition of congruence

$\angle 1 \cong \angle 3$

Transitive Property of Congruence

Paragraph Proof

It is given that $m\angle 2 = m\angle 3$. From the definition of congruence, $\angle 2 \cong \angle 3$. It is also given that $\angle 1 \cong \angle 2$. Therefore, by the Transitive Property of Congruence, $\angle 1 \cong \angle 3$.

CHECK YOUR KNOWLEDGE

For questions 1–5, state the property of equality or congruence that represents the given statement.

1. If $4x = 16$, then $x = 4$.

2. $2x + 1 = 2x + 1$

3. If $y = 3x + 4$ and $y = 5$, then $5 = 3x + 4$.

4. If $\overline{AB} \cong \overline{CD}$ and $\overline{CD} \cong \overline{EF}$, then $\overline{AB} \cong \overline{EF}$.

5. If $\angle P \cong \angle Q$, then $\angle Q \cong \angle P$.

6. Complete the two-column proof below.

Given: $m\angle BAD = 97°$,
   $m\angle CAD = 32°$
Prove: $m\angle BAC = 65°$

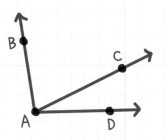

STATEMENTS	REASONS
1. _____	1. _____
2. $m\angle BAC + m\angle CAD = m\angle BAD$	2. Angle Addition Postulate
3. $m\angle BAC + 32° = 97°$	3. _____
4. _____	4. Subtraction Property of Equality

7. Fill in the missing steps in the flowchart proof to prove that m∠GFH = m∠IFJ.

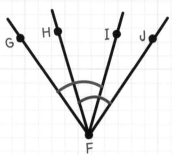

Given: m∠GFI = m∠HFJ
Prove: m∠GFH = m∠IFJ

Given

m∠GFI = m∠GFH + m∠HFI		
Angle Addition Postulate

Angle Addition Postulate

Substitution

m∠HFI = m∠HFI
Reflexive Property

m∠GFH = m∠IFJ

_____

8. Fill in the missing blanks in the paragraph proof.

Given: ℓ bisects $\overline{SU}$
Prove: $ST = \dfrac{1}{2}SU$

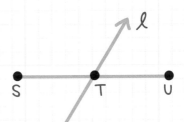

We are given that ℓ bisects $\overline{SU}$. By the Segment Addition Postulate, _____. By the definition of _____, $\overline{ST} \cong \overline{TU}$. Congruent segments have equal length, so _____. Substituting this into $ST + TU = SU$ gives $ST = \dfrac{1}{2}SU$.

9. Fill in the missing blanks in the paragraph proof.

Given: $\angle 2 \cong \angle 3$, $\angle 1$ and $\angle 2$ are vertical angles
Prove: $m\angle 1 = m\angle 3$

Since $\angle 1$ and $\angle 2$ are vertical angles, _____. It is given that $\angle 2 \cong \angle 3$. By the _____, $\angle 1 \cong \angle 3$. Congruent angles have equal measure, so _____.

CHECK YOUR ANSWERS

1. Division Property of Equality (or Multiplication Property of Equality)

2. Reflexive Property of Equality

3. Substitution Property of Equality (or Transitive Property of Equality)

4. Transitive Property of Congruence

5. Symmetric Property of Congruence

6.

STATEMENTS	REASONS
1. $m\angle BAD = 97°$, $m\angle CAD = 32°$	1. Given
2. $m\angle BAC + m\angle CAD = m\angle BAD$	2. Angle Addition Postulate
3. $m\angle BAC + 32° = 97°$	3. Substitution Property of Equality
4. $m\angle BAC = 65°$	4. Subtraction Property of Equality

7.

$$m\angle GFI = m\angle HFJ$$

Given

$$m\angle GFI = m\angle GFH + m\angle HFI$$

Angle Addition Postulate

$$m\angle HFJ = m\angle HFI + m\angle IFJ$$

Angle Addition Postulate

$$m\angle GFH + m\angle HFI = m\angle HFI + m\angle IFJ$$

Substitution

$$m\angle HFI = m\angle HFI$$

Reflexive Property

$$m\angle GFH = m\angle IFJ$$

Subtraction Property of Equality

8. We are given that ℓ bisects $\overline{SU}$. By the Segment Addition Postulate, $ST + TU = SU$. By the definition of segment bisector, $\overline{ST} \cong \overline{TU}$. Congruent segments have equal length, so $ST = TU$. Substituting this into $ST + TU = SU$ gives $ST = \frac{1}{2}SU$.

9. Since $\angle 1$ and $\angle 2$ are vertical angles, $\angle 1 \cong \angle 2$. It is given that $\angle 2 \cong \angle 3$. By the Transitive Property of Congruence, $\angle 1 \cong \angle 3$. Congruent angles have equal measure, so $m\angle 1 = m\angle 3$.

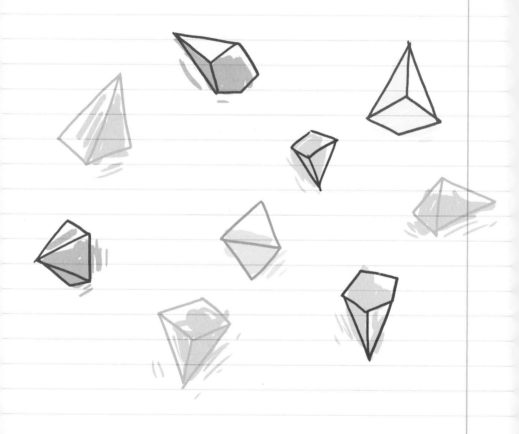

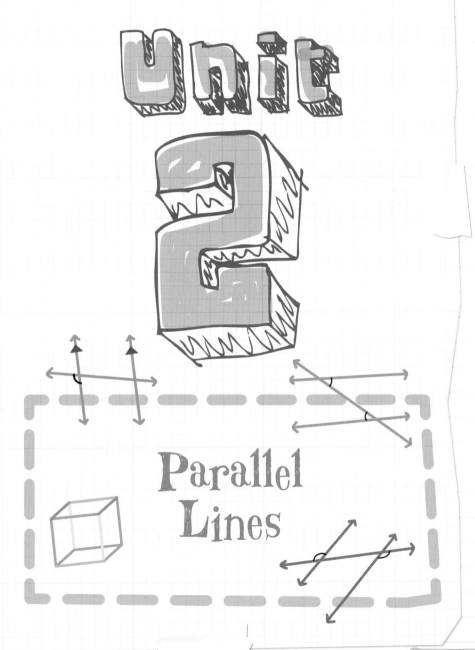

Unit 2

Parallel Lines

Chapter 7

PARALLEL LINES AND TRANSVERSALS

PARALLEL LINES are lines on the same plane that never meet (intersect). They're indicated with arrows.

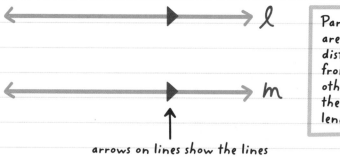

arrows on lines show the lines are parallel

Parallel lines are the same distance from each other over their entire lengths.

This notation $\parallel$ is used to show parallel lines: $\ell \parallel m$

$\parallel$ is the symbol for "is parallel to"

$\nparallel$ is the symbol for "is not parallel to"

SKEW LINES are two lines, on different planes, that never meet.

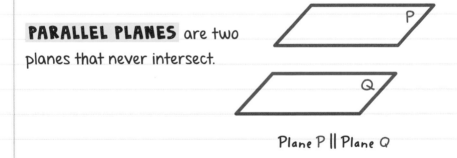

I JUST WANT TO MEET YOU.

IT'S JUST NOT MEANT TO BE.

n and m are skew lines

PARALLEL PLANES are two planes that never intersect.

Plane P $\parallel$ Plane Q

Two segments or rays are parallel if the lines that contain them are parallel, and they are skew if the lines that contain them are skew.

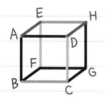

Parallel Segments

$\overline{AE} \parallel \overline{DH}$

$\overline{EF} \parallel \overline{DC}$

$\overline{BC} \parallel \overline{EH}$

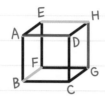

Skew Segments

$\overline{AD}$ and $\overline{HG}$

$\overline{BF}$ and $\overline{EH}$

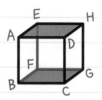

Parallel Planes

Plane AEH $\parallel$ Plane BCG

TRANSVERSALS

A **TRANSVERSAL** is a line that intersects two or more lines.

The angles that are formed by a transversal and the lines it intersects have special names.

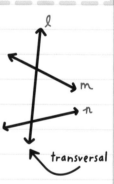

INTERIOR ANGLES are all the angles between the lines intersected by the transversal.

> Interior angles:
> ∠3, ∠4, ∠5, ∠6

EXTERIOR ANGLES are all the angles that are not between the lines intersected by the transversal.

> Exterior angles:
> ∠1, ∠2, ∠7, ∠8

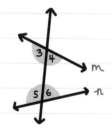

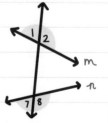

TRANSVERSAL ANGLE PAIRS

ANGLE PAIR	EXAMPLE	CHARACTERISTICS
ALTERNATE INTERIOR ANGLES	∠3 and ∠6 ∠4 and ∠5	interior angles on opposite sides of the transversal
SAME-SIDE INTERIOR ANGLES (CORRESPONDING INTERIOR ANGLES)	∠3 and ∠5 ∠4 and ∠6	interior angles on the same side of the transversal
ALTERNATE EXTERIOR ANGLES	∠1 and ∠8 ∠2 and ∠7	exterior angles on opposite sides of the transversal

TRANSVERSAL ANGLE PAIRS

ANGLE PAIR	EXAMPLE	CHARACTERISTICS
CORRESPONDING ANGLES	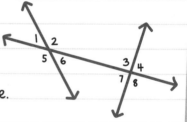 ∠1 and ∠5 ∠2 and ∠6 ∠3 and ∠7 ∠4 and ∠8	in the same relative position on each line on the same side of the transversal

EXAMPLE: Name all pairs of alternate interior, same-side interior, alternate exterior, and corresponding angles in the figure.

Alternate interior angles: ∠2 and ∠7, ∠3 and ∠6

Same-side interior angles: ∠2 and ∠3, ∠6 and ∠7

Alternate exterior angles: ∠1 and ∠8, ∠4 and ∠5

Corresponding angles: ∠1 and ∠3, ∠2 and ∠4, ∠5 and ∠7, ∠6 and ∠8

Two or More Transversals

This figure shows four transversals. Every line is a transversal to two other lines:

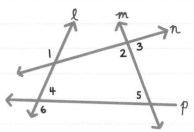

ℓ is a transversal intersecting *n* and *p*.

m is a transversal intersecting *n* and *p*.

n is a transversal intersecting *ℓ* and *m*.

p is a transversal intersecting *ℓ* and *m*.

Some special angle pairs formed by a transversal in the figure above are:

- ∠1 and ∠6: alternate exterior angles, connected by transversal *ℓ*.

- ∠1 and ∠3: alternate exterior angles connected by transversal *n*.

- ∠3 and ∠5: alternate interior angles connected by transversal *m*.

- ∠4 and ∠5: same-side interior angles connected by transversal *p*.

- ∠2 and ∠5: same-side interior angles connected by transversal *m*.

EXAMPLE: Name all the transversal angle pairs in the figure.

Each line is a transversal that connects the other two lines.

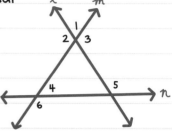

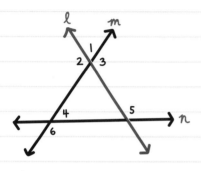

l is a transversal connecting *m* and *n*.

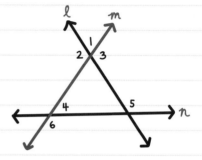

m is a transversal connecting *l* and *n*.

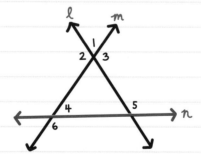

n is a transversal connecting *l* and *m*.

The transversal angle pairs are:

Alternate interior angles:
$\angle2$ and $\angle4$, transversal m
($\angle2$ and $\angle4$ are between lines ℓ and n)

Same-side interior angles:
$\angle3$ and $\angle5$, transversal ℓ
($\angle3$ and $\angle5$ are between lines m and n)

Alternate exterior angles:
$\angle1$ and $\angle6$, transversal m
($\angle1$ and $\angle6$ are outside lines ℓ and n)

Corresponding angles:
$\angle1$ and $\angle5$, transversal ℓ
$\angle3$ and $\angle4$, transversal m
$\angle4$ and $\angle5$, transversal n

For questions 1–3, use the figure below.

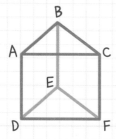

1. Name two segments parallel to $\overline{AD}$.

2. Name three segments skew to $\overline{AC}$.

3. Name two parallel planes.

For questions 4–7, use the figure below.

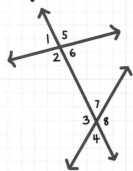

4. Name all alternate interior angle pairs.

5. Name all same-side interior angle pairs.

6. Name all alternate exterior angle pairs.

7. Name all corresponding angle pairs.

For questions 8–11, use the figure below.

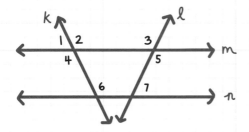

8. Name the transversal that connects ∠1 and ∠5, and name the angle pair.

9. Name the transversal that connects ∠5 and ∠7, and name the angle pair.

10. Find the alternate interior angle pair that is numbered. Name the transversal that connects it.

11. Find all corresponding angles that are numbered. Name the transversal that connects each pair.

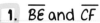

CHECK YOUR ANSWERS

1. $\overline{BE}$ and $\overline{CF}$

2. $\overline{BE}$, $\overline{DE}$, and $\overline{EF}$

3. Plane ABC and plane DEF

4. $\angle 2$ and $\angle 7$, $\angle 3$ and $\angle 6$

5. $\angle 2$ and $\angle 3$, $\angle 6$ and $\angle 7$

6. $\angle 1$ and $\angle 8$, $\angle 4$ and $\angle 5$

7. $\angle 1$ and $\angle 3$, $\angle 2$ and $\angle 4$, $\angle 5$ and $\angle 7$, $\angle 6$ and $\angle 8$

8. Transversal m, alternate exterior angles

9. Transversal ℓ, same-side interior

10. $\angle 4$ and $\angle 6$, transversal k

11. $\angle 1$ and $\angle 3$, transversal m
$\angle 2$ and $\angle 6$, transversal k
$\angle 6$ and $\angle 7$, transversal n

Chapter 8

PROVING SPECIAL ANGLE PAIRS

Special angle pairs in parallel lines have specific properties, and can be used to prove that two lines are parallel.

CORRESPONDING ANGLES POSTULATE

If two parallel lines are cut by a transversal, their corresponding angles are congruent.

lie on the same side of the transversal

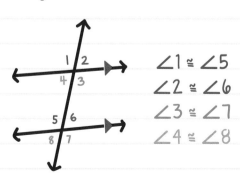

$$\angle 1 \cong \angle 5$$
$$\angle 2 \cong \angle 6$$
$$\angle 3 \cong \angle 7$$
$$\angle 4 \cong \angle 8$$

Important: The lines must be parallel.

PARALLEL   NOT PARALLEL

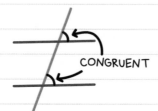   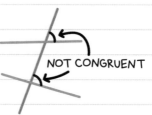

CONGRUENT   NOT CONGRUENT

EXAMPLE: In the figure below, m∠2 = 81°. Find all other angles with a measure of 81°.

Since the lines are parallel, we know:

Corresponding angles ∠2 and ∠6 are congruent, so: m∠6 = 81°

Vertical angles ∠2 and ∠4 are congruent, so: m∠4 = 81°

Corresponding angles ∠4 and ∠8 are congruent, so: m∠8 = 81°

ALTERNATE INTERIOR ANGLES THEOREM

If two parallel lines are cut by a transversal, then their alternate interior angles are congruent.

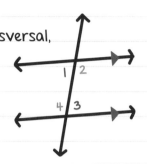

$$\angle 1 \cong \angle 3$$
$$\angle 2 \cong \angle 4$$

EXAMPLE:

Given: $k \parallel \ell$
Prove: $\angle 5 \cong \angle 3$

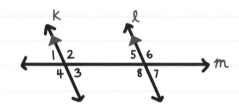

STATEMENTS	REASONS
1. $k \parallel \ell$	1. Given
2. $\angle 3 \cong \angle 7$	2. Corresponding Angles Postulate
3. $\angle 7 \cong \angle 5$	3. Definition of vertical angles
4. $\angle 3 \cong \angle 5$	4. Transitive Property of Congruence
5. $\angle 5 \cong \angle 3$	5. Symmetric Property of Congruence

ALTERNATE EXTERIOR ANGLES THEOREM

If two parallel lines are cut by a transversal, then their alternate exterior angles are congruent.

$$\angle 1 \cong \angle 3$$
$$\angle 2 \cong \angle 4$$

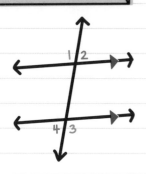

EXAMPLE: Find m∠1, m∠2, and m∠3 in the figure below.

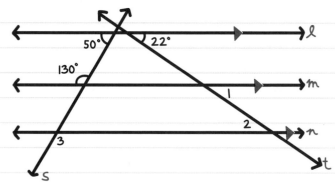

m∠1 = 22° from the CORRESPONDING ANGLES POSTULATE with lines ℓ and m and transversal t.

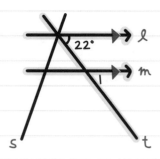

m∠2 = 22° from the ALTERNATE
INTERIOR ANGLES THEOREM, with
lines m and n and transversal t.

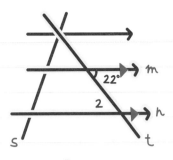

m∠3 = 130° from the ALTERNATE
EXTERIOR ANGLES THEOREM, with
lines m and n and transversal s.

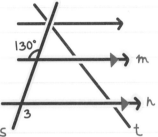

SAME-SIDE INTERIOR ANGLES THEOREM

When two parallel lines are intersected by a transversal,
then their same-side interior angles are supplementary.

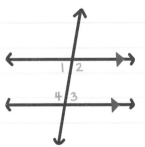

$$m\angle 1 + m\angle 4 = 180°$$
$$m\angle 2 + m\angle 3 = 180°$$

Find the values for x and y in the figure.

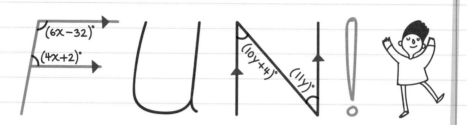

On **F**, we know the labeled angles are supplementary (from the SAME-SIDE INTERIOR ANGLES THEOREM):

$6x - 32 + 4x + 2 = 180$

$10x - 30 = 180$ Simplify.

$10x = 210$ Add 30 to both sides.

$x = 21$ Divide both sides by 10.

On **N**, we know the labeled angles are congruent (from the ALTERNATE INTERIOR ANGLES THEOREM):

$10y + 4 = 11y$

$y = 4$ Subtract $10y$ from both sides.

PARALLEL LINE POSTULATE AND THEOREMS

CORRESPONDING ANGLES POSTULATE	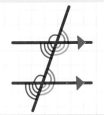	Corresponding angles are congruent if the lines are parallel.
ALTERNATE INTERIOR ANGLES THEOREM	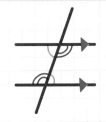	Alternate interior angles are congruent if the lines are parallel.
SAME-SIDE INTERIOR ANGLES THEOREM	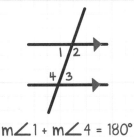 $m\angle 1 + m\angle 4 = 180°$ $m\angle 2 + m\angle 3 = 180°$	Same-side interior angles are supplementary if the lines are parallel.
ALTERNATE EXTERIOR ANGLES THEOREM	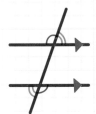	Alternate exterior angles are congruent if the lines are parallel.

1. Can the Alternate Interior Angles Theorem be used to find the value of x?

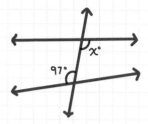

For questions 2–5, find m∠1. What theorem or postulate did you use?

2.

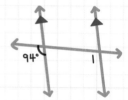

3.

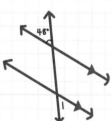

4.

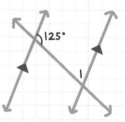

5.

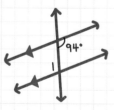

6. In the figure to the right m∠11 = 103°. Name all the other angles that have a measure of 103°.

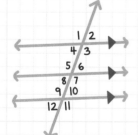

For questions 7 and 8, use the figure below.

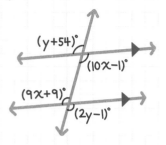

7. Find the value of x. What theorem or postulate did you use to find the value?

8. Find the value of y.

For questions 9 and 10, use the figure below.

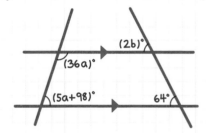

9. Find the value of a. What theorem or postulate did you use?

10. Find the value of b. What theorem or postulate did you use?

CHECK YOUR ANSWERS

1. No, the lines are not parallel.

2. m∠1 = 94°, using the Corresponding Angles Postulate

3. m∠1 = 48°, using the Alternate Exterior Angles Theorem

4. m∠1 = 55°, using the Same-Side Interior Angles Theorem

5. m∠1 = 94°, using the Alternate Interior Angles Theorem

6. ∠1, ∠3, ∠5, ∠7, ∠9

7. x = 10, using the Alternate Interior Angles Theorem

8. y = 55

9. a = 2, using the Same-Side Interior Angles Theorem

10. b = 32, using the Corresponding Angles Postulate

Chapter 9

PROVING LINES PARALLEL

The converses of the parallel line theorems and postulates are true.

CONVERSE OF CORRESPONDING ANGLES POSTULATE	If corresponding angles are CONGRUENT, then the lines are PARALLEL.
CONVERSE OF ALTERNATE INTERIOR ANGLES THEOREM	If alternate interior angles are CONGRUENT, then the lines are PARALLEL.
CONVERSE OF SAME-SIDE INTERIOR ANGLES THEOREM	If same-side interior angles are SUPPLEMENTARY, then the lines are PARALLEL.
CONVERSE OF ALTERNATE EXTERIOR ANGLES THEOREM	If alternate exterior angles are CONGRUENT, then the lines are PARALLEL.

Use these theorems to determine if lines are parallel:

CONVERSE OF SAME-SIDE INTERIOR ANGLES THEOREM

Same-side interior angles are supplementary (101° + 79° = 180°), so lines r and s are parallel.

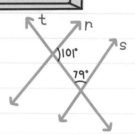

CONVERSE OF ALTERNATE EXTERIOR ANGLES THEOREM

Alternate exterior angles are **not** congruent, so lines e and f are **not** parallel.

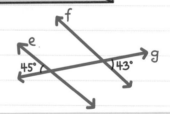

CONVERSE OF CORRESPONDING ANGLES POSTULATE

Corresponding angles are **not** congruent, so lines h and i are **not** parallel.

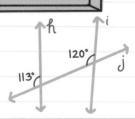

CONVERSE OF ALTERNATE INTERIOR ANGLES THEOREM

Alternate interior angles are congruent, so lines v and w are parallel.

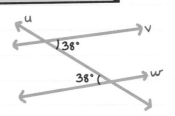

EXAMPLE: If i ∥ j and i ∥ k, prove j ∥ k.

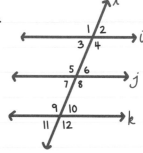

Given: i ∥ j, i ∥ k
Prove: j ∥ k

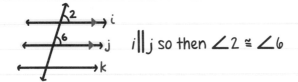

i ∥ j so then ∠2 ≅ ∠6

i ∥ k so then ∠2 ≅ ∠10

∠6 ≅ ∠10

STATEMENTS	REASONS
1. $i \parallel j$, $i \parallel k$	1. Given
2. $\angle 2 \cong \angle 6$	2. Corresponding Angles Postulate
3. $\angle 2 \cong \angle 10$	3. Corresponding Angles Postulate
4. $\angle 6 \cong \angle 10$	4. Transitive Property of Congruence
5. $j \parallel k$	5 Converse of Corresponding Angles Postulate

EXAMPLE: Is line ℓ parallel to line m?

Since 31° + 57° = 88°, the alternate interior angles are congruent.

By the CONVERSE OF ALTERNATE INTERIOR ANGLES THEOREM, we know ℓ is parallel to m.

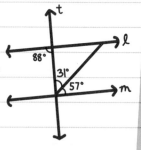

EXAMPLE:

Write a paragraph proof to show
that if m∠2 + m∠7 = 180°, then
ℓ ‖ m.

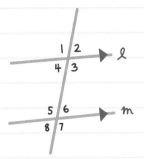

Given: m∠2 + m∠7 = 180°
Prove: ℓ ‖ m

Given: m∠2 + m∠7 = 180°. Because vertical angles
have equal measure, m∠2 = m∠4 and m∠7 = m∠5.
Substituting these two values into the given equation
gives m∠4 + m∠5 = 180°.

By the CONVERSE OF SAME-SIDE INTERIOR ANGLES
THEOREM, ℓ ‖ m.

Complete each sentence.

1. If alternate interior angles are congruent, then the lines are _____.

2. If same-side interior angles are _____, then the lines are parallel.

For questions **3–6**, determine whether lines l and m are parallel and state the reasoning.

3.

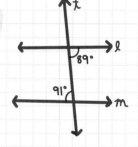

4.

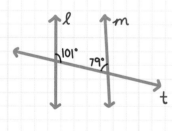

5.

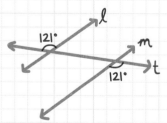

6.

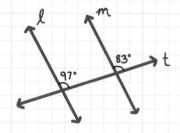

7. Is $d \parallel \ell$?

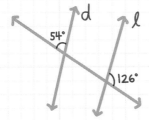

8. Which of the following lines are parallel? Explain your reasoning.

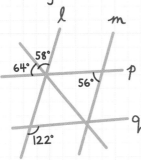

9. Fill in the blanks in the paragraph proof to show that if $m\angle 1 + m\angle 6 = 180°$, then $\ell \parallel m$.

Given $m\angle 1 + m\angle 6 = 180°$. Because _____ have equal measure, $m\angle 1 = m\angle 3$. Substituting into the given equation gives _____. By the _____, $\ell \parallel m$.

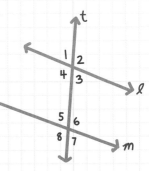

10. Complete each statement and reason for the following proof.

Given: $n \parallel o$, $m\angle 1 + m\angle 4 = 180°$
Prove: $\ell \parallel m$

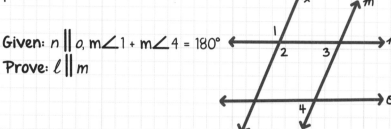

STATEMENTS	REASONS
1. $n \parallel o$, $m\angle 1 + m\angle 4 = 180°$	1. Given
2. $\angle 3 \cong \angle 4$	2. _____
3. $m\angle 3 = m\angle 4$	3. Definition of congruence
4. _____	4. Definition of vertical angles
5. $m\angle 1 = m\angle 2$	5. _____
6. $m\angle 2 + m\angle 3 = 180°$	6. Substitution
7. $\ell \parallel m$	7. _____

1. parallel

2. supplementary

3. No, alternate interior angles are not congruent.

4. Yes, Converse to Same-Side Interior Angles Theorem.

5. Yes, Converse to Alternate Exterior Angles Theorem.

6. No, corresponding angles are not congruent.

7. Yes. (Since 180° – 126° = 54°, d ∥ e by Converse to Corresponding Angles Postulate or Converse to Alternate Exterior Angles Postulate.)

8. p is parallel to q. Since 64° + 58° = 122°, p ∥ q by Converse to Alternate Exterior Angles Theorem (with transversal ℓ).

9. Given m∠1 + m∠6 = 180°. Because vertical angles have equal measure, m∠1 = m∠3. Substituting into the given equation gives m∠3 + m∠6 = 180°. By the Converse of Same-Side Interior Angles Theorem, ℓ ∥ m.

10.

STATEMENTS	REASONS
1. $n \parallel o$, $m\angle 1 + m\angle 4 = 180°$	1. Given
2. $\angle 3 \cong \angle 4$	2. Corresponding Angles Postulate
3. $m\angle 3 = m\angle 4$	3. Definition of congruence
4. $\angle 1 \cong \angle 2$	4. Definition of vertical angles
5. $m\angle 1 = m\angle 2$	5. Definition of congruence
6. $m\angle 2 + m\angle 3 = 180°$	6. Substitution
7. $\ell \parallel m$	7. Converse of Same-Side Interior Angles Theorem

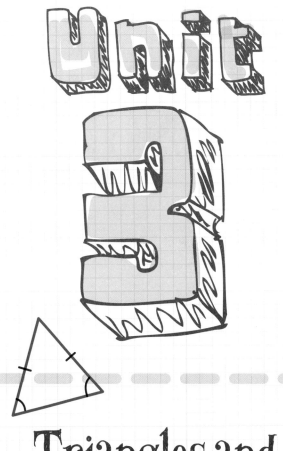

Unit 3

Triangles and Congruence

Chapter 10

TYPES OF TRIANGLES

A **POLYGON** is a TWO-DIMENSIONAL (flat) closed figure with at least three straight sides.

A **TRIANGLE** is a polygon with three sides and three angles. The symbol for a triangle is △.

To name a triangle, write the △ symbol followed by the letters of the three vertices.

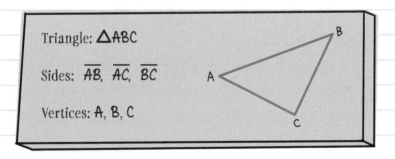

Triangle: △ABC

Sides: $\overline{AB}$, $\overline{AC}$, $\overline{BC}$

Vertices: A, B, C

CLASSIFYING TRIANGLES

We can CLASSIFY (or organize) triangles by their sides:

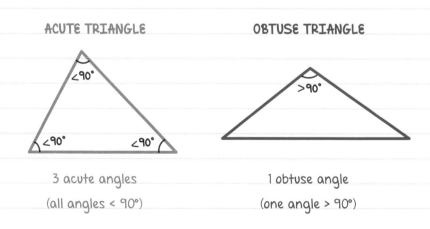

EQUILATERAL TRIANGLE	ISOSCELES TRIANGLE	SCALENE TRIANGLE

These marks mean the sides are equal.

These marks mean the angles are equal.

3 congruent sides
3 congruent angles

2 congruent sides
2 congruent angles

0 congruent sides
0 congruent angles

We can also classify triangles by their types of angles:

ACUTE TRIANGLE	OBTUSE TRIANGLE

<90°

<90°   <90°

>90°

3 acute angles
(all angles < 90°)

1 obtuse angle
(one angle > 90°)

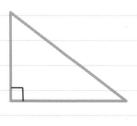

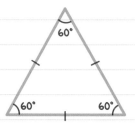

1 right angle (90°)   3 congruent angles

If a triangle is equilateral, then it is equiangular.

If a triangle is equiangular, then it is equilateral.

If a triangle is equilateral, then it has three 60° angles.

EQUILATERAL ⟷ **EQUIANGULAR**

We can combine both systems of classification to describe a triangle more precisely.

EXAMPLE: Classify the triangle.

ANGLES: There is one obtuse angle.
SIDES: No congruent sides
TYPE: An obtuse scalene triangle

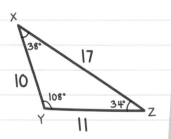

EXAMPLE: $\overrightarrow{AC}$ bisects $\angle$ BAD.
Determine if $\triangle$ABD is acute,
obtuse, right, or equiangular.

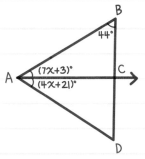

Step 1: Find the value of x.

Since $\overrightarrow{AC}$ bisects $\angle$ BAD, that means it divides $\angle$ BAD
into two congruent angles with equal measure.

m$\angle$ BAC = m$\angle$ CAD

$7x + 3 = 4x + 21$	Substitute.
$3x + 3 = 21$	Subtract 4x from both sides.
$3x = 18$	Subtract 3 from both sides.
$x = 6$	Divide both sides by 3.

Step 2: Find m$\angle$ BAC, m$\angle$ CAD, and m$\angle$ BAD

m$\angle$ BAC = $(7x + 3)° = [7(6) + 3]° = 45°$
m$\angle$ CAD = $(4x + 21)° = [4(6) + 21]° = 45°$
m$\angle$ BAD = m$\angle$ BAC + m$\angle$ CAD
$\qquad = 45° + 45°$
$\qquad = 90°$

Since $\angle$ BAD measures 90°, it is a right angle,
so $\triangle$ABD is a right triangle.

Isosceles Triangles

In an ISOSCELES TRIANGLE, the sides that are equal in length are called the LEGS. The third side is called the BASE. The angles opposite the legs are called the BASE ANGLES.

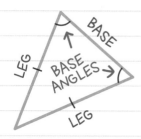

In this isosceles triangle:

∠A is opposite $\overline{BC}$.

∠B is opposite $\overline{AC}$.

∠C is opposite $\overline{AB}$.

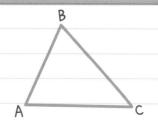

ISOSCELES TRIANGLE THEOREM

If two sides of a triangle are congruent, then the angles opposite those sides are congruent.

If $\overline{AB} \cong \overline{BC}$, then ∠A ≅ ∠C.

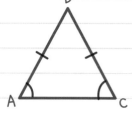

The converse of this is also true.

CONVERSE OF ISOSCELES TRIANGLE THEOREM

If two angles of a triangle are congruent, then the sides opposite those angles are also congruent.

If $\angle A \cong \angle C$, then $\overline{AB} \cong \overline{BC}$.

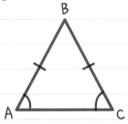

EXAMPLE: Find the value of x in $\angle$LMN.

Since $\overline{LM} \cong \overline{MN}$, we know that $\angle$L is congruent to $\angle$N (from the ISOSCELES TRIANGLE THEOREM).

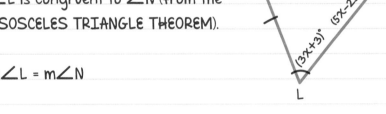

$m\angle L = m\angle N$

$3x + 3 = 5x - 23$	Substitute.
$3 = 2x - 23$	Subtract $3x$ from both sides.
$26 = 2x$	Add 23 to both sides.
$x = 13$	Divide both sides by 2.

Complete each statement.

1. An isosceles triangle has _____ congruent sides.

2. A scalene triangle has _____ congruent sides.

3. An acute triangle has _____ acute angles.

4. The measure of ∠A is _____°.

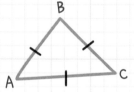

For questions 5–7, classify each triangle by its angle and side measurements.

5.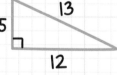

6.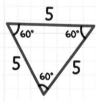

7.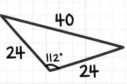

8. $\overrightarrow{QS}$ bisects $\angle PQR$. Determine if $\triangle PQR$ is acute, obtuse, or right.

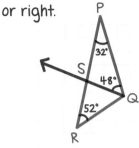

9. Find the value of x in the triangle below.

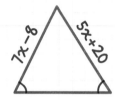

10. Find the value of y in the triangle below.

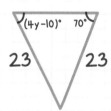

11. Find the values of x, y, and z in the figure below.

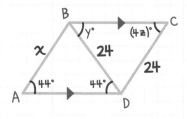

CHECK YOUR ANSWERS

1. two

2. zero

3. three

4. 60

5. right scalene

6. acute, equiangular, and equilateral

7. obtuse isosceles

8. obtuse

9. $7x - 8 = 5x + 20$; therefore, $x = 14$

10. $70 = 4y - 10$, so $y = 20$

11. $x = 24$, $y = 44$, $z = 11$

Chapter 11

INTERIOR AND EXTERIOR ANGLES

INTERIOR ANGLES

The angles inside a triangle are the
INTERIOR ANGLES.

Interior angles: ∠1, ∠2, ∠3

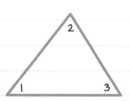

TRIANGLE ANGLE-SUM THEOREM

The sum of the measures of the three
interior angles is 180°.

m∠1 + m∠2 + m∠3 = 180°

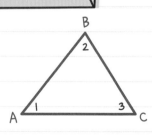

EXAMPLE: Find m∠A in △ABC.

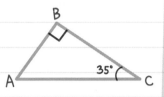

∠B is a right angle, so m∠B = 90°.

From the TRIANGLE ANGLE-SUM
THEOREM, the measures of the angles
in a triangle add up to 180°:

m∠A + m∠B + m∠C = 180°

m∠A + 90° + 35° = 180°

m∠A + 125° = 180°

m∠A = 55°

EXAMPLE: Find the measures
of each angle in △GHI.

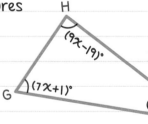

All three interior angles
add up to 180°:

m∠G + m∠H + m∠I = 180°

$(7x + 1) + (9x - 19) + 2x = 180$

$18x - 18 = 180$

$18x = 198$

$x = 11$

Substituting $x = 11$ into each angle measure gives:

$m\angle G = (7x + 1)° = [7(11) + 1]° = 78°$

$m\angle H = (9x - 19)° = [9(11) - 19]° = 80°$

$m\angle I = (2x)° = 2(11)° = 22°$

CHECK YOUR WORK

$m\angle G + m\angle H + m\angle I = 78° + 80° + 22° = 180°$ ✓

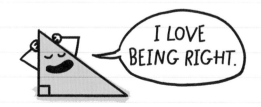

I LOVE BEING RIGHT.

EXTERIOR ANGLES

The angles on the outside of
the triangle are the EXTERIOR
ANGLES.

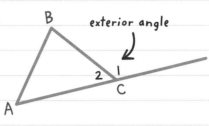

$\angle 1$ is an exterior angle
of $\triangle ABC$.

$\angle 1$ and $\angle 2$ are supplementary to each other.

$m\angle 1 + m\angle 2 = 180°$

EXAMPLE: In $\triangle PQR$, $m\angle Q$ is
45° and $m\angle R$ is 85°. Find $m\angle 1$.

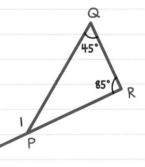

First, find the measure of $\angle QPR$.

All three interior angles add
up to 180°:

$m\angle QPR + m\angle Q + m\angle R = 180°$

$m\angle QPR + 45° + 85° = 180°$

$m\angle QPR = 50°$

Then, use that information to find m∠1.
∠1 and ∠QPR are supplementary,

m∠1 + m∠QPR = 180°

m∠1 + 50° = 180°

m∠1 = 130°

The measurement of an exterior angle is equal to the sum of the two nonadjacent interior angles.

m∠1 = m∠2 + m∠3

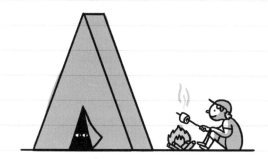

Given: △ABC with exterior angle ∠4
Prove: m∠1 + m∠2 = m∠4

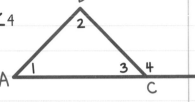

ΔABC with exterior angle ∠4
Given

m∠1 + m∠2 + m∠3 = 180°
Triangle Angle-Sum Theorem

m∠3 + m∠4 = 180°
Definition of linear pair

m∠1 + m∠2 + m∠3 = m∠3 + m∠4
Substitution

m∠1 + m∠2 = m∠4
Subtraction Property of Equality

EXAMPLE: Find m∠1.

Because 72° is the same value
as the sum of m∠1 and 27°,

$72° = m∠1 + 27°$
$72° - 27° = m∠1 + 27° - 27°$
$45° = m∠1$
$m∠1 = 45°$

EXAMPLE: Find the value of x in the figure.

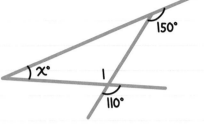

Since vertical angles are congruent,

$m\angle 1 = 110°$

Since 150° is the same value as the sum of $m\angle 1$ and $x°$,

$150 = m\angle 1 + x$

$150 = 110 + x$

$x = 40$

CHECK YOUR KNOWLEDGE

1. Find the value of x in $\triangle PQR$.

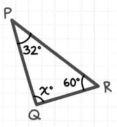

2. Find the value of x in $\triangle TUV$.

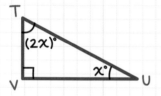

3. Find the measures of $\angle A$, $\angle B$, and $\angle C$.

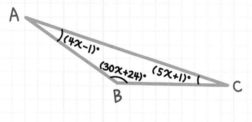

4. Find $m\angle 1$ in $\triangle JKL$.

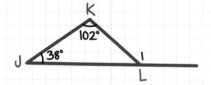

5. Find m∠F in △DEF.

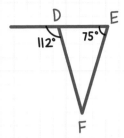

6. Find the value of *b* in the figure below.

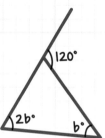

7. Find the value of *r* in the figure below.

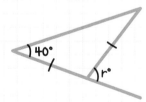

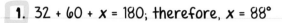

1. $32 + 60 + x = 180$; therefore, $x = 88°$

2. $2x + x + 90 = 180$; therefore, $x = 30°$

3. $(4x - 1) + (30x + 24) + (5x + 1) = 180$;
therefore, $m\angle A = 15°$, $m\angle B = 144°$, $m\angle C = 21°$

4. $38 + 102 = m\angle 1$; therefore, $m\angle 1 = 140°$

5. $112 = 75 + m\angle F$; therefore, $m\angle F = 37°$

6. $120 = 2b + b$; therefore, $b = 40°$

7. $40 + 40 = r$; therefore, $r = 80°$

Chapter 12

SIDE-SIDE-SIDE AND SIDE-ANGLE-SIDE CONGRUENCE

CONGRUENCE

Congruent polygons have the same shape and size. Their
CORRESPONDING ANGLES (angles in the same relative
position on each figure) and CORRESPONDING SIDES
are congruent.

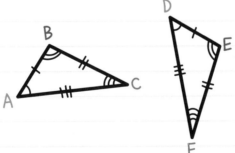

If △ABC and △DEF are congruent, the corresponding
angles are congruent:

∠A ≅ ∠D   ∠B ≅ ∠E   ∠C ≅ ∠F

And the corresponding sides are congruent:

$$\overline{AB} \cong \overline{DE} \qquad \overline{BC} \cong \overline{EF} \qquad \overline{AC} \cong \overline{DF}$$

The congruence statement is $\triangle ABC \cong \triangle DEF$.

IMPORTANT: Make sure the corresponding congruent angles are listed in the same order. For example, writing $\triangle ABC \cong \triangle DEF$ means that $\angle A \cong \angle D$, $\angle B \cong \angle E$, and $\angle C \cong \angle F$. We can't write $\triangle ABC \cong \triangle EFD$ because $\angle A$ is not congruent to $\angle E$.

EXAMPLE: Determine if $\triangle GHI$ is congruent to $\triangle JKL$. If it is, write a congruence statement.

Find the missing angle measures.

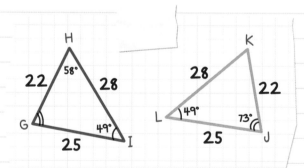

By the TRIANGLE ANGLE-SUM THEOREM,

$m\angle G + m\angle H + m\angle I = 180°$
$m\angle G + 58° + 49° = 180°$
$m\angle G = 73°$

Also, $m\angle J + m\angle K + m\angle L = 180°$
$73° + m\angle K + 49° = 180°$
$m\angle K = 58°$

The triangles are congruent because they have congruent angles . . .

$\angle G \cong \angle J$ $\angle H \cong \angle K$ $\angle I \cong \angle L$

. . . and their corresponding sides are congruent.

$\overline{GH} \cong \overline{JK}$ $\overline{HI} \cong \overline{KL}$ $\overline{GI} \cong \overline{JL}$

The congruence statement is $\triangle GHI \cong \triangle JKL$.

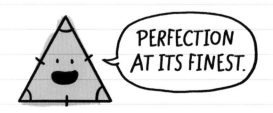

PERFECTION AT ITS FINEST.

SIDE-SIDE-SIDE (SSS) CONGRUENCE

SIDE-SIDE-SIDE (SSS) CONGRUENCE POSTULATE

If the three sides of one triangle are congruent to the three sides of another triangle, then the triangles are congruent.

If we know the corresponding sides are congruent, then the angles will also be congruent.

If $\overline{AB} \cong \overline{DE}$, $\overline{BC} \cong \overline{EF}$ and $\overline{AC} \cong \overline{DF}$

Then △ABC ≅ △DEF.

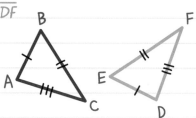

In this triangle,
$\overline{KM}$ bisects $\overline{JL}$ and $\overline{JK} \cong \overline{KL}$.
Determine whether △JKM is
congruent to △LKM.

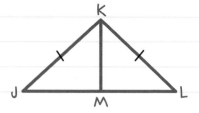

Since $\overline{KM}$ bisects $\overline{JL}$, $\overline{JM} \cong \overline{ML}$.

Corresponding sides are congruent:

$\overline{JK} \cong \overline{KL}$

$\overline{JM} \cong \overline{ML}$

$\overline{KM} \cong \overline{KM}$ ← a line segment is congruent to itself

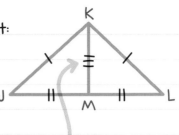

Therefore, $\triangle JKM \cong \triangle LKM$.

EXAMPLE: Write a two-column proof to prove the two triangles are congruent.

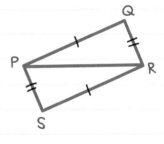

Given: $\overline{PQ} \cong \overline{RS}$ and $\overline{QR} \cong \overline{SP}$
Prove: $\triangle PQR \cong \triangle RSP$

STATEMENTS	REASONS
1. $\overline{PQ} \cong \overline{RS}$, $\overline{QR} \cong \overline{SP}$	1. Given
2. $\overline{PR} \cong \overline{PR}$	2. Reflexive Property of Congruence
3. $\triangle PQR \cong \triangle RSP$	3. Side-Side-Side Congruence Postulate

SIDE-ANGLE-SIDE (SAS) CONGRUENCE

SIDE-ANGLE-SIDE (SAS) CONGRUENCE POSTULATE

If two sides and the **INCLUDED ANGLE** of one triangle are congruent to two sides and the included angle of another triangle, then the triangles are congruent.

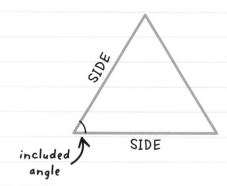

SIDE

SIDE

included angle

INCLUDED ANGLE
the angle between two sides of a triangle.

If $\overline{AB} \cong \overline{DE}$, $\angle A \cong \angle D$, and $\overline{AC} \cong \overline{DF}$

Then $\triangle ABC \cong \triangle DEF$.

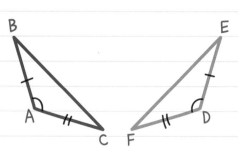

EXAMPLE: Which of the following triangles are congruent by Side Angle Side?

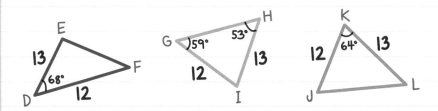

Each triangle has side lengths of 12 and 13. If the included angles are congruent, then the triangles are congruent.

First, find the missing included angle in the second triangle:

Since the sum of the angles in a triangle add up to 180°,

$m\angle G + m\angle H + m\angle I = 180°$

$59° + 53° + m\angle I = 180°$

$m\angle I = 68°$

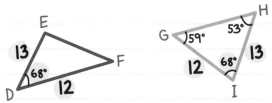

△JKL is not congruent to the other two triangles because the included angle, ∠K, is not congruent to ∠I or ∠D (m∠K = 64°).

Corresponding sides: $\overline{DE} \cong \overline{HI}$ and $\overline{DF} \cong \overline{GI}$

Included angle: $\angle D \cong \angle I$

Then by the SAS CONGRUENCE POSTULATE,

$\triangle DEF \cong \triangle IHG$ ←

EXAMPLE: Prove the two triangles are congruent.

Given: QR = 15 and RT = 15
PR = 28 and RS = 28

Prove: $\triangle PQR \cong \triangle STR$

QR = 15	RT = 15	PR = 28	RS = 28
Given	Given	Given	Given

$\overline{QR} \cong \overline{RT}$	$\overline{PR} \cong \overline{RS}$	$\angle QRP \cong \angle TRS$
Definition of congruence	Definition of congruence	Definition of vertical angles

$\triangle PQR \cong \triangle STR$
SAS Congruence Postulate

146

We can also solve problems with triangles (and other shapes) on a coordinate plane.

A triangle is formed by three points on the coordinate plane. The points are the vertices of the triangle. If a segment on a coordinate plane is horizontal or vertical, we can count the squares to find its length in units.

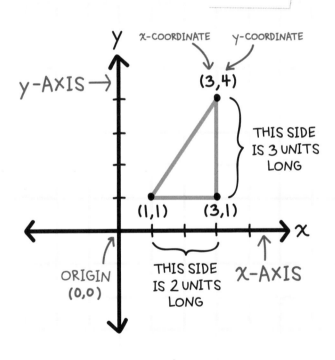

Determine if the two
triangles are congruent.

Corresponding sides:

Since AB = 2 units and
AE = 2 units

$\overline{AB} \cong \overline{AE}$

Since BC = 3 units and DE = 3 units,

$\overline{DE} \cong \overline{BC}$

Included angle:

m∠DEA = 90° and m∠CBA = 90°, so

∠DEA ≅ ∠CBA

Therefore, by the SIDE-ANGLE-SIDE CONGRUENCE
POSTULATE, △DEA ≅ △CBA.

CHECK YOUR KNOWLEDGE

1. Given △ABC ≅ △DEF, state the congruent corresponding sides and angles.

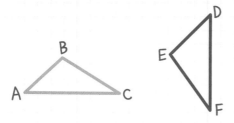

For questions 2–6, determine if the given triangles are congruent. If so, write a congruence statement and include the postulate (SSS or SAS) it demonstrates.

2. △JKL and △LMJ

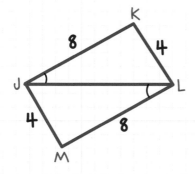

MORE QUESTIONS

3. △ABD and △DCA

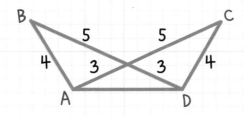

4. △PQR and △STU

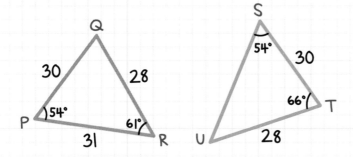

5. △ABC and △DEF

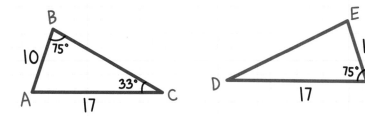

6. △PQR and △STR

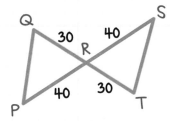

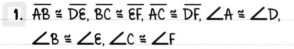

1. $\overline{AB} \cong \overline{DE}$, $\overline{BC} \cong \overline{EF}$, $\overline{AC} \cong \overline{DF}$, $\angle A \cong \angle D$, $\angle B \cong \angle E$, $\angle C \cong \angle F$

2. Yes, $\triangle JKL \cong \triangle LMJ$, SSS

3. Yes, $\triangle ABD \cong \triangle DCA$, SSS

4. No

5. No

6. Yes, $\triangle PQR \cong \triangle STR$, SAS

Chapter 13

ANGLE-SIDE-ANGLE AND ANGLE-ANGLE-SIDE CONGRUENCE

There are additional ways to determine if triangles are congruent:

ANGLE-SIDE-ANGLE (ASA) CONGRUENCE

ANGLE-SIDE-ANGLE (ASA) CONGRUENCE POSTULATE

If two angles and the **INCLUDED SIDE** of one triangle are congruent to two angles and the included side of another triangle, then the triangles are congruent.

If $\angle A \cong \angle D$, $\overline{AC} \cong \overline{DF}$, and $\angle C \cong \angle F$

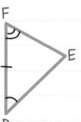

Then $\triangle ABC \cong \triangle DEF$.

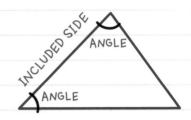

INCLUDED SIDE
the side between
two angles of a triangle.

EXAMPLE: Which of the following triangles are congruent by angle-side-angle (ASA)?

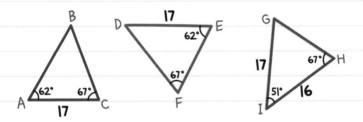

Each triangle has a side length of 17. Those will be the included sides.

First find the missing adjacent angle measures.

m∠D + m∠E + m∠F = 180°	m∠G + m∠H + m∠I = 180°
m∠D + 62° + 67° = 180°	m∠G + 67° + 51° = 180°
m∠D = 51°	m∠G = 62°

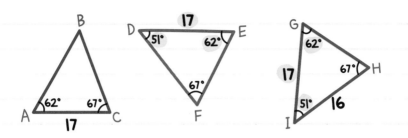

$\angle D \cong \angle I$, $\overline{DE} \cong \overline{IG}$, and $\angle E \cong \angle G$, therefore $\triangle DEF \cong \triangle IGH$ by the ANGLE-SIDE-ANGLE CONGRUENCE POSTULATE.

Even without knowing the exact measures of the angles and sides, we can prove that these triangles are congruent.

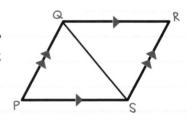

We know that $\overline{QR} \parallel \overline{PS}$ (given).

Use $\overline{PS}$ and $\overline{QR}$ as the parallel lines and $\overline{QS}$ as the transversal.

Which means $\angle SQR \cong \angle QSP$ (Alternate interior angles are congruent).

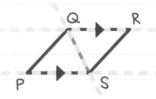

$\overline{QP} \parallel \overline{RS}$ (given)

∠PQS ≅ ∠QSR (Alternate interior angles are congruent.)

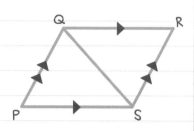

$\overline{QS} \cong \overline{QS}$ (This is the side that's shared by both triangles.)

Paragraph proof:

We are given that $\overline{QR} \parallel \overline{PS}$ and $\overline{QP} \parallel \overline{RS}$. ∠SQR ≅ ∠QSP and ∠PQS ≅ ∠QSR by the ALTERNATE INTERIOR ANGLES THEOREM. Also, $\overline{QS} \cong \overline{QS}$ by the REFLEXIVE PROPERTY OF CONGRUENCE.

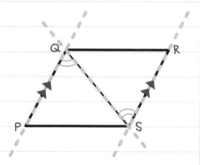

So, by the ANGLE-SIDE-ANGLE CONGRUENCE POSTULATE (ASA), △PQS ≅ △RSQ.

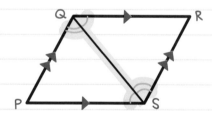

ANGLE-ANGLE-SIDE (AAS) CONGRUENCE

If two angles and a nonincluded side of one triangle are congruent to two angles and the corresponding nonincluded side of another triangle, then the triangles are congruent.

If $\angle A \cong \angle D$, $\angle B \cong \angle E$, and $\overline{BC} \cong \overline{EF}$

Then $\triangle ABC \cong \triangle DEF$.

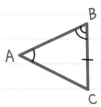
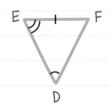

EXAMPLE: Prove $\triangle ABC \cong \triangle FDE$.

$\angle A \cong \angle F$

$\angle B \cong \angle D$

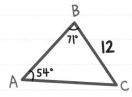
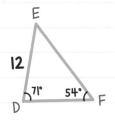

$\overline{BC} \cong \overline{DE}$

So, by the ANGLE-ANGLE-SIDE (AAS) CONGRUENCE POSTULATE, $\triangle ABC \cong \triangle FDE$.

EXAMPLE: Prove the two triangles below are congruent.

Given: $\angle P \cong \angle S$

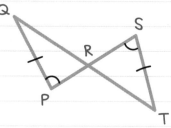

$\overline{QP} \cong \overline{TS}$

$\angle QRP \cong \angle SRT$ (Vertical angles are congruent.)

By the ANGLE-ANGLE-SIDE CONGRUENCE POSTULATE, $\triangle PQR \cong \triangle STR$.

HYPOTENUSE-LEG (HL) THEOREM

This congruence theorem is specifically for right triangles.

If the hypotenuse and a leg of one right triangle are congruent to the hypotenuse and a leg of another right triangle, then the triangles are congruent.

If $\angle A$ and $\angle D$ are right angles, $\overline{BC} \cong \overline{EF}$, and $\overline{AB} \cong \overline{DE}$

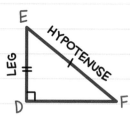

Then $\triangle ABC \cong \triangle DEF$.

TRIANGLE CONGRUENCE SUMMARY

Side Side Side	
	all sides congruent
Side Angle Side	
	two sides and included angle congruent
Angle Side Angle	
	two angles and included side congruent
Angle Angle Side	
	two angles and a nonincluded side congruent
Hypotenuse Leg	
	hypotenuse and leg of two right triangles congruent

DOES SIDE SIDE ANGLE WORK TO CONFIRM THAT THE TRIANGLES MUST BE CONGRUENT?

These triangles have two pairs of corresponding sides congruent to each other and a pair of nonincluded angles that are congruent, but they are different shapes.

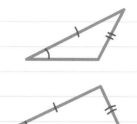

SSA is not a way to show congruence.

DOES ANGLE ANGLE ANGLE WORK TO CONFIRM THAT THE TRIANGLES MUST BE CONGRUENT?

These triangles have three pairs of corresponding angles congruent to each other, but they are different shapes.

AAA is not a way to show congruence.

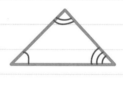

CHECK YOUR KNOWLEDGE

For questions 1–5, state the congruence postulate or theorem that would be used to prove the triangles are congruent. If none exists, answer "none."

1.
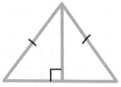

2.
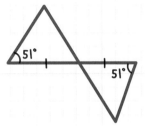

3.
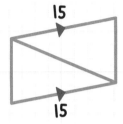

4.
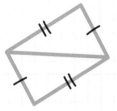

5.

6. Find the value of x that would make △GHI ≅ △JKI.

CHECK YOUR ANSWERS

1. SAS

2. ASA

3. HL

4. SSS

5. AAS

6. $x = 7$

Chapter 14

TRIANGLE BISECTORS

PERPENDICULAR BISECTORS

Perpendicular bisectors always cross a line segment at right angles (90°), cutting it into two equal parts.

PERPENDICULAR BISECTOR THEOREM

If a point is on the perpendicular bisector of a line segment, then the point is **EQUIDISTANT** to the segment's endpoints.

← at equal distances

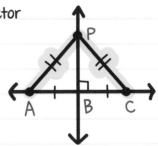

If point P is on the perpendicular bisector of $\overline{AC}$, then AP = PC.

The converse of this theorem is also true.

CONVERSE OF PERPENDICULAR BISECTOR THEOREM

If a point is equidistant to the endpoints of a segment, then it is on the perpendicular bisector of that segment.

If $AP = PC$, then point P is on the perpendicular bisector of $\overline{AC}$.

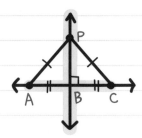

EXAMPLE: Find the value of x in the figure.

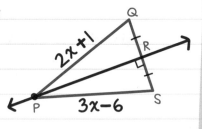

Since $\overleftrightarrow{PR}$ is a perpendicular bisector of $\overline{QS}$, P is equidistant to Q and S.

$PQ = PS$

$2x + 1 = 3x - 6$

$x = 7$

When three or more lines intersect at one point, they are CONCURRENT. Their point of intersection is called the POINT OF CONCURRENCY.

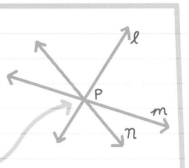

Lines ℓ, m, and n are concurrent. P is their point of concurrency.

CIRCUMCENTER

In a triangle, there are three perpendicular bisectors that all meet at one point, the CIRCUMCENTER.

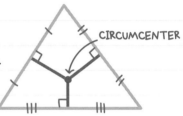

The circumcenter can be outside or inside the triangle.

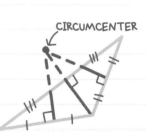

We can draw a circle through the three vertices of any triangle. The circumcenter of the triangle will be the center of the circle.

THINK CIRCLE CENTER!

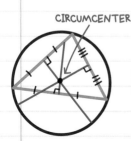
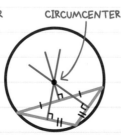
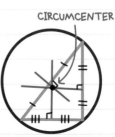

The circumcenter of a triangle is equidistant to the vertices.

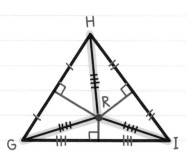

If R is the circumcenter of △GHI, then HR = GR = RI.

EXAMPLE: In △GHI, HR = 3x – 7, GR = x + 3.

Find the value of RI.

Since the circumcenter is equidistant to the vertices, HR = GR = RI.

Step 1: Find the value of x.

HR = GR
3x – 7 = x + 3
2x – 7 = 3
2x = 10
x = 5

Step 2: Calculate HR (or GR—they are the same length).

HR = 3x − 7 = 3(5) − 7 = 8

Since HR = RI,

RI = 8

INCENTER

In a triangle, the angle bisectors of the three interior angles all meet at one point. This point is at the center of the triangle and is called the **INCENTER**.

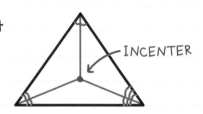

INCENTER

INCENTER THEOREM

The incenter is equidistant to the sides of the triangle.

If P is the incenter, then PT = PU = PV.

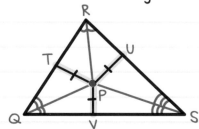

EXAMPLE: If M is the incenter of $\triangle JKL$, MN = $3x + 16$, and MP = $7x + 12$, find MO.

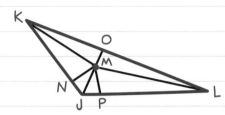

From the incenter theorem,
MN = MP = MO.

Step 1: Find the value of x.

MN = MP

$3x + 16 = 7x + 12$

$16 = 4x + 12$

$4 = 4x$

$x = 1$

Step 2: Find the value of MO.
Substituting the value of x into MN,

MN = $3x + 16 = 3(1) + 16 = 19$

Since MN = MO,

MO = 19

MEDIAN AND CENTROID

A **MEDIAN** of a triangle is a line from a vertex to the midpoint of the opposite side.

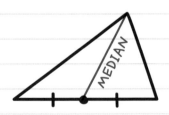

Every triangle has three medians which meet at a point called the **CENTROID**.

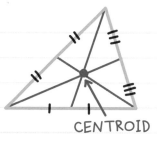

CENTROID

CENTROID THEOREM

The centroid is $\frac{2}{3}$ of the distance from each vertex to the midpoint of the opposite side.

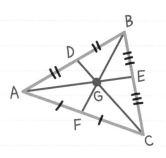

If G is the centroid of $\triangle ABC$, then

$$BG = \frac{2}{3} BF, \quad AG = \frac{2}{3} AE, \quad CG = \frac{2}{3} CD$$

EXAMPLE: In $\triangle ABC$ above, BG = 8. Find the measures of GF and BF.

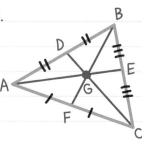

From the Centroid Theorem,

$$BG = \frac{2}{3} BF$$

$$8 = \frac{2}{3} BF$$

$8 \times 3 = \dfrac{2}{3} BF \times \cancel{3}$ Multiply both sides by 3.

$24 = 2 \times BF$ Divide both sides by 2.

$BF = 12$

We can now find GF using the SEGMENT ADDITION POSTULATE:

$BF = BG + GF$

$12 = 8 + GF$

$GF = 4$

If you wanted to balance a triangle plate on one finger, you would need to place your finger on the centroid to balance it. This point is called the **center of gravity**—the point where the weight is equally balanced.

ALTITUDE AND ORTHOCENTER

The **ALTITUDE** of a triangle is the line segment from a vertex to the opposite side, and perpendicular to that side. An altitude can be outside or inside the triangle.

perpendicular to the side opposite the vertex

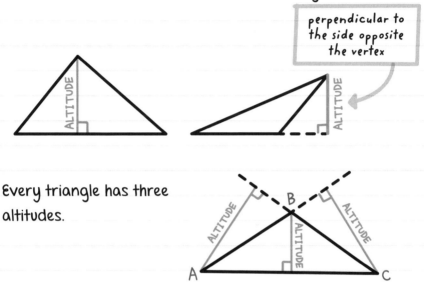

Every triangle has three altitudes.

The point where the altitudes of a triangle meet is the **ORTHOCENTER**.

The orthocenter can be outside or inside the triangle.

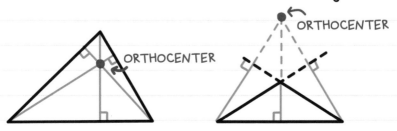

Triangle bisectors and their points of concurrencies:

TERM	POINT OF CONCURRENCY (P)	THEOREM
perpendicular bisector	circumcenter	The circumcenter of a triangle is equidistant to the vertices.
angle bisector	incenter	The incenter is equidistant to the sides of the triangle.
median	centroid	If P is the centroid of △ABC, then $BP = \frac{2}{3}BF$, $AP = \frac{2}{3}AE$, $CP = \frac{2}{3}CD$

TERM	POINT OF CONCURRENCY (P)	THEOREM
altitude	orthocenter	No theorem for this one.

A way to help remember the term that matches each point of concurrency:

Median—Centroid, Altitude—Orthocenter,

Perpendicular Bisector—Circumcenter, Angle Bisector—Incenter.

My cat ate old peanut butter cookies and became ill.

1. Find the value of x.

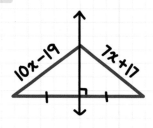

2. Find the measure of MN.

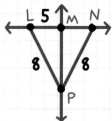

3. For triangles in illustrations a, b, and c below, state whether AB is a perpendicular bisector, median, or altitude.

a.

b.

c.

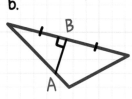

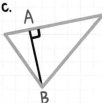

For questions 4–7, determine if point P is the incenter, circumcenter, centroid, or orthocenter of the triangle.

4.

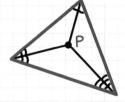

5.

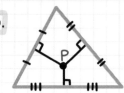

6.

7.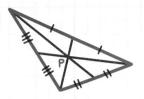

8. Find the measure of JI in △GHI below.

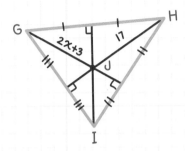

9. In △ABC, DG = 2x + 3 and GF = 3x − 7. Find the value of x.

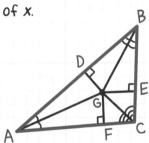

10. In the triangle below, EI = 135. Find the measures of EK and KI.

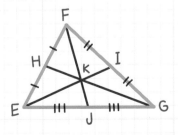

CHECK YOUR ANSWERS

1. $10x - 19 = 7x + 17$; therefore, $x = 12$

2. MN = 5

3. a. median; b. perpendicular bisector; c. altitude

4. incenter

5. circumcenter

6. orthocenter

7. centroid

8. JI = 17

9. $2x + 3 = 3x - 7$; therefore, $x = 10$

10. $EK = \frac{2}{3}(135)$; therefore, EK = 90, KI = 45

Chapter 15

TRIANGLE INEQUALITIES

COMPARING SIDES AND ANGLES

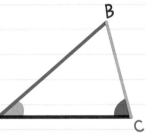

When comparing two sides of a triangle, the angle opposite the longer side is larger than the angle opposite the shorter side.

> If $\overline{AB} > \overline{BC}$, then $m\angle C > m\angle A$.

When comparing two angles of a triangle, the side opposite the larger angle is longer than the side opposite the smaller angle.

> If $m\angle C > m\angle A$, then $\overline{AB} > \overline{BC}$.

EXAMPLE: Since 6 > 5, then y > x.

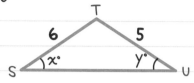

EXAMPLE: Since 62° > 56°, then a > b.

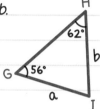

EXAMPLE: List the angles in △JKL from *largest* to *smallest*.

Since $\overline{JK} > \overline{KL} > \overline{JL}$ (24 > 21 > 15),
Then m∠L > m∠J > m∠K.

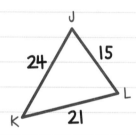

EXAMPLE: List the sides in △GHI from *longest* to *shortest*.

Since m∠I > m∠H > m∠G
(126° > 33° > 21°),
Then $\overline{GH} > \overline{GI} > \overline{HI}$

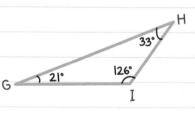

178

The sum of the lengths of any two sides in a triangle is greater than the length of the third side. In other words, add the length of two sides. That sum will be greater than the length of the third side.

$AB + BC > AC$

$BC + AC > AB$

$AB + AC > BC$

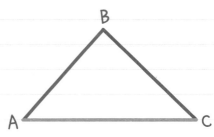

These three sticks will never form a triangle because the sum of the lengths of the smaller sticks is less than the length of the longer stick.

3 cm + 4 cm < 10 cm

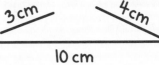

EXAMPLE: Is it possible to have a triangle with side lengths of 14, 21, and 30?

Check that any two sides are greater than the third side.

14 + 21 > 30

35 > 30 ✔

14 + 30 > 21

44 > 21 ✔

21 + 30 > 14

51 > 14 ✔

Since this satisfies the Triangle Inequality Theorem, these side lengths form a triangle.

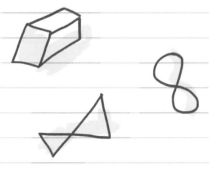

EXAMPLE: Becky is building a triangular planter for her vegetable garden. She has two lengths of wood: 12 ft and 5 ft. What is the range of values for the length of the third side?

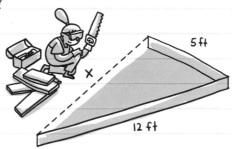

Assign the variable x for the third side. According to the Triangle Inequality Theorem, x has to satisfy these conditions:

$x + 5 > 12$	$5 + 12 > x$	$12 + x > 5$
$x > 7$	$17 > x$	$x > -7$
	(or $x < 17$)	Since $x > -7$ has a negative number, we can ignore this.

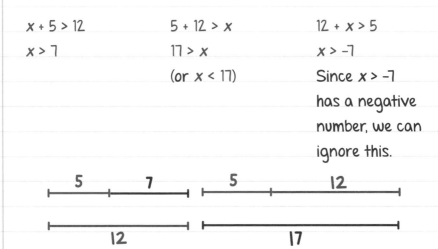

The length of the third side must be greater than 7 ft and less than 17 ft.

For questions 1 and 2, complete the statements. Fill in the blanks.

1. Since PR > QR, _____ > _____.

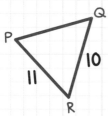

2. Since m∠X < m∠2, _____ ∠ _____.

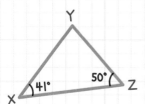

3. List the angles in △XYZ from *largest* to *smallest.*

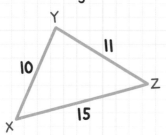

4. List the sides in △DEF from *shortest* to *longest*.

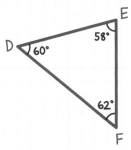

In questions 5–8, state whether it is possible to form a triangle with the given side lengths.

5. 7, 10, 15

6. 21, 30, 76

7. 5, 5, 9

8. 10, 23, 40

9. A triangle has two sides with lengths of 6 and 17. Find the range of possible values for the third side.

10. A triangle has two sides with a length of 22 each. Find the range of possible values for the third side.

ANSWERS

1. $m\angle Q > m\angle P$

2. $YZ < XY$

3. $\angle Y, \angle X, \angle Z$

4. $\overline{DF}, \overline{EF}, \overline{DE}$

5. yes

6. no

7. yes

8. no

9. $11 < x < 23$

10. $0 < x < 44$

Unit 4

Quadrilaterals and Polygons

Chapter 16

PARALLELOGRAMS

QUADRILATERALS

A **QUADRILATERAL** is a shape with four sides.

QUADRI = 4

LATERAL = SIDES

We name a quadrilateral using the four letters of its vertices.

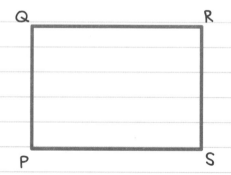

This quadrilateral is called PQRS.

Common quadrilaterals:

NAME	EXAMPLE	CHARACTERISTICS
Parallelogram		Opposite sides are parallel and equal in length.
Rectangle		A parallelogram where all four sides form right angles
Rhombus		A parallelogram where all sides are equal in length
Square		A parallelogram where all sides are equal in length and all sides form right angles
Trapezoid	b_1 b_2	Has exactly two parallel sides. Sides do **NOT** have to be equal in length.

PROPERTIES OF PARALLELOGRAMS

Parallelograms have the following properties:

- congruent opposite sides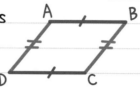

- congruent opposite angles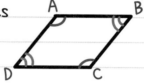

- consecutive angles that are supplementary

  SUPPLEMENTARY

- diagonals bisect each other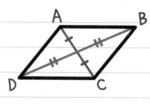

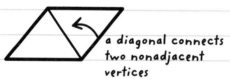
a diagonal connects two nonadjacent vertices

- each diagonal divides the parallelogram into two congruent triangles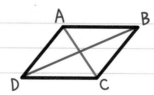

EXAMPLE: ABCD is a parallelogram.

Find the length of $\overline{BD}$.

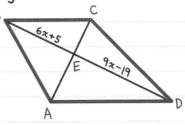

Step 1: Find the value of x.

Diagonals bisect each other in parallelograms, so $\overline{AC}$ divides $\overline{BD}$ into two congruent segments.

$\overline{BE} \cong \overline{ED}$

$BE = ED$

$6x + 5 = 9x - 19$

$5 = 3x - 19$

$24 = 3x$

$x = 8$

Step 2: Find the values of BE and ED.

$BE = 6x + 5$ $ED = 9x - 19$

$\quad = 6(8) + 5$ $\quad = 9(8) - 19$

$\quad = 48 + 5$ $\quad = 72 - 19$

$\quad = 53$ $\quad = 53$ ← Since BE = ED, we know the calculations are correct.

Step 3: Find the length of BD.

$BD = BE + ED$

$\quad = 53 + 53$

$\quad = 106$

THEOREMS TO PROVE A PARALLELOGRAM

We can prove a quadrilateral is a parallelogram by using any of the following theorems.

If both pairs of opposite sides are congruent, then it is a parallelogram.

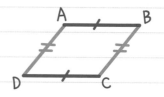

$$\overline{AB} \cong \overline{DC} \text{ and } \overline{AD} \cong \overline{BC}$$

If both pairs of opposite angles are congruent, then it is a parallelogram.

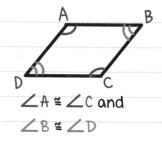

$$\angle A \cong \angle C \text{ and}$$
$$\angle B \cong \angle D$$

If an angle is supplementary to both of its consecutive angles, then it is a parallelogram.

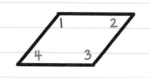

$$m\angle 1 + m\angle 2 = 180°$$
$$\text{and } m\angle 1 + m\angle 4 = 180°$$

If a quadrilateral has diagonals that bisect each other, then it is a parallelogram.

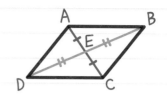

$\overline{AE} \cong \overline{EC}$ and $\overline{DE} \cong \overline{EB}$

If a quadrilateral has one pair of sides that is both congruent and parallel, then it is a parallelogram.

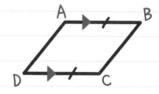

$\overline{AB} \cong \overline{DC}$ and $\overline{AB} \parallel \overline{DC}$

EXAMPLE: Find the values of
x and y that would make ABCD
a parallelogram.

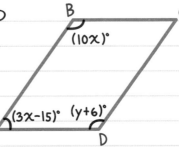

For ABCD to be
a parallelogram

1. ∠A and ∠B must
be supplementary.

m∠A + m∠B = 180°
(3x − 15) + (10x) = 180
13x − 15 = 180
13x = 195
x = 15°

2. ∠A and ∠D must be supplementary.

m∠A + m∠D = 180°
(3x − 15) + (y + 6) = 180
3(15) − 15 + y + 6 = 180
36 + y = 180
y = 144°

Prove that EFGH is a parallelogram.

Since m∠E + m∠H = 180°, then by the <u>Converse of Same-Side Interior Angles Theorem</u>, $\overline{EF} \parallel \overline{HG}$. Since EF = HG = 8, $\overline{EF} \cong \overline{HG}$.

EFGH has one pair of sides that is both congruent and parallel, so it is a parallelogram.

> If two lines are cut by a transversal and the same side interior angles are supplementary, then the lines are parallel.

CHECK YOUR KNOWLEDGE

1. Complete the sentence.

   If a quadrilateral is a parallelogram, then its opposite sides are _____ and _____.

2. Complete the sentence.

   If a quadrilateral is a parallelogram, then its consecutive angles are _____.

3. ABCD is a parallelogram. Find the value of x.

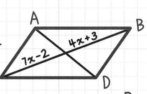

4. Find the missing angle measures in parallelogram ABCD.

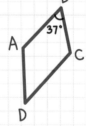

5. Find the values of x, m∠A, and m∠C in the parallelogram.

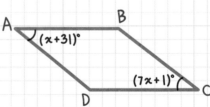

6. Find the values of x, m∠A, and m∠D.

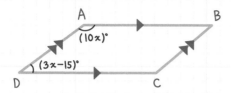

For questions 7-9, state whether there is enough information given to determine if the quadrilateral is a parallelogram.

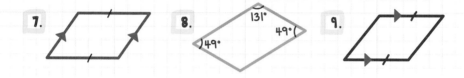

7.

8. 131° 49°

)49°

9.

10. Find the values of x and y so that ABCD is a parallelogram.

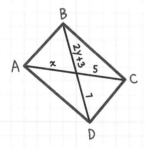

CHECK YOUR ANSWERS

1. Congruent, parallel

2. Supplementary

3. $7x - 2 = 4x + 3$; therefore, $x = \dfrac{5}{3}$

4. $m\angle A = 143$, $m\angle C = 143$, $m\angle D = 37$

5. $x + 31 = 7x + 1$; therefore, $x = 5$, $m\angle A = 36$, $m\angle C = 36$

6. $3x - 15 + 10x = 180$;
therefore, $x = 15$, $m\angle A = 150$, $m\angle D = 30$

7. No

8. Yes

9. Yes

10. $2y + 3 = 7$; therefore, $y = 2$, $x = 5$

Chapter 17

RHOMBUSES, RECTANGLES, AND SQUARES

Rhombuses, rectangles, and squares are quadrilaterals that are also parallelograms.

RHOMBUSES

A **RHOMBUS** is a parallelogram with four congruent sides.

Rhombuses have all the properties that a parallelogram has, plus a couple more.

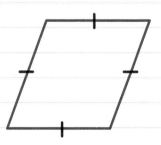

Rhombuses have diagonals that are perpendicular.	Each diagonal in a rhombus bisects a pair of opposite angles.

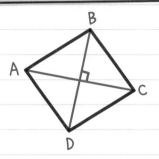

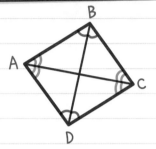

$\overline{AC}$ is perpendicular to $\overline{BD}$.
Write this as: $\overline{AC} \perp \overline{BD}$

$\overline{AC}$ bisects $\angle A$ and $\angle C$.
$\overline{BD}$ bisects $\angle B$ and $\angle D$.

EXAMPLE: Find m$\angle$UVW in rhombus TUVW.

$\angle$UVT is 30°.

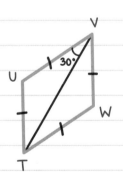

$\overline{TV}$ bisects $\angle$UVW.

Therefore, m$\angle$TVW is also 30°.

m$\angle$UVW = m$\angle$UVT + m$\angle$TVW

= 30° + 30° = 60°

EXAMPLE: Rhombus DEFG has m∠EDG = 104°. Find the value of x.

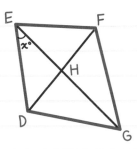

Since diagonals are perpendicular in a rhombus,

m∠DHE = 90°

Since each diagonal bisects a pair of opposite angles in a rhombus,

$\overline{DF}$ bisects ∠EDG

$m\angle EDF = \dfrac{1}{2}m\angle EDG$

$\qquad = \dfrac{1}{2}(104°)$

$\qquad = 52°$

Since the angle measures in a triangle add to 180°,

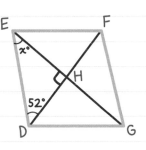

$x + 52 + 90 = 180$

$x + 142 = 180$

$x = 38°$

THEOREMS TO PROVE A RHOMBUS

Use these theorems to determine if a parallelogram is a rhombus.

If a parallelogram has perpendicular diagonals, then it is a rhombus.

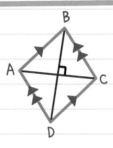

$$\overline{AC} \perp \overline{BD}$$

If a parallelogram has one diagonal that bisects a pair of opposite angles, then it is a rhombus.

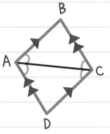

$\overline{AC}$ bisects $\angle A$ and $\angle C$

If a parallelogram has one pair of consecutive congruent sides, then it is a rhombus.

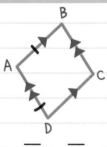

$$\overline{AB} \cong \overline{AD}$$

EXAMPLE: Determine if GHIJ is a rhombus.

GHIJ is a parallelogram, since its opposite sides are parallel. If diagonal $\overline{HJ}$ bisects $\angle$GHI and $\angle$GJI, then it is a rhombus.

Step 1: Prove that GHIJ is a parallelogram.

Since $\overline{GH} \parallel \overline{JI}$ and $\overline{HI} \parallel \overline{GJ}$, both pairs of opposite sides are parallel, making GHIJ a parallelogram.

Step 2: Prove that GHIJ is a rhombus.

Since the angle measures in a triangle add to 180°, and GJH is a triangle:

m$\angle$GJH + 50° + 65° = 180°
m$\angle$GJH = 65°

Therefore, $\overline{HJ}$ bisects $\angle$GJI.

Since the total angle measures in a triangle equal 180°, and JHI is a triangle:

$m\angle JHI + 50° + 65° = 180°$

$m\angle JHI = 65°$

Therefore, $\overline{HJ}$ bisects $\angle GHI$.

Since a diagonal of GHIJ bisects a pair of opposite angles, it is a rhombus.

RECTANGLES

A **RECTANGLE** is a parallelogram with four right angles.

If a parallelogram is a rectangle, then its diagonals are congruent.

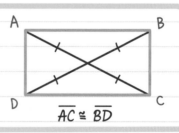

$\overline{AC} \cong \overline{BD}$

The converse of this is also true:

If a parallelogram has congruent diagonals, then it is a rectangle.

EXAMPLE: Two wooden braces on a rectangular fence have lengths of LN = (5x + 2) ft and KM = (20x – 18) ft. Find the approximate lengths of the braces.

close, but not exact

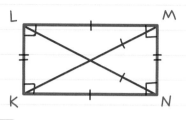

Since the fence is in the shape of a rectangle, the diagonals are congruent.

LN = KM

$5x + 2 = 20x - 18$

$20 = 15x$

$x = \dfrac{20}{15}$

$= \dfrac{(20 \div 5)}{(15 \div 5)}$ Reduce by dividing numerator and denominator by 5.

$x = \dfrac{4}{3}$

The lengths of the diagonals are:

LN = 5x + 2	KM = 20x − 18
$= 5(\frac{4}{3}) + 2$	$= 20(\frac{4}{3}) − 18$
$= \frac{26}{3} \approx 8.7$	$= \frac{26}{3} \approx 8.7$

The lengths of the wooden braces are approximately 8.7 ft.

SQUARES

A **SQUARE** is a parallelogram with four right angles and four congruent sides.

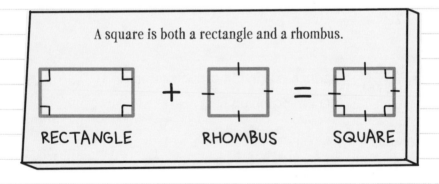

A square is both a rectangle and a rhombus.

RECTANGLE + RHOMBUS = SQUARE

EXAMPLE: Find the values of x and y in square ABCD.

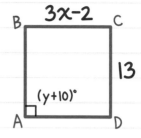

Since squares have four congruent sides,

BC = CD

$3x - 2 = 13$

$3x = 15$

$x = 5$

Since squares also have four right angles,

$m\angle A = 90°$

$y + 10 = 90$

$y = 80$

CHECK YOUR KNOWLEDGE

For questions 1-5, state whether the parallelograms are rectangles, rhombuses, and/or squares.

1.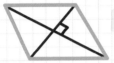

2.

3.

4.

5.

6. Determine if ABCD is a rhombus.

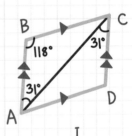

7. Find the value of x in rhombus GHIJ.

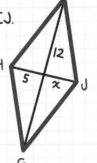

8. Find the value of x in rhombus ABCD.

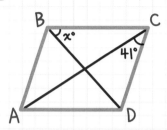

9. LN = 24x – 30 and KM = 17x – 2 in rectangle KLMN. Find the values of x, LN, and KM.

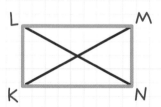

10. Find the values of x and y in square TUVW.

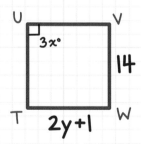

ANSWERS

CHECK YOUR ANSWERS

1. rhombus

2. rhombus and rectangle

3. rhombus, rectangle, and square

4. rhombus

5. rectangle

6. Yes. It is a parallelogram and has one diagonal that bisects a pair of opposite angles.

7. $x = 5$

8. $x = 49$

9. $24x - 30 = 17x - 2$; therefore, $x = 4$, LN = 66, KM = 66

10. $3x = 90$; therefore, $x = 30$
$2y + 1 = 14$; therefore, $y = \dfrac{13}{2}$

Chapter 18

TRAPEZOIDS AND KITES

Trapezoids and kites are quadrilaterals that are not parallelograms.

TRAPEZOIDS

A **TRAPEZOID** is a quadrilateral with exactly one pair of parallel sides.

The parallel sides are called bases, and the nonparallel sides are called legs.

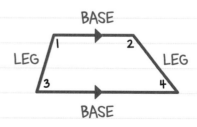

The angles adjacent to a base are called base angles. ∠1 and ∠2 are base angles to the top base and ∠3 and ∠4 are base angles to the bottom base.

The **MIDSEGMENT** of a trapezoid is a line segment that bisects both legs.

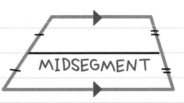

MIDSEGMENT

The midsegment of a trapezoid is parallel to the bases. Its length is found by averaging the lengths of the two bases (adding up the lengths of the two bases and dividing by two).

Length of midsegment = $\dfrac{b_1 + b_2}{2}$

b_1

MIDSEGMENT

b_2

OR, LIKE THIS: $\dfrac{1}{2}(b_1 + b_2)$

EXAMPLE: The beams of a bridge are constructed in the shape of a trapezoid. The base measures 230 ft and the center beam is 150 ft long. What is the length of the top beam?

Top beam = b_1
Bottom beam = b_2

b_2 = 230 ft

The midsegment = 150 ft

Length of midsegment = $\frac{b_1 + b_2}{2}$

$150 = \frac{b_1 + 230}{2}$

$150 \times 2 = \frac{b_1 + 230}{2} \times 2$ Multiply both sides by 2.

$300 = b_1 + 230$

$b_1 = 70$

The top beam is 70 ft long.

ISOSCELES TRAPEZOIDS

An **ISOSCELES TRAPEZOID** has congruent legs.

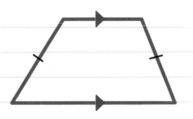

> If a trapezoid is isosceles, then it has two pairs of congruent base angles.

If $\overline{AB} \cong \overline{CD}$, then $\angle B \cong \angle C$ and $\angle A \cong \angle D$.

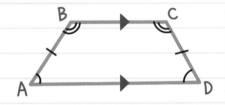

EXAMPLE: Find m$\angle$Q, m$\angle$R, and m$\angle$S.

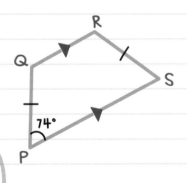

Since $\overleftrightarrow{QR} \parallel \overleftrightarrow{PS}$, $\angle Q$ and $\angle P$ are supplementary (Same-Side Interior Angles Theorem).

m$\angle$Q + m$\angle$P = 180°
m$\angle$Q + 74° = 180°
m$\angle$Q = 106°

When two lines that are parallel are intersected by a transversal, the same-side interior angles are supplementary.

Since base angles are congruent in isosceles trapezoids,

$m\angle R = m\angle Q = 106°$
$m\angle S = m\angle P = 74°$

A trapezoid is isosceles if and only if its diagonals are congruent.

$\overline{AB} \cong \overline{CD}$ if and only if $\overline{AC} \cong \overline{BD}$.

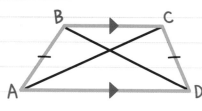

EXAMPLE: Determine if trapezoid WXYZ is isosceles.

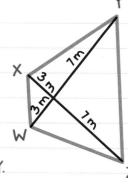

$XZ = 3 + 7 = 10$

$WY = 3 + 7 = 10$

Since $XZ = 10$ and $WY = 10$, $XZ = WY$.

Since the diagonals are congruent, the trapezoid is isosceles.

KITES

A **KITE** is a quadrilateral with two pairs of adjacent congruent sides.

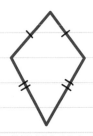

If a quadrilateral is a kite, then its diagonals are perpendicular.

If a quadrilateral is a kite, then at least one pair of opposite angles are congruent.

EXAMPLE: Given kite ABCD, where $\overline{AB} \cong \overline{BC}$ and $\overline{AD} \cong \overline{CD}$, prove $\angle A \cong \angle C$.

It is given that $\overline{AB} \cong \overline{BC}$ and $\overline{AD} \cong \overline{CD}$. Also $\overline{BD} \cong \overline{BD}$. By SSS, $\triangle ABD \cong \triangle CBD$. Since congruent triangles have corresponding congruent angles, $\angle A \cong \angle C$.

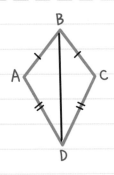

side-side-side triangle theorem

TYPES OF QUADRILATERALS

QUADRILATERALS
Polygons with 4 sides

PARALLELOGRAMS

Opposite sides are ∥
Opposite sides are ≅
Opposite angles are ≅
Consecutive angles are supplementary
Diagonals bisect each other
Diagonals form two ≅ triangles

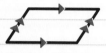

RHOMBUSES
4 ≅ sides
Diagonals are ⊥
Diagonals bisect opposite angles

SQUARES
A rhombus and a rectangle

RECTANGLES
4 right angles
Diagonals are ≅

TRAPEZOIDS
1 pair of ∥ sides

KITES
2 pairs of adjacent ≅ sides
1 pair of opposite angles are ≅
Diagonals are ⊥

ISOSCELES TRAPEZOIDS
Legs are ≅
Base angles are ≅
Diagonals are ≅

CHECK YOUR KNOWLEDGE

1. Name the bases, legs, base angles, and midsegment in quadrilateral PQRS.

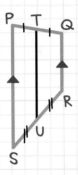

2. Find the value of b.

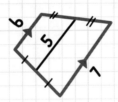

3. Find the value of x.

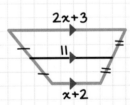

4. Find m∠P and m∠R.

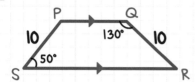

5. Find the missing angle measures in isosceles trapezoid GHIJ.

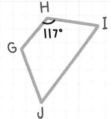

6. The diagonals of an isosceles trapezoid have lengths 7x + 23 and 15x + 19. Find the value of x.

7. Find the value of y.

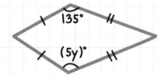

ANSWERS

CHECK YOUR ANSWERS

1. Bases: $\overline{PS}$ and $\overline{QR}$; legs: $\overline{PQ}$ and $\overline{SR}$; base angles: $\angle P$ and $\angle S$, $\angle Q$ and $\angle R$; midsegment: $\overline{TU}$

2. $\dfrac{b+7}{2} = 5$; therefore, $b = 3$

3. $\dfrac{2x+3+x+2}{2} = 11$; therefore, $x = \dfrac{17}{3}$

4. $m\angle P = 130°$, $m\angle R = 50°$

5. $m\angle G = 117°$, $m\angle I = 63°$, $m\angle J = 63°$

6. $7x + 23 = 15x + 19$; therefore, $x = \dfrac{1}{2}$

7. $135 = 5y$; therefore, $y = 27$

Chapter 19

ANGLE MEASURES IN POLYGONS

A **POLYGON** is a closed plane figure with at least three straight sides. Polygons are named by the number of sides they have.

# OF SIDES	NAME	# OF SIDES	NAME
3	Triangle	7	Heptagon
4	Quadrilateral	8	Octagon
5	Pentagon	9	Nonagon
6	Hexagon	10	Decagon

INTERIOR ANGLE MEASURES

The interior angles of a polygon are
found inside the boundaries of the shape.

The interior angles of a triangle add
up to 180°.

This works for all triangles.

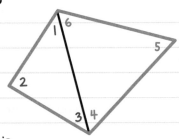

45°

90°

45°

90 + 45 + 45 = 180

We can use this information to find the sum of the angle
measures in other polygons.

A quadrilateral can be made from two triangles.

The interior angles of each triangle is:

$m\angle 1 + m\angle 2 + m\angle 3 = 180°$

$m\angle 4 + m\angle 5 + m\angle 6 = 180°$

The sum of all the interior angles is:

$180° + 180° = 360°$ or $2 \times 180° = 360°$

The interior angles of a quadrilateral add up to 360°.
This is true for all quadrilaterals.

Rule: Each time you add a side to a polygon add another 180° to the total of the interior angle.

The same process can be used for any number of sides.

# OF SIDES	# OF TRIANGLES	SUM OF THE MEASURES OF INTERIOR ANGLES
3	1	$1 \times 180°$
4	2	$2 \times 180°$
5	3	$3 \times 180°$
n	$n - 2$	$(n - 2) \times 180°$

Subtract 2 from the number of sides and the difference tells how many triangles make up the polygon.

Sum of Interior Angles = $(n - 2) \times 180°$

This means "the number of triangles that make up the polygon times 180°."

EXAMPLE: Find the sum of the measures of the interior angles of a decagon.

A DECAGON has 10 sides.

The sum of the measures of the interior angles is:

$(n - 2)180° = (10 - 2)180° = (8)180° = 1440°$

EXAMPLE: Find m∠k in the pentagon.

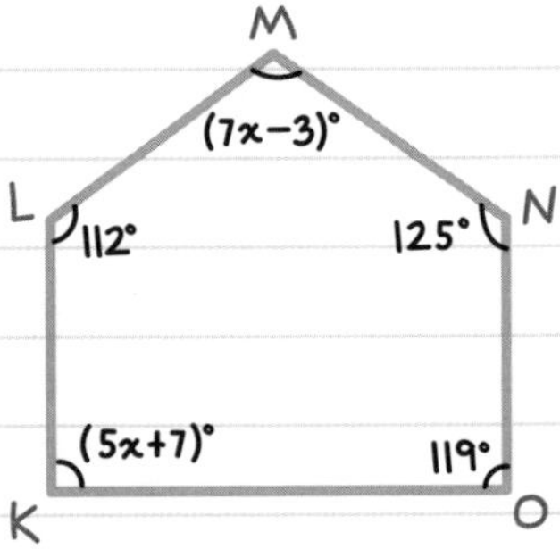

First find the sum of the angle measures of a pentagon:

$(n - 2)180° = (5 - 2)180° = (3)180 = 540°$

Since the angles' measures in the pentagon add up to 540°:

m∠K + m∠L + m∠M + m∠N + m∠O = 540°
$(5x + 7) + 112 + (7x - 3) + 125 + 119 = 540$
$12x + 360 = 540$
$12x = 180$
$x = 15$

Therefore, m∠k = $(5x + 7)° = [5(15) + 7]° = 82°$

EXTERIOR ANGLE MEASURE

The exterior angle is the angle between the side of
a polygon and a line extended from the next side.

POLYGON EXTERIOR ANGLE-SUM THEOREM

The sum of the exterior angles always stays the same,
no matter how many sides the polygon has.

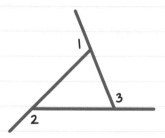

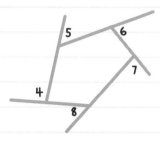

$m\angle 1 + m\angle 2 + m\angle 3 = 360°$

$m\angle 4 + m\angle 5 + m\angle 6 +$
$m\angle 7 + m\angle 8 = 360°$

The exterior angles of a polygon add up to 360°.

Note: Use only one exterior angle at each vertex.

The two exterior angles at each vertex have the same measure.

∠2 and ∠3 are both exterior angles for ∠1.

∠2 ≅ ∠3

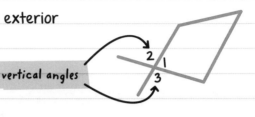

vertical angles

EXAMPLE: Find the value of x.

Since exterior angle measures add to 360°,

$(10x+4)°$

$35°$

$(3x-14)°$

$59°$

$35 + (10x + 4) + 59 + (3x - 14) = 360$

$13x + 84 = 360$

$13x = 276$

$x = 21.2°$

A REGULAR POLYGON has all congruent angles and all congruent sides. To find the measure of each interior angle in a regular polygon, divide the total angle measure by the number of sides.

EXAMPLE: Find the measure of each interior angle in a regular heptagon.

FIND THE TOTAL ANGLE MEASURE AND DIVIDE BY 7!

A heptagon has 7 sides, the interior angle measures add to:

$(n - 2)180° = (7 - 2)180° = (5)180° = 900°$

A regular heptagon has 7 congruent angles, each angle has a measure of:

$$\frac{900°}{7} \approx 128.6°$$

1. Find the sum of the measures of the interior angles of a 13-sided polygon.

2. Find the sum of the measures of the interior angles of the following polygon.

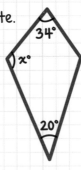

3. Find the value of x.

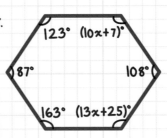

123° (10x+7)°

87°   108°

163° (13x+25)°

4. Find the value of x in the kite.

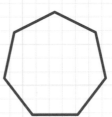

34°

x°

20°

5. What is the measure of the sum of the exterior angles in a pentagon?

6. What is the measure of the sum of the exterior angles in the quadrilateral?

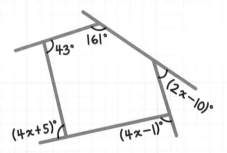

7. Find the value of x.

43°   161°

$(4x+5)°$

$(4x-1)°$

$(2x-10)°$

8. Find the measure of each interior angle in a regular pentagon.

1. (13 − 2)180 = 1980°

2. (7 − 2)180 = 900°

3. 87 + 123 + 10x + 7 + 108 + 13x + 25 + 163 = (6 − 2)180; therefore, x = 9

4. 34 + x + 20 + x = (4 − 2)180; therefore, x = 153°

5. 360°

6. 360°

7. 4x + 5 + 137 + 19 + 2x − 10 + 4x − 1 = 360; therefore, x = 21°

8. $\dfrac{(5-2)180}{5}$; therefore, each angle measures 108°

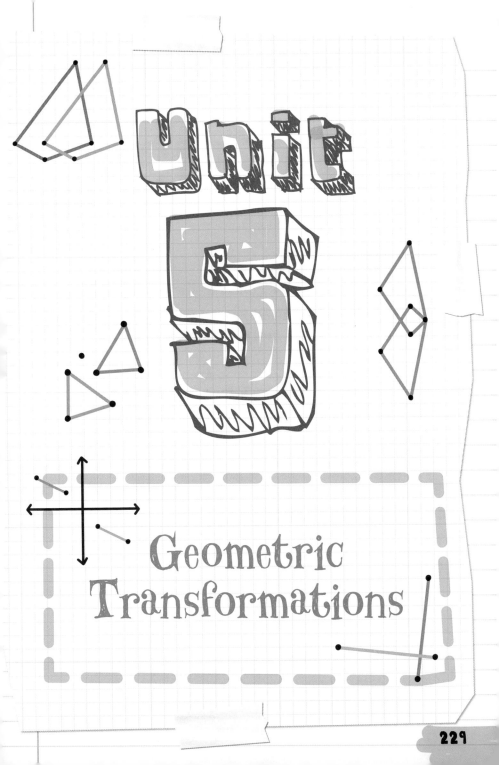

Unit 5

Geometric Transformations

Chapter 20

REFLECTIONS

RIGID MOTIONS

Figures on a coordinate plane can be moved in any direction, which results in new figures and new positions. The action of moving a figure is called a **TRANSFORMATION**.

In a transformation, the original figure is called the **PREIMAGE**, and the new figure is called the **IMAGE**.

If the shape and the size of a figure remain the same in a transformation, the movement is called a **RIGID MOTION** or **CONGRUENCE TRANSFORMATION**.

There are three types of rigid motions:

REFLECTIONS

TRANSLATIONS

ROTATIONS

A **REFLECTION** is a type
of transformation that flips
an image over a line, so that
the image appears backward,
like in a mirror.

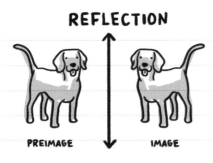

REFLECTION

PREIMAGE   IMAGE

A reflection is a rigid motion: The shape and size of the
image do not change.

> ## REFLECTION
> a movement that maps (moves) all points of a
> shape so that each point on the image moves to
> the opposite side of the reflecting line and is the
> same distance from its point in the preimage.

△ABC is the **preimage**.
△A'B'C' is the **image**.

The mark (') is called
PRIME.

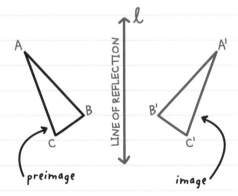

preimage   image

The prime mark (') represents the new mapping point of
the preimage.

△A'B'C' is read: "triangle A prime, B prime, C prime."

Line ℓ is the LINE OF REFLECTION. We say △ABC is reflected across line ℓ.

If we were to fold our paper along the line of reflection, the two triangles would match up perfectly.

The reflection MAPS each point on △ABC to a corresponding point on △A'B'C'.

matches

A maps to A'   B maps to B'   C maps to C'

Reflections have OPPOSITE ORIENTATIONS (reverse arrangement of points). For example, if A to B to C are arranged in a clockwise order in the preimage, then A' to B' to C' are arranged in a counterclockwise (opposite) order in the image.

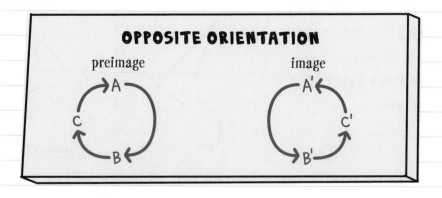

REFLECTIONS ON THE COORDINATE PLANE

Reflections can be shown on the coordinate plane.

In an ordered pair, x, y names the coordinates of a point in the coordinate system.

The x position names the location along the x-axis (horizontal), and the y position gives the location along the y-axis (vertical).

For example, to plot $(3, 4)$:

1. Start at the origin, location $(0, 0)$.

2. Move 3 units horizontally (to the right). This is the x-coordinate.

3. Move 4 units vertically (up). This is the y-coordinate.

*If the x-coordinate is negative, move left, and if the y-coordinate is negative, move down.

The red line is the line of reflection. This line of reflection is written as $x = 1$.

$x = 1$ means that all points on this line of reflection have an x-coordinate of 1.

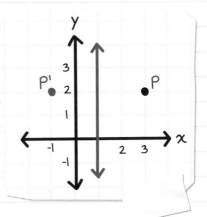

For example $(1, -1)$, $(1, 0)$, $(1, 2)$

Point P, written as P(3, 2), is 2 units to the right of the line of reflection. Point P', written as P'(-1, 2), is 2 units to the left of the line of reflection.

P(3, 2) maps to P'(-1, 2). This is written as:

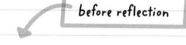
before reflection

P(3, 2) → P'(-1, 2)   The arrow is read as "maps to":
                         P(3, 2) **maps to** P'(-1, 2).

after reflection

The line of reflection is the PERPENDICULAR BISECTOR of the line segment that connects the corresponding points of the image and preimage.

$\overline{PP'}$ connects the points of the image and preimage.

The line $x = 1$ (the line of reflection) is the perpendicular bisector of $\overline{PP'}$.

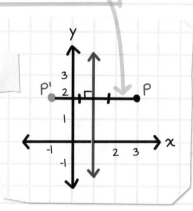

In this image lines $\overline{RR'}$, $\overline{SS'}$, and $\overline{TT'}$ connect the corresponding points of the image and preimage.

$\triangle RST \rightarrow \triangle R'S'T'$, the line of reflection, line k is the PERPENDICULAR BISECTOR of $\overline{RR'}$, $\overline{SS'}$, and $\overline{TT'}$.

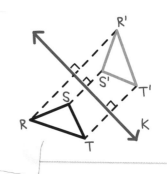

EXAMPLE: Reflect the quadrilateral on the coordinate plane across line $y = 3$.

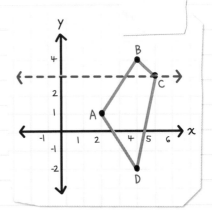

REFLECT EACH VERTEX POINT, AND THEN CONNECT THE VERTICES.

The line $y = 3$ is a horizontal line. All points on the line have a y-coordinate of 3.

Since the line of reflection is the perpendicular bisector of $\overline{AA'}$, it will be an equal distance from A and A'.

Count the number of units from A to the line of reflection, and place point A' the same number of units on the opposite side of the line.

- A is at point (2, 1), 2 units **below** the line of reflection.
  A' will be at point (2, 5), 2 units **above** the line of reflection.
    A(2, 1) → A'(2, 5).

- B is at point (4, 4), 1 unit **above** the line of reflection.
  B' will be 1 unit **below** the line of reflection.
    B(4, 4) → B'(4, 2).

Each point maps to the opposite side of the line of reflection.

- Point C(5, 3), is on the line of reflection. Since there is no distance, C' will be at the same point.
    C(5, 3) → C'(5, 3).

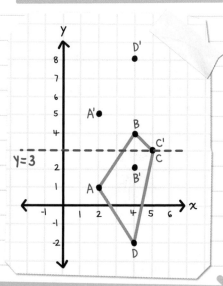

- Point D(4, –2) is 5 units *below* the line of reflection. D' will be 5 units *above* the line of reflection.

  D(4, –2) → D(4, 8).

Connect the vertices.

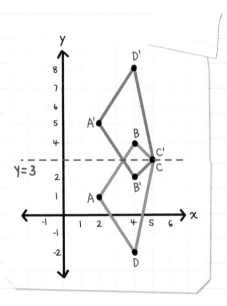

There are three common lines of reflection: the x-axis, y-axis, and line $y = x$. Each has a rule that can be used to plot points in an image.

LINE OF REFLECTION	RULE	EXAMPLE
x-axis	$(x, y) \rightarrow (x, -y)$ Multiply the y-coordinate by –1.	
y-axis	$(x, y) \rightarrow (-x, y)$ Multiply the x-coordinate by –1.	
$y = x$ the same as $y = 1x + 0$	$(x, y) \rightarrow (y, x)$ Reverse the order of the coordinates.	

EXAMPLE: Reflect $\overline{AB}$ across the x-axis.

Rule: $(x, y) \rightarrow (x, -y)$

$A(1, 1) \rightarrow A'(1, -1)$

$B(4, 3) \rightarrow B'(4, -3)$

1. Plot the image points.

2. Draw a line to connect the points.

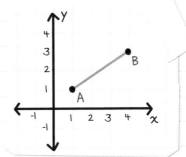

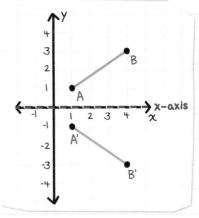

EXAMPLE: Reflect $\overline{AB}$ across the line $y = x$.

Rule: $(x, y) \rightarrow (y, x)$

$A(1, 1) \rightarrow A'(1, 1)$

$B(4, 3) \rightarrow B'(3, 4)$

1. Plot the image points.

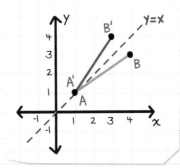

2. Draw a line to connect the points.

239

CHECK YOUR KNOWLEDGE

1. What is a geometric transformation?

2. What is a reflection?

3. Complete the sentence.

   In a reflection, a point P and its image P' are the same distance to the _____.

For questions 4 and 5, draw the image of $\overline{PQ}$, where P(-1, -2) and Q(-2, 0) are reflected across the following lines.

4. $x = 1$

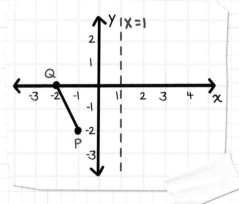

5. $y = -1$

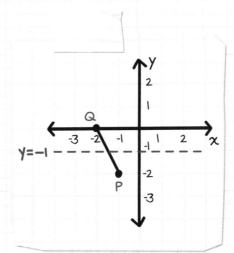

CHECK YOUR ANSWERS

1. A geometric transformation changes the shape, size, or position of a figure (preimage) to create a new figure (the image).

2. A reflection is a type of rigid motion that flips an image over a line.

3. Line of reflection

4.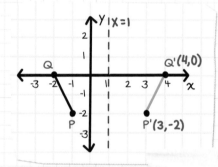

5.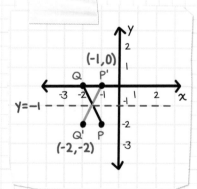

Chapter 21

TRANSLATIONS

A **TRANSLATION** is a type
of rigid motion that slides
a figure a certain distance
to the left or right, up or down,
or both horizontally and
vertically.

Each point in the figure
slides the same distance
in the same direction.

The figure's shape, size,
and orientation remain
the same.

TRANSLATIONS ON A COORDINATE PLANE

A translation on the coordinate plane moves all the points in the image the same distance and in the same direction. In △ABC, each point moves 4 units right (*x*-axis) and 2 units up (*y*-axis).

moves 2 units along the *y*-axis

moves 4 units along the *x*-axis

Translations can be defined (described) using a TRANSLATION VECTOR, which states how many units each point in the graph moves in the translation.

The translation vector is (4, 2).

4 units in the x-direction

2 units in the y-direction

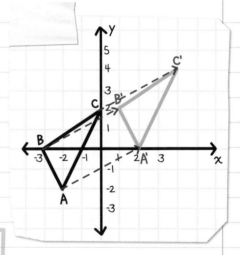

> If a translation vector moves a point a units
> along the x-axis and b units along the y-axis,
> then the translation vector is (a, b).
>
> The **translation rule** is:
>
> $(x, y) \rightarrow (x + a, y + b)$,
> where (a, b) is the translation vector.

For example: A translation vector of $(-1, 3)$ has a translation rule of $(x, y) \rightarrow (x - 1, y + 3)$. This moves each point 1 unit to the left and 3 units up.

With that translation vector, the point $(5, -2)$ maps to:

$(5, -2) \rightarrow (5 - 1, -2 + 3)$ which is $(4, 1)$

$5 - 1 = 4$
$-2 + 3 = 1$

The point $(-4, 7)$ maps to:

$(-4, 7) \rightarrow (-4 - 1, 7 + 3)$ or $(-5, 10)$

$-4 - 1 = -5$
$7 + 3 = 10$

EXAMPLE: What are the translation vector and translation rule that describe the translation of P → P'?

P moves 3 units right and 2 units up to P':

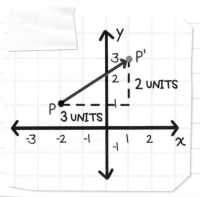

The translation vector is (3, 2).

The translation rule is:
$(x, y) \rightarrow (x + 3, y + 2)$.

EXAMPLE: What are the translation vector and translation rule that describe the translation of quadrilateral FGHI → F'G'H'I'?

Each point moves 4 units right and 3 units up.

The translation vector is (4, 3).

The translation rule is $(x, y) \rightarrow (x + 4, y + 3)$.

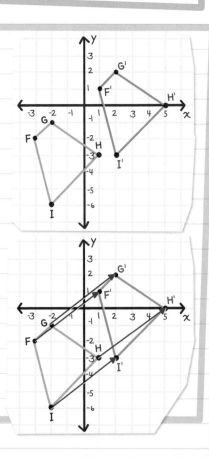

EXAMPLE: Graph the translation of △LMN, given a translation vector of (–2, 5).

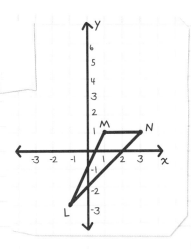

Move each vertex 2 units to the left and 5 units up.

Rule: $(x, y) \rightarrow (x - 2, y + 5)$

Plot the points.

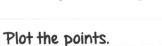

$$\begin{matrix} & (-1 - 2) & (-3 + 5) \\ L(-1, -3) & \rightarrow & L'(-3, 2) \end{matrix}$$

$$\begin{matrix} & (1 - 2) & (1 + 5) \\ M(1, 1) & \rightarrow & M'(-1, 6) \end{matrix}$$

$$\begin{matrix} & (3 - 2) & (1 + 5) \\ N(3, 1) & \rightarrow & N'(1, 6) \end{matrix}$$

Connect the points.

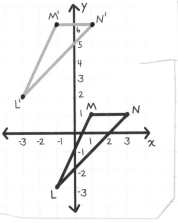

HELP ME! I'M IN MATH CLASS AND HAVE TO TRANSLATE A TRIANGLE.

THAT'S EASY. TRIANGULO.

NO! I MEAN THE GEOMETRICAL TRANSLATION.

GEOMETRICO.

FORGET IT.

1. After translating any figure, what always remains the same about the figure?

2. What is the translation vector that translates D to D'?

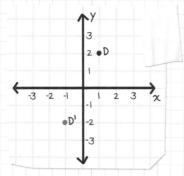

For questions 3-6, state whether the following graph shows a translation or not.

3.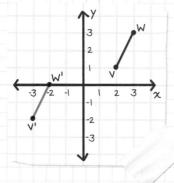

4.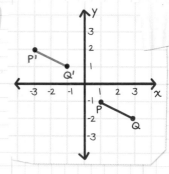

5.

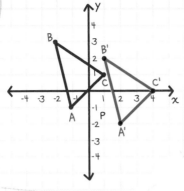

6.

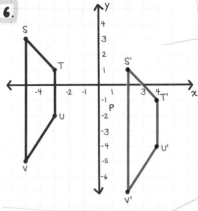

7. What is the translation vector in question 6?

8. What is the translation rule that describes the translation in question 6?

9. Graph the translation of △EFG, given a translation vector of (–3, 1).

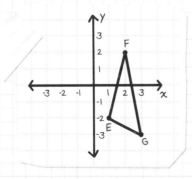

10. Graph the translation of the quadrilateral below, given a translation vector of (2, 0).

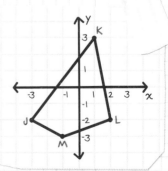

ANSWERS

CHECK YOUR ANSWERS

1. The figure's shape, size, and orientation

2. (−2, −4)

3. Yes, (−5, −3)

4. Yes, (−4, 3)

5. Yes, (3, −1)

6. Yes

7. (7, −2)

8. $(x, y) \to (x + 7, y − 2)$

9.

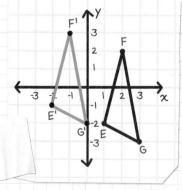

10.

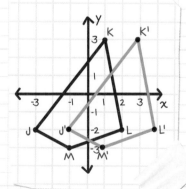

Chapter 22

ROTATIONS

ROTATIONS are transformations that turn a figure around a fixed point. Rotations are rigid motions. The shape, size, and measures of angles of the figure stay the same, but the orientation changes.

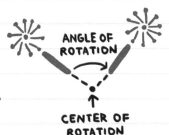

A rotation includes a:

- **CENTER OF ROTATION** —the point around which a figure is turned. The center of rotation can be located outside the figure or anywhere inside or along the figure.

- **ANGLE OF ROTATION** —the number of degrees each point on the figure is turned. Rotation can be clockwise or counterclockwise.

> clockwise = turns right
> counterclockwise = turns left

Any point and its image are the same distance from
the center of rotation.

EXAMPLE: Point T is rotated $x°$ counterclockwise
about point R.

The center of rotation is R.
The angle of rotation is $x°$.

T and T' are the same distance
from the center of rotation, R.

This is written as: RT = RT'.

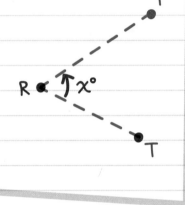

DRAWING ROTATIONS

You can use a protractor and a ruler to draw a rotation about a point.

To rotate point K 70° counterclockwise about point P:

Step 1: Draw a line from P to K.

Step 2: Use a protractor to draw a 70° angle counterclockwise, left, from $\overline{PK}$.

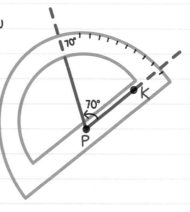

Step 3: Measure the length of $\overline{PK}$. Draw a new point labeled K' the same distance from P on the new line.

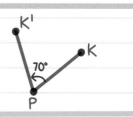

Rotating a Square

To rotate a square 90° clockwise about the center of rotation, P, each point on the square must rotate 90° clockwise.

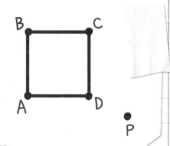

Distance of A to P is the same as distance of A' to P.

Since AP = A'P, think of the line AP rotating 90° clockwise.

Use a protractor to draw a 90° angle.

Plot a point at the location.

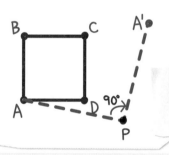

Repeat the same for vertices B, C, and D. Then connect the points.

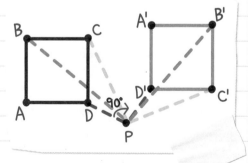

EXAMPLE: Draw the image of △ABC rotated 110° counterclockwise about point Q.

• Q

Rotate each vertex, one at a time, using a protractor and ruler.

To rotate Point A:

1. Draw a line from point Q to point A.

2. Use a protractor to draw a 110° angle.

3. Measure the length of $\overline{QA}$.

4. Draw a point A' the same distance on the new line.

Rotate points B and C in the same way. Connect points A', B', and C'.

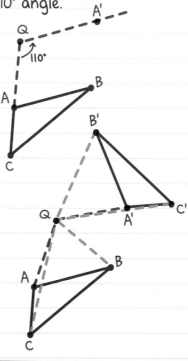

FINDING THE ANGLE OF ROTATION

You can find an angle of rotation with a protractor and ruler. A figure is rotated counterclockwise about a point located at (–1, 0). Point (2, 2) is rotated to (–3, 3).

To find the angle of rotation:

1. Draw a line from the center of rotation through each point (2, 2) and (–3, 3).

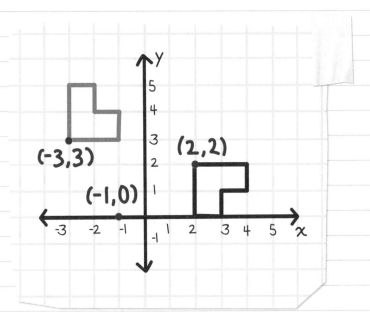

2. Use a protractor to measure the angle.

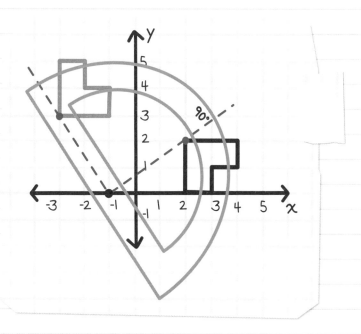

The angle of rotation is 90°.

ROTATIONS ON THE COORDINATE PLANE

Three common rotation angles used on a coordinate plane are 90°, 180°, and 270°. There are rules that we can use for these rotations about the origin.

The origin is the point (0, 0). It's where the *x*-axis and *y*-axis meet.

ANGLE OF ROTATION	RULE	EXAMPLE counterclockwise about the origin
90°	$(x, y) \rightarrow (-y, x)$ Multiply the y-coordinate by –1, and reverse the order of the coordinates.	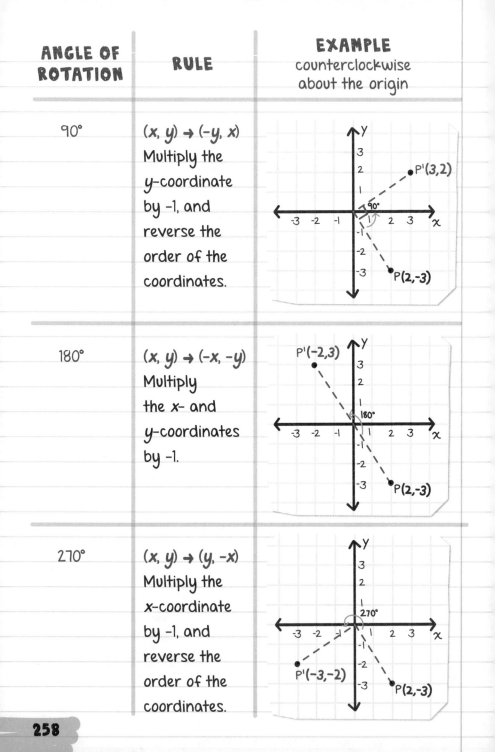
180°	$(x, y) \rightarrow (-x, -y)$ Multiply the x- and y-coordinates by –1.	
270°	$(x, y) \rightarrow (y, -x)$ Multiply the x-coordinate by –1, and reverse the order of the coordinates.	

EXAMPLE: Rotate the triangle 180° about the origin.

First rotate each point 180° about the origin:

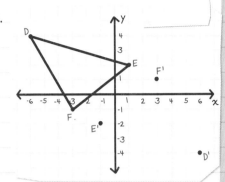

Rule: $(x, y) \rightarrow (-x, -y)$

$D(-6, 4) \rightarrow D'(6, -4)$

$E(1, 2) \rightarrow E'(-1, -2)$

$F(-3, -1) \rightarrow F'(3, 1)$

Multiply the x and y coordinates by -1.

Next plot the new points.

Then connect all the points.

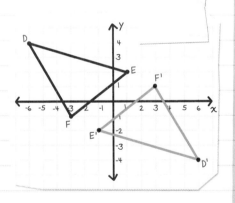

When the rotation is 180°, it doesn't matter if the direction is clockwise or counterclockwise, because the image will end up in the same place.

FINDING THE CENTER OF ROTATION

Steps for finding the center of rotation:

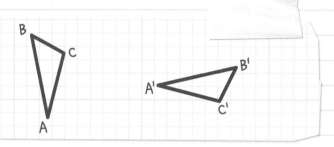

---

1. Draw a line to connect A and A'.

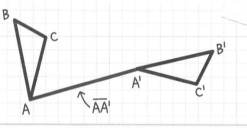

---

2. Construct a perpendicular bisector through $\overline{AA'}$.

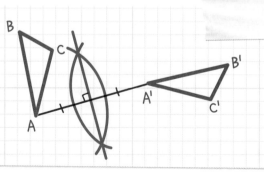

3. Repeat steps 1 and 2 on points B and B!

The intersection of the two perpendicular bisectors is
the center of rotation.

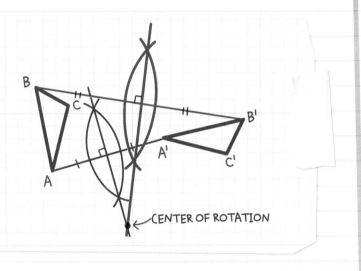

If we draw the perpendicular bisector of $\overline{CC'}$, it will also
pass through the point of rotation.

1. **True or False:** In a rotation, the shape, size, and orientation of a figure remain the same.

2. Rotate the triangle 90° counterclockwise about the center of rotation, R.

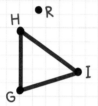

3. Use a protractor to draw the rotation of △GHI 60° counterclockwise about point R.

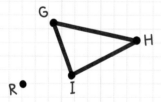

4. Draw the center of rotation that rotates △ABC to △A'B'C.

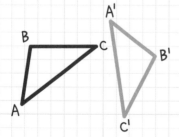

Use the graphed line below to answer questions **5** and **6**:

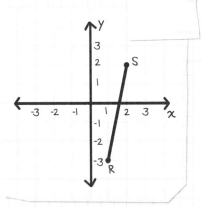

5. $\overline{RS}$ is rotated 180° counterclockwise about the origin. What are the coordinates of R' and S'?

6. Draw the rotation of $\overline{RS}$ 270° counterclockwise about the origin.

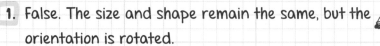

CHECK YOUR ANSWERS

1. False. The size and shape remain the same, but the orientation is rotated.

2.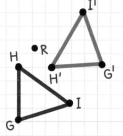

3.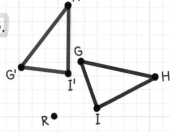

4.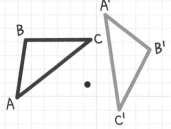

5. R'(-1, 3), S'(-2, -2)

6.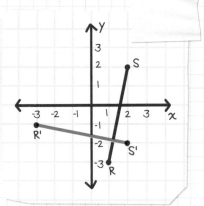

Chapter 23

COMPOSITIONS

COMPOSITIONS OF TRANSFORMATIONS

COMPOSITIONS OF TRANSFORMATIONS combine two or more transformations to form a new transformation.

In a composition, you perform each transformation on the image from the previous transformation.

Example of a composition of transformation: The green fish is reflected to the pink fish, and then translated to the yellow fish.

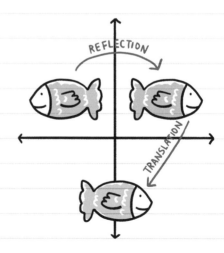

EXAMPLE: Draw the graph of $\overline{JK}$ rotated 90° counterclockwise about the origin, and then reflected across line $y = 1$.

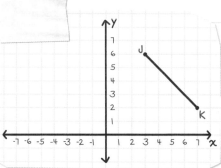

Step 1: Rotate $\overline{JK}$ 90° counterclockwise about the origin.

Use the rule $(x, y) \rightarrow (-y, x)$ to find the endpoints.

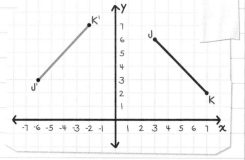

- $J(3, 6) \rightarrow J'(-6, 3)$
- $K(7, 2) \rightarrow K'(-2, 7)$

Connect the endpoints.

Label the points with double prime (″) when an image is reflected a second time.

Step 2: Reflect $\overline{J'K'}$ across line $y = 1$.

J' is 2 units above $y = 1$, so place J″ 2 units below $y = 1$.

K' is 6 units above $y = 1$, so place K″ 6 units below $y = 1$.

Connect the endpoints.

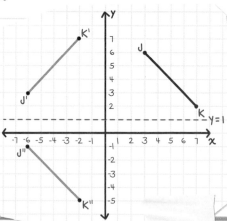

COMPOSITIONS OF TRANSLATIONS

A **COMPOSITION OF TRANSLATIONS** combines two or more translations.

Example of a composition of translations: The yellow dog is translated to the pink dog, and then translated to the blue dog.

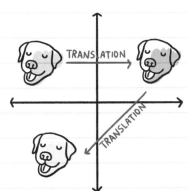

In this image:

△A is translated to △B.
△B is translated to △C.

SO, △A IS TRANSLATED TO △C.

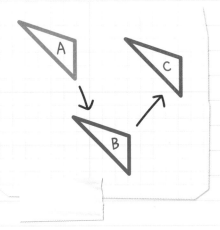

The composition of two translations is another translation.

EXAMPLE: Describe the transformation from $\overline{DE}$ to $\overline{D''E''}$.

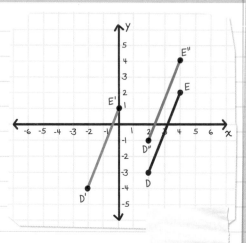

$\overline{DE}$ is translated along vector (−4, −1) to $\overline{D'E'}$.

$\overline{D'E'}$ is translated along vector (4, 3) to $\overline{D''E''}$.

This is a composition of two translations, so the result is a translation.

To find the translation vector, we can either:

- Count the units from D to D″ (or E to E″):

    D moves 0 units left/right and 2 units up to map to D″ (0, 2).

                        OR

- Add the coordinates of translation vectors (−4, −1) and (4, 3):

    (−4 + 4, −1 + 3) = (0, 2).

The transformation from $\overline{DE}$ to $\overline{D''E''}$ is a translation along vector (0, 2).

268

GLIDE REFLECTIONS

A **GLIDE REFLECTION** is a **translation** followed by a **reflection**. The reflection line is parallel to the direction of the translation.

Example of glide reflection:
The gray cat translates to
the purple cat, then reflects
to the green cat.

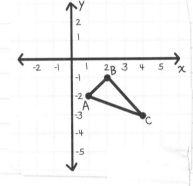

EXAMPLE: Draw the glide reflection where △ABC is translated along vector (−4, 0) and then reflected across the x-axis.

Translate along vector (−4, 0):

A(1, −2) → A'(−3, −2)

B(2,−1) → B'(−2, −1)

C(4, −3) → C'(0, −3)

Plot the points and connect the vertices.

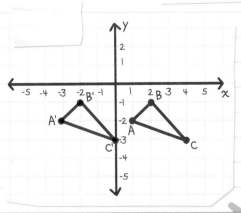

Reflect △A'B'C' across the x-axis:

A'(−3, −2) ➔ A''(−3, 2)

B'(−2, −1) ➔ B''(−2, 1)

C'(0, −3) ➔ C''(0, 3)

Plot the points and connect the vertices.

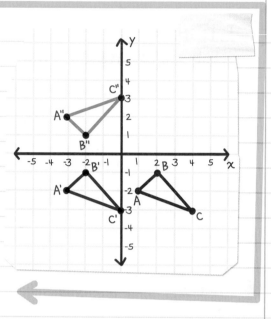

KEY PROPERTIES OF RIGID MOTIONS

Rigid Motion	Size stays the same?	Angle measure stays the same?	Orientation stays the same?
Reflection	Yes	Yes	No
Translation	Yes	Yes	Yes
Rotation	Yes	Yes	No
Glide reflection	Yes	Yes	No

COMPOSITIONS OF REFLECTIONS

Compositions of reflections have different rules, depending on whether the lines of reflection are parallel or intersect.

Parallel

A composition of **two reflections** across **two parallel lines** forms a translation.

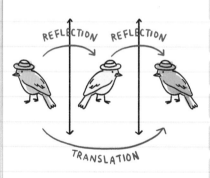

Intersect

A composition of **two reflections** across **two intersecting** lines forms a rotation about the point of intersection.

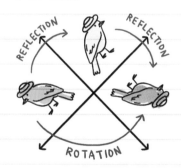

EXAMPLE: Reflect △LMN across the y-axis and then across x = 5. What is the single transformation that maps △LMN to △L"M"N"?

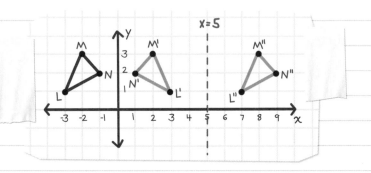

Reflecting across the y-axis gives △L'M'N'.

Reflecting △L'M'N' across x = 5 gives △L"M"N".

△LMN moves 10 units to the right to △L"M"N". Therefore, a translation along vector (10, 0) maps △LMN to △L"M"N".

THE Y-AXIS AND X = 5 ARE PARALLEL LINES. REFLECTING ACROSS TWO PARALLEL LINES FORMS A TRANSLATION.

EXAMPLE: Reflect quadrilateral PQRS across line ℓ and then m. What's the single transformation that maps PQRS to P"Q"R"S"?

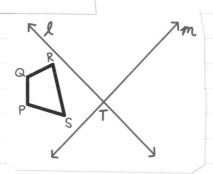

Reflecting PQRS across line ℓ gives P'Q'R'S'. Reflecting P'Q'R'S' across line m gives P"Q"R"S".

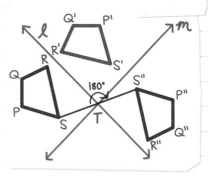

The result is a rotation around point T.

To find the angle of rotation, draw a line from S to T and S" to T. The angle between these two lines is 180°.

REFLECTING ACROSS TWO INTERSECTING LINES FORMS A ROTATION ABOUT THE POINT OF INTERSECTION.

The transformation is a rotation with center of rotation T and angle of rotation 180°.

SYMMETRY

If a figure is reflected across a line and the new figure
is unchanged, then the figure has **LINE SYMMETRY**.
The line of reflection is called the **LINE OF SYMMETRY**.
A line of symmetry divides a figure into two mirror images.

line of
symmetry

Sometimes a figure can have more than one line of
symmetry.

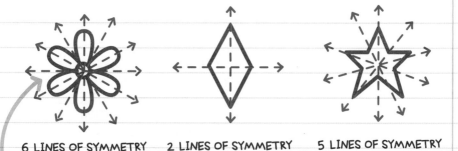

6 LINES OF SYMMETRY   2 LINES OF SYMMETRY   5 LINES OF SYMMETRY

There are six different lines along which you can reflect
the figure of the flower, and it will still look the same.

If a figure is rotated between 0° and 360° about its center and the figure remains the same, then it has **ROTATIONAL SYMMETRY**. The point of rotation is called the **CENTER OF ROTATION**.

This figure has rotational symmetry because it still looks the same after a rotation of 180°, which is less than one full turn (360°).

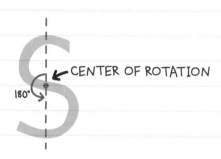

This figure has rotational symmetry because when rotated 90°, 180°, or 270°, it still looks the same. It maps to itself.

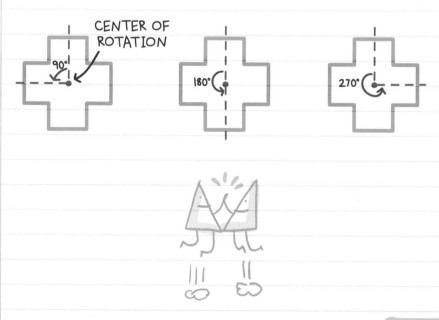

CHECK YOUR KNOWLEDGE

1. Graph the composition of point P(4, 1), rotated 270° counterclockwise about the origin to P', and then reflected across $y = -1$ to P".

2. **True or False:** If figure A is translated to figure B and figure B is translated to figure C, then figure A to figure C is a translation.

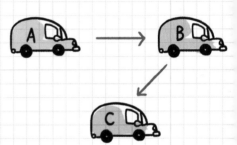

3. △GHI is translated along vector (7, –3) to △G'H'I'. △G'H'I' is translated along vector (–2, 13) to △G"H"I". Describe the transformation from △GHI to △G"H"I".

4. What is the composition of two reflections across two parallel lines?

5. Complete the sentence.
   A composition of two reflections across two _____ lines forms a rotation about the point of _____.

6. Graph the reflection of △PQR across l and then m. Describe the single transformation that maps △PQR to △P"Q"R".

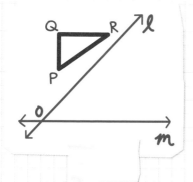

7. Does this figure have line symmetry? If so, how many lines of symmetry does it have?

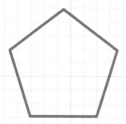

CHECK YOUR ANSWERS

1.

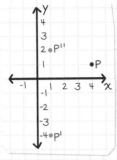

2. True

3. Translation along vector (5, 10) ← (Hint: Add the coordinates of translation vectors.)

4. A translation

5. intersecting, intersection

6. A rotation with center of rotation 0 and angle of rotation 270° counterclockwise (or 90° clockwise).

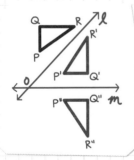

7. Yes, 5 lines of symmetry

Chapter 24

CONGRUENCE

Two figures are **CONGRUENT** if there is a sequence of rigid motions that maps one figure directly onto the other.

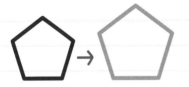

Not a rigid motion
(Side lengths get larger)
→ Not Congruent

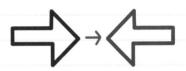

A rigid motion
(Reflection)
→ Congruent

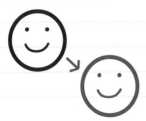

A rigid motion
(Translation)
→ Congruent

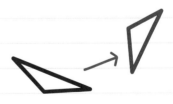

Not a rigid motion
(Angles and side
lengths change size)
→ Not Congruent

EXAMPLE: Is △ABC congruent to △DEF?

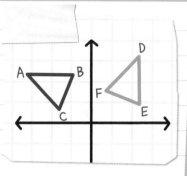

If there is a rigid motion that takes △ABC to △DEF, then the triangles are congruent.

A rotation of 270° counterclockwise maps △ABC to △DEF.

Therefore, △ABC is congruent to △DEF.

△ABC ≅ △DEF

Order is important when writing congruence statements.

△ABC ≅ △DEF means that A maps to D, B maps to E, and C maps to F.

△ABC ≅ △EFD is incorrect because A does not map to E.

Equivalent to △ABC ≅ △DEF:

△ACB ≅ △DFE   △DEF ≅ △ABC
△BAC ≅ △EDF   △EDF ≅ △BAC

EXAMPLE: Determine whether the two figures in the graph are congruent. If they are, write a congruence statement.

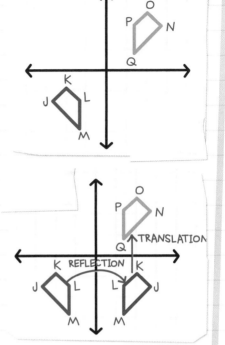

JKLM maps to NOPQ by a reflection across the y-axis, followed by a translation along vector.

Because a sequence of rigid motions maps JKLM to NOPQ, the figures are congruent.

The congruence statement is JKLM ≅ NOPQ.

EXAMPLE: Determine if △XYZ is congruent to △GHI.

If you trace △XYZ, and rotate, reflect, and/or translate it, you'll see it is not possible to map to △GHI. Because there is no sequence of rigid motions that maps △XYZ to △GHI, these triangles are not congruent.

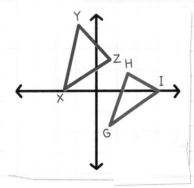

1. **True or False:** Two figures are congruent if there is a sequence of transformations that maps one figure onto another.

For questions 2 and 3, determine if the following images are congruent.

2.

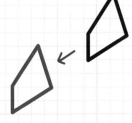

3.

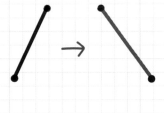

4. Write a congruence statement for the following congruent figures.

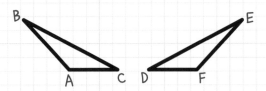

For questions 5–7, determine if the figures are congruent.
If they are, write a congruence statement.

5.

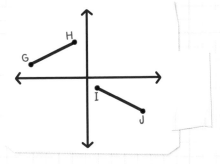

6.

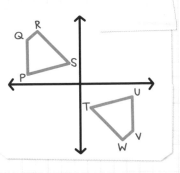

7.

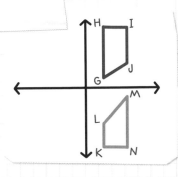

CHECK YOUR ANSWERS

1. False. Two figures are congruent if there is a sequence of **rigid motions** that maps one figure onto another. (Not all transformations are rigid motions.)

2. Yes. There is a rigid motion (translation) that maps one figure onto the other.

3. No. There is not a sequence of rigid motions that maps one line segment onto the other.

4. $\triangle ABC \cong \triangle FED$ (or $\triangle ACB \cong \triangle FDE$, $\triangle BAC \cong \triangle EFD$, $\triangle BCA \cong \triangle EDF$, $\triangle CAB \cong \triangle DFE$)

5. Yes, $\overline{GH} \cong \overline{IJ}$ or $\overline{HG} \cong \overline{JI}$

6. Yes, PQRS $\cong$ UVWT (or QRSP $\cong$ VWTU, RSPQ $\cong$ WTUV, SPQR $\cong$ TUVW, SRQP $\cong$ TWVU, RQPS $\cong$ WVUT, QPSR $\cong$ VUTW, PSRQ $\cong$ UTWV)

7. No. There is not a sequence of rigid motions that maps one figure onto the other.

Unit 6

Similarity

Chapter 25

RATIO AND PROPORTION

RATIO

A **RATIO** is a comparison of two or more quantities. It can be written in different ways.

When comparing a to b, we can write:

$$a \text{ to } b \quad \text{or} \quad a{:}b \quad \text{or} \quad \frac{a}{b}$$

a represents the first quantity.
b represents the second quantity.

The ratio 4 to 8 can be written 4 to 8 or 4:8 or $\frac{4}{8}$.

Note: We can multiply or divide a or b by any value (except zero), and the ratio a to b remains the same (equivalent).

For example, ratios that are equivalent to 6:10:

18:30	3:5	120:200	6x:10x	$\frac{6}{x}:\frac{10}{x}$
(6 x 3 : 10 x 3)	$\left(\frac{6}{2}:\frac{10}{2}\right)$	(6 x 20 : 10 x 20)	(x ≠ 0)	(x ≠ 0)

Ratios can also be used to compare measures.

EXAMPLE: What is the ratio of the length AB to the length XY?

32   •B
A•   •Y
        •Y
              24
    X•

Simplify.

$$\frac{AB}{XY} = \frac{32}{24} = \frac{32 \div 8}{24 \div 8} = \frac{4}{3}$$

The ratio is 4 to 3 or 4:3 or $\frac{4}{3}$.

Extended Ratio

An **EXTENDED RATIO** compares more than two quantities.

It is written in the form $a:b:c$.

EXAMPLE: A recipe for chocolate pudding requires 2 cups of sugar, 1 cup of cocoa, and 8 cups of milk.

Write an extended ratio for the ingredients.

How many cups of each ingredient would you need to double the recipe?

The ratio of sugar to cocoa to milk is $2:1:8$.

To double the recipe, multiply each value by 2.

$2 \cdot 2 = 4$ $1 \cdot 2 = 2$ $8 \cdot 2 = 16$

The ratio for the doubled recipe is $4:2:16$.

We need 4 cups of sugar, 2 cups of cocoa, and 16 cups of milk to double the recipe.

PROPORTION

A **PROPORTION** is an equation where two ratios are equal.

It can be written as: $\dfrac{a}{b} = \dfrac{c}{d}$ or $a{:}b = c{:}d$

For example, $\dfrac{1}{2} = \dfrac{2}{4}$

In the proportion $\dfrac{a}{b} = \dfrac{c}{d}$ multiply $a \cdot d$ and $b \cdot c$ and set them equal to each other.

$$\dfrac{a}{b} \bowtie \dfrac{c}{d}$$

$$ad = bc$$

> Two ratios that form a proportion are called **EQUIVALENT FRACTIONS**.

You can check if two ratios form a proportion by using CROSS PRODUCTS. To find cross products, set the two ratios next to each other, then multiply diagonally. If both products are equal to each other, then the two ratios are equal and form a proportion.

For example, $\dfrac{2}{3} \bowtie \dfrac{8}{12}$

this is also known as cross multiplication

$$2 \times 12 = 24$$
$$3 \times 8 = 24$$

cross products

The cross products are equal, so $\dfrac{2}{3} = \dfrac{8}{12}$.

EXAMPLE: Are $\frac{3}{4}$ and $\frac{5}{6}$ proportional?

Multiply: $\frac{3}{4} \diagdown\!\!\!\!\diagup \frac{5}{6}$

$3 \times 6 = 18$

$5 \times 4 = 20$ The cross products are 18 and 20.

$18 \neq 20$

The cross products are not equal, so $\frac{3}{4} \neq \frac{5}{6}$.

You can also use a proportion to find an unknown quantity.
Use x to represent the unknown quantity.

EXAMPLE: Solve: $\frac{3}{4} = \frac{x}{12}$

$\frac{3}{4} \diagdown\!\!\!\!\diagup \frac{x}{12}$ cross multiply

$3 \cdot 12 = 4 \cdot x$

$36 = 4x$

$\frac{36}{4} = \frac{4x}{4}$

$x = 9$

The proportion is: $\frac{3}{4} = \frac{9}{12}$

EXAMPLE: Solve: $\dfrac{5}{6} = \dfrac{15}{2x}$

$\dfrac{5}{6} \bowtie \dfrac{15}{2x}$ cross multiply

$5 \cdot 2x = 6 \cdot 15$

$10x = 90$

$x = 9$

The proportion is: $\dfrac{5}{6} = \dfrac{15}{18}$

CHECK YOUR WORK:

$\dfrac{15}{2x} = \dfrac{15}{2(9)} = \dfrac{15}{18} = \dfrac{15 \div 3}{18 \div 3} = \dfrac{5}{6}$ ✓

EXAMPLE: On average, Tim spends \$3 for every 19 miles he drives. Tim is planning a 570-mile road trip. How much money should he budget for gas?

Write a proportion that compares *the dollar cost for gas* to *the number of miles*.

average   trip

$\dfrac{\$3}{19 \text{ mi}} = \dfrac{\$x}{570 \text{ mi}}$ ← gas
    ← miles

$3 \cdot 570 = 19 \cdot x$

$1710 = 19x$

$x = 90$

Tim should budget $90 for gas.

CHECK YOUR KNOWLEDGE

Find the value of x.

1. $\dfrac{3}{2x} = \dfrac{9}{24}$

2. $\dfrac{3}{15} = \dfrac{x}{25}$

3. $-\dfrac{5}{8} = \dfrac{20}{4x}$

4. $\dfrac{7x}{14} = 1$

5. The average length of a Brachiosaurus was 84 feet, and a Velociraptor was 6 feet. Josh has a toy Brachiosaurus that is 28 inches long. What length toy Velociraptor should he buy so that it is proportional in size to the Brachiosaurus?

6. It takes Greg 16 minutes to trim 6 rosebushes. How many minutes will it take him to trim 30 rosebushes?

ANSWERS

CHECK YOUR ANSWERS

1. 3 · 24 = 9 · 2x; therefore, x = 4

2. 3 · 25 = x · 15; therefore, x = 5

3. −5 · 4x = 20 · 8; therefore, x = −8

4. 7x · 1 = 14 · 1; therefore, x = 2

5. $\frac{84}{6} = \frac{28}{x}$; therefore, the length is 2 inches

6. $\frac{16}{6} = \frac{x}{30}$; therefore, it will take him 80 minutes

Chapter 26

DILATIONS

SCALE FACTOR

A **DILATION** is a transformation that is not a rigid motion. Dilations change the size of a figure. The shape remains the same.

A dilation is either:

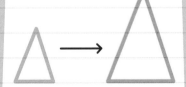

an **enlargement** or **magnification**— the image is larger than the preimage

PREIMAGE → IMAGE

OR

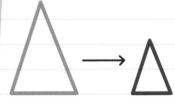

a **reduction**— the image is smaller than the preimage

PREIMAGE → IMAGE

Dilations have a center, O, which is a (fixed point). All the points expand or shrink from the center by a **SCALE FACTOR**.

SCALE FACTOR (r)
a ratio that determines how much bigger or smaller the image is compared to the preimage.

the location from which all points shrink or are expanded

When you **enlarge a figure**, the scale factor is **greater than** 1.

When you **shrink a figure**, the scale factor is **less than** 1. (The new, dilated figure will be a fraction of the original size.)

A scale factor of 1 means the figure stays the same size: 100%. A scale factor of 2 means the figure is 200% larger.

Finding the Scale Factor

We can find the scale factor from the ratio of corresponding side lengths of a pair of figures.

EXAMPLE: Find the scale factor.

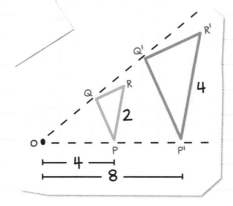

One Way

Divide a side length of the image, $\triangle P'Q'R'$, by the corresponding side length of the preimage, $\triangle PQR$:

Scale factor $r = \dfrac{P'R'}{PR} = \dfrac{8}{4} = 2$

Scale factor $r = 2$

Another Way

Divide the distance from the center, O to P, by the distance from O to P'.

$r = \dfrac{OP'}{OP} = \dfrac{8}{4} = 2$

Don't forget to simplify.

EXAMPLE: △ABC maps to (corresponds to) △A'B'C'.
Determine the scale factor.

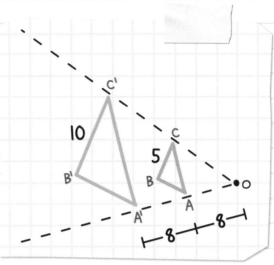

One Way

Find the ratio of corresponding side lengths:

$$r = \frac{B'C'}{BC}$$

$$r = \frac{10}{5} = 2$$

Another Way

Find the ratio using the distance from the center:

$$r = \frac{OA'}{OA}$$

$$r = \frac{8+8}{8} = \frac{16}{8}$$

$$r = 2$$

The scale factor is 2.
The image is an enlargement.

EXAMPLE: Quadrilateral GHIJ maps to G'H'I'J'. Determine the scale factor.

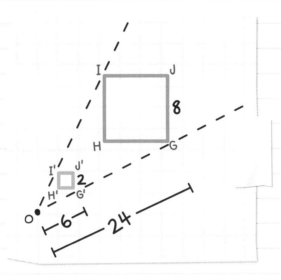

One Way	Another Way
Find the ratio of corresponding side lengths:	Find the ratio using the distance from the center:
$r = \dfrac{G'J'}{GJ}$	$r = \dfrac{O'G'}{OG}$
$r = \dfrac{2}{8}$	$r = \dfrac{6}{24}$
$r = \dfrac{1}{4}$	$r = \dfrac{1}{4}$
Scale factor $= \dfrac{1}{4}$	

The scale factor is $\dfrac{1}{4}$. The image is a reduction.

DRAWING A DILATION

EXAMPLE: Draw the image of △PQR under a dilation with center O and scale factor 3.

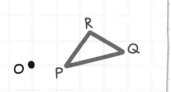

Step 1: Draw rays from O through each vertex.

Step 2: Draw P'.

Use a ruler or compass to measure the length of OP,

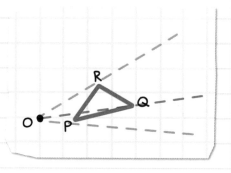

OP = 1 cm

Multiply OP by scale factor 3 to get OP'.

$3 \cdot OP' = 3 \cdot (1 \text{ cm}) = 3 \text{ cm}$

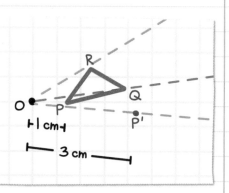

OP' = 3 cm

On the ray OP, draw P' 3 cm from O.

Step 3: Repeat step 2 for points Q and R.

OR' = 3 · OR = 3 · (2 cm) = 6 cm

OQ' = 3 · OQ = 3 · (3 cm) = 9 cm

Step 4: Connect the points to draw the new triangle.

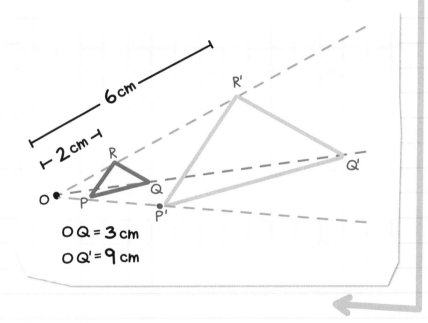

Corresponding sides are parallel in a dilation as long as they don't pass through the center, O.

So, QP ∥ Q'P', QR ∥ Q'R', and PR ∥ P'R'.

DILATIONS ON THE COORDINATE PLANE

To find the image of a dilation on the coordinate plane with the center at the origin (0, 0), <u>multiply each x-coordinate and y-coordinate by the scale factor, r.</u>

$P(x, y) \rightarrow P'(rx, ry)$

If a dilation has a scale factor, r, then $P(x, y)$ maps to $P'(rx, ry)$.

EXAMPLE: P(3, 2) maps to P' under a dilation with a scale factor of $\frac{3}{2}$ and the center at the origin.

Find the coordinates of P' after the dilation.

$P(x, y) \rightarrow P'(rx, ry)$

x-coordinate

$P(3, 2) \rightarrow P'(\frac{3}{2} \cdot 3, \frac{3}{2} \cdot 2)$

y-coordinate   scale factor

$$\frac{3}{2} \cdot 3 = \frac{9}{2}$$

$$\frac{3}{2} \cdot 2 = 3$$

$P'(\frac{9}{2}, 3)$ Simplify.

$P'(4\frac{1}{2}, 3)$

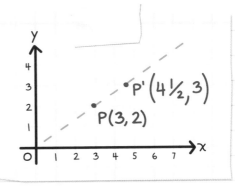

EXAMPLE: Catherine is editing a portrait on her computer. The editing software places the image on a grid. She enlarges the height of the portrait to 200% through a dilation with center O. What are the coordinates of the vertices of the enlarged picture?

An enlargement of 200% is a scale factor of 2.

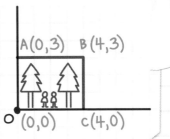

The new coordinates are:

$A(0, 3) \rightarrow A'(2 \cdot 0, 2 \cdot 3)$ new coordinate $A'(0, 6)$

$B(4, 3) \rightarrow B'(2 \cdot 4, 2 \cdot 3)$ new coordinate $B'(8, 6)$

$C(4, 0) \rightarrow C'(2 \cdot 4, 2 \cdot 0)$ new coordinate C'(8, 0)

$O(0, 0) \rightarrow O'(2 \cdot 0, 2 \cdot 0)$ new coordinate O'(0, 0)

The center
of a dilation
maps to itself.

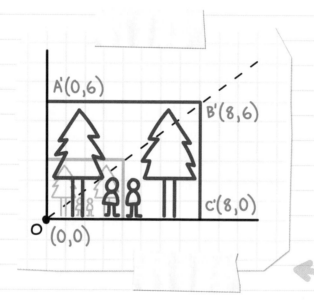

1. State whether each sentence is true or false:
   A. Dilations are rigid motions.
   B. Dilations are transformations.
   C. Dilations preserve shape but not size.
   D. The dilation of a line maps it to a parallel line.

For questions 2–5, determine the scale factor of the dilation that maps P to P' with center O. State whether the dilation is an enlargement or a reduction.

2.

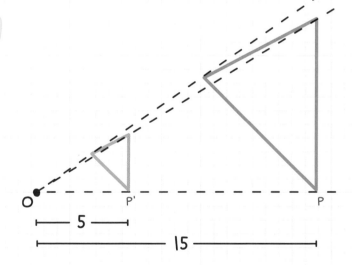

3.

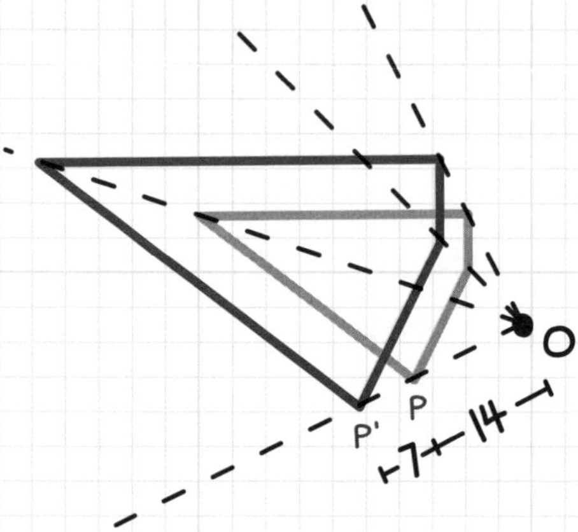

4.

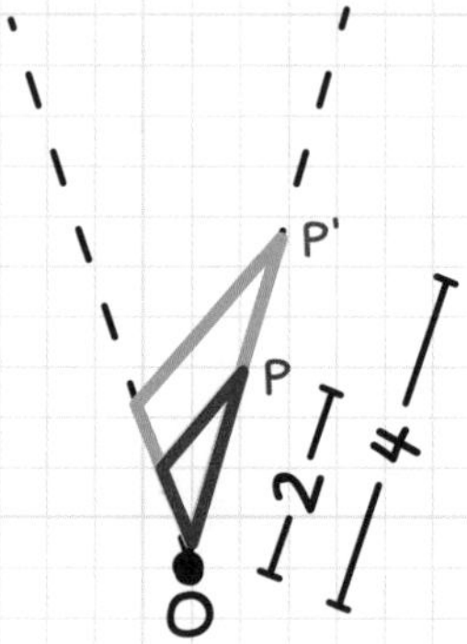

5.

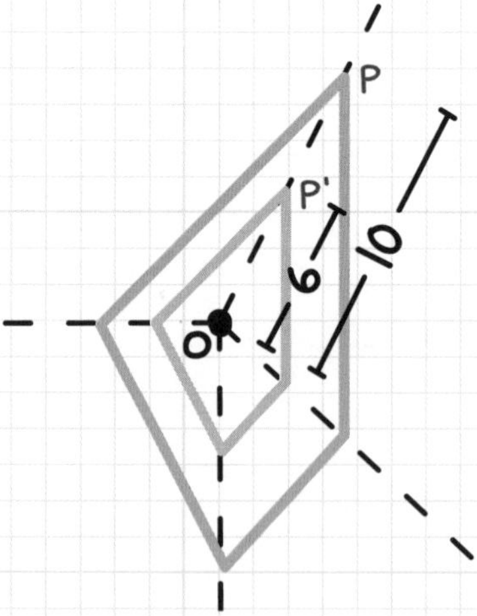

For questions 6 and 7, copy the figure and point O. Draw the dilation of the figure through point O with the given scale factor, r.

6. r = 2

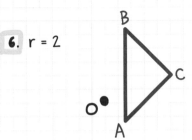

7. $r = \dfrac{1}{2}$

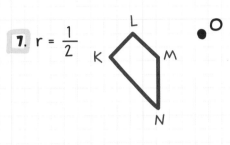

8. P(4, 3) maps to P' under a dilation with a scale factor of 4 and the center at the origin. What are the coordinates of P'?

9. Quadrilateral OPQR maps to O'P'Q'R' under a dilation with a scale factor of $\dfrac{1}{3}$ and the center at the origin. Find the coordinates of the vertices after the dilation.

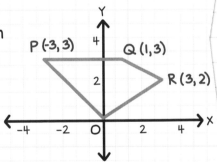

10. Draw the dilation of OPQR in question 9.

1. A. False
   B. True
   C. True
   D. True

2. $\frac{1}{3}$, reduction

3. $\frac{3}{2}$, enlargement

4. 2, enlargement

5. $\frac{3}{5}$, reduction

6.

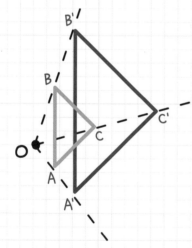

7.

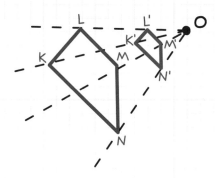

8. P'(16, 12)

9. O'(0, 0), P'(−1, 1), Q'($\frac{1}{3}$, 1),
R'(1, $\frac{2}{3}$)

10.

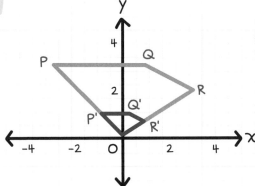

Chapter 27

SIMILAR FIGURES

Two figures are **SIMILAR** if they have the same shape but not necessarily the same size.

> SIMILAR FIGURES ARE DILATIONS, BUT CAN ALSO BE ROTATED, TRANSLATED, OR REFLECTED.

Similar figures have

CORRESPONDING ANGLES (angles that are in the same relative position on each figure) that are congruent,

and

CORRESPONDING SIDES (sides that are in the same relative position on each figure) that are proportional in size.

Similar Figures

SIMILAR POLYGONS

Two polygons are SIMILAR if all corresponding angles are congruent and all corresponding side lengths are proportional.

EXAMPLE: The polygons are similar because they have congruent angles . . .

∠A ≅ ∠E
∠C ≅ ∠G
∠B ≅ ∠F
∠D ≅ ∠H

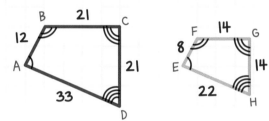

. . . and their corresponding sides are proportional.

$\dfrac{AB}{EF} = \dfrac{12}{8} = \dfrac{3}{2}$ $\dfrac{CD}{GH} = \dfrac{21}{14} = \dfrac{3}{2}$

$\dfrac{BC}{FG} = \dfrac{21}{14} = \dfrac{3}{2}$ $\dfrac{AD}{EH} = \dfrac{33}{22} = \dfrac{3}{2}$

The symbol for similarity is (~).

The similarity statement is ABCD ~ EFGH.

Note: The order in a similarity statement is important.

Write ABCD ~ EFGH in that order because ∠A ≅ ∠E, ∠B ≅ ∠F, ∠C ≅ ∠G, and ∠D ≅ ∠H.

The **SCALE FACTOR** of two similar polygons is the ratio of the lengths of the corresponding sides.

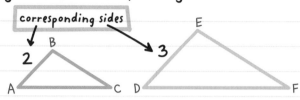

If △ABC ~ △DEF,

then the scale factor of △ABC to △DEF is $\frac{2}{3}$.

The scale factor of △DEF to △ABC is $\frac{3}{2}$.

EXAMPLE: Determine if the triangles are similar. If they are similiar, write a similarity statement and give the scale factor.

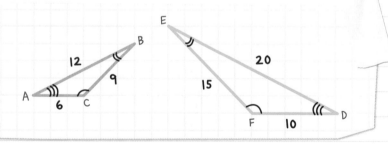

The triangles are similar because they have congruent angles . . .

∠A ≅ ∠D   ∠B ≅ ∠E   ∠C ≅ ∠F

. . . and their corresponding sides are proportional.

Longest sides: $\dfrac{AB}{DE} = \dfrac{12}{20} = \dfrac{3}{5}$

Shortest sides: $\dfrac{AC}{DF} = \dfrac{6}{10} = \dfrac{3}{5}$

> In a triangle, the corresponding sides touch the same two angle pairs.

Remaining sides: $\dfrac{BC}{EF} = \dfrac{9}{15} = \dfrac{3}{5}$

When the orientation of the shapes is different, we can compare proportions of the longest and shortest sides to help match up the correct corresponding sides.

The similarity statement is:

$\triangle ABC \sim \triangle DEF$

The scale factor of $\triangle ABC$ to $\triangle DEF$ is $\dfrac{3}{5}$.

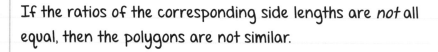

If the ratios of the corresponding side lengths are *not* all equal, then the polygons are not similar.

EXAMPLE: △PQR is not similar to △TUV. This is because the corresponding side lengths are *not* all proportional.

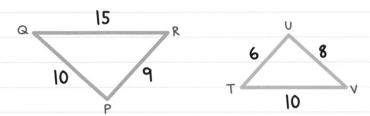

Longest sides: $\dfrac{QR}{TV} = \dfrac{15}{10} = \boxed{\dfrac{3}{2}}$

Shortest sides: $\dfrac{RP}{TU} = \dfrac{9}{6} = \boxed{\dfrac{3}{2}}$

Remaining sides: $\dfrac{PQ}{UV} = \dfrac{10}{8} = \dfrac{\cancel{5}}{\cancel{4}}$ $\boxed{\dfrac{5}{4} \neq \dfrac{3}{2}}$

If we know two figures are similar figures, we can use their proportionality to find unknown measurements.

EXAMPLE: △VWX ~ △VYZ. Find the value of a.

Because the triangles are similar, the corresponding side lengths are proportional:

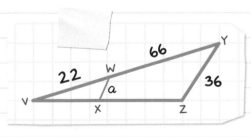

$$\frac{VW}{VY} = \frac{WX}{YZ}$$

$$\frac{22}{22+66} = \frac{a}{36}$$

$$\frac{22}{88} = \frac{a}{36}$$

$$\frac{1}{4} \diagdown\diagup \frac{a}{36}$$ Reduce $\frac{22}{88}$ to $\frac{1}{4}$.

$$1 \cdot 36 = 4 \cdot a$$

$$36 = 4a$$

$$a = \frac{36}{4}$$

$$a = 9$$

WHAT? THEY'RE SIMILAR.

CHECK YOUR KNOWLEDGE

1. State whether each sentence is true or false:
   A. Similar figures have corresponding congruent angles.
   B. Similar figures have corresponding congruent sides.

2. Write a similarity statement for the similar polygons in the given figure.

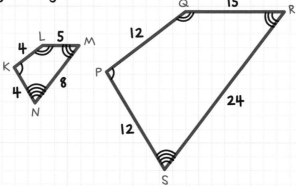

3. What is the scale factor of KLMN to PQRS in question 2?

4. Find the value of x.
   $\triangle GHI \sim \triangle LKJ$

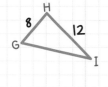

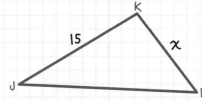

For questions **5-7**, determine if the following polygons are similar. If so, write a similarity statement and give the scale factor.

5.

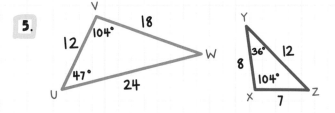

6.

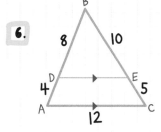

7.

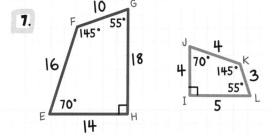

CHECK YOUR ANSWERS

1. **A.** True

   B. False (Corresponding side lengths are proportional.)

2. KLMN ~ PQRS. There's more than one correct answer: LMNK ~ QRSP would be another one—the congruent angles just have to line up in the statement.

3. 3

4. $\frac{8}{12} = \frac{x}{15}$; therefore, $x = 10$

5. No. The angle measures are not congruent.

6. Yes: △ABC ~ △DBE, $\frac{3}{2}$ (or △DBE ~ △ABC $\frac{2}{3}$). (The letters in the similarity statements can be rearranged, as long as the corresponding letters line up.)

7. No

Chapter 28

SIMILAR TRIANGLES

ANGLE-ANGLE (AA) SIMILARITY

We can compare angles to prove that triangles are similar.

ANGLE-ANGLE (AA) SIMILARITY POSTULATE

If two angles of one triangle are congruent to two angles of another triangle, then those two triangles are similar.

If $\angle B \cong \angle E$ and $\angle C \cong \angle F$

Then $\triangle ABC \sim \triangle DEF$

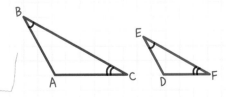

EXAMPLE: Since ∠H ≅ ∠L and ∠I ≅ ∠J,

Then by the Angle-Angle (AA) Similarity Postulate,
△GHI ~ △KLJ.

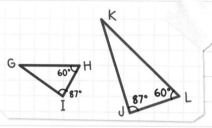

EXAMPLE: Determine if △JKM is similar to △LMK.

Since $\overline{KL} \parallel \overline{JM}$, the alternate interior angles are congruent.

Therefore, ∠JMK ≅ ∠LKM.

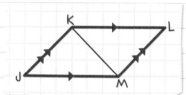

Since $\overline{JK} \parallel \overline{ML}$, the alternate interior angles are congruent too.

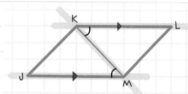

So, ∠JKM ≅ ∠LMK.

By the Angle-Angle (AA) Similarity Postulate,
△JKM ≅ △LMK.

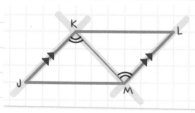

EXAMPLE: Beverly is $5\frac{1}{2}$ feet tall. Her shadow is 3 feet long. She measures the shadow of a nearby tree to be 36 feet long. How tall is the tree?

Step 1: Draw a sketch.

Step 2: Determine similarity.

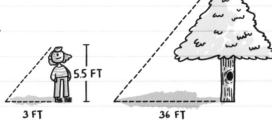

5.5 FT

3 FT   36 FT

Beverly and the tree both form right triangles (90°) with their own shadows and the sun's rays.

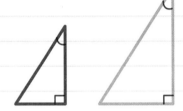

The angles that the sun's rays make with both Beverly and the tree are congruent. The sun is shining down on both of them at the same angle.

Therefore, by the Angle-Angle (AA) Similarity Postulate, the triangles are similar.

Step 3: Write a proportion. Then solve.

Let h = height of the tree.

$$\frac{\text{Beverly's shadow}}{\text{Tree's shadow}} = \frac{\text{Beverly's height}}{\text{Tree's height}}$$

$$\frac{3}{36} \diagdown \frac{5.5}{h}$$

$3 \cdot h = 36 \cdot 5.5$

$3h = 198$

$h = 66$

The tree is 66 feet tall.

SIDE-ANGLE-SIDE (SAS) SIMILARITY

We can compare corresponding sides and included angles to determine if triangles are similar.

SIDE-ANGLE-SIDE (SAS) SIMILARITY THEOREM

If two corresponding sides of two triangles are proportional and the included angles of those sides are congruent, then the triangles are similar.

If $\angle A \cong \angle D$ and $\dfrac{AB}{DE} = \dfrac{AC}{DF}$

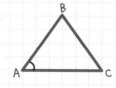

Then $\triangle ABC \sim \triangle DEF$.

EXAMPLE: Show how the triangles are similar.

$\triangle PRT \sim \triangle QRS$

Two corresponding side lengths
are proportional.

$\dfrac{RQ}{RP} = \dfrac{18}{18+6}$

$\phantom{\dfrac{RQ}{RP}} = \dfrac{18}{24} = \boxed{\dfrac{3}{4}}$

$\dfrac{RS}{RT} = \dfrac{15}{15+5}$

$\phantom{\dfrac{RS}{RT}} = \dfrac{15}{20} = \boxed{\dfrac{3}{4}}$

Included angles are
congruent.

An angle is
congruent
to itself.

$\angle R \cong \angle R$ (by the Reflexive Property)

SIDE-SIDE-SIDE (SSS) SIMILARITY

We can compare corresponding sides to determine if two triangles are similar.

SIDE-SIDE-SIDE (SSS) SIMILARITY THEOREM

If the corresponding sides of two triangles are proportional, then the triangles are similar.

If $\dfrac{AB}{DE} = \dfrac{BC}{EF} = \dfrac{AC}{DF}$,

Then $\triangle ABC \sim \triangle DEF$.

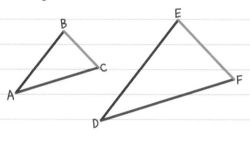

EXAMPLE: Is $\triangle UVW$ similar to $\triangle XZY$?

Compare the proportions from longest to shortest sides.

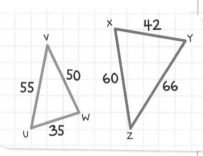

Longest sides: $\dfrac{UV}{YZ} = \dfrac{55}{66} = \boxed{\dfrac{5}{6}}$

Shortest sides: $\dfrac{UW}{XY} = \dfrac{35}{42} = \boxed{\dfrac{5}{6}}$

Remaining sides: $\dfrac{VW}{ZX} = \dfrac{50}{60} = \boxed{\dfrac{5}{6}}$

The triangles are similar because the corresponding side lengths are proportional.

△UVW ~ △YZX

To determine the order that the vertices should be listed in the similarity statement, use the angle size to identify corresponding congruent angles.

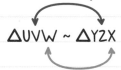

smallest angles (*opposite shortest side*)

△UVW ~ △YZX

largest angles (*opposite longest side*)

Triangle Similarity Summary

Angle-Angle (AA) Similarity Postulate

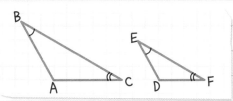

If ∠B ≅ ∠E and ∠C ≅ ∠F
Then △ABC ~ △DEF.

Side-Angle-Side (SAS)
Similarity Theorem

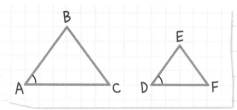

If $\angle A \cong \angle D$ and $\dfrac{AB}{DE} = \dfrac{AC}{DF}$

Then $\triangle ABC \sim \triangle DEF$.

Side-Side-Side (SSS)
Similarity Theorem

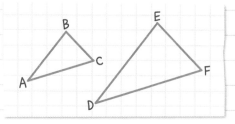

If $\dfrac{AB}{DE} = \dfrac{BC}{EF} = \dfrac{AC}{DF}$

Then $\triangle ABC \sim \triangle DEF$.

For questions 1–4, state the similarity theorem or postulate you would use to determine whether the triangles are similar.

1.

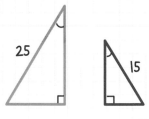

25 15

2.

20 6 8 15

3.

10 20 20 25 16 8

4.

For questions 5–8, determine whether the triangles are similar. If so, write a similarity statement.

5. △GHI and △PQR

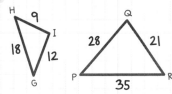

H 9 I 18 12 G Q 28 21 P 35 R

6. △LMO and △ONM

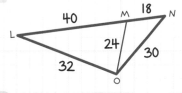

40 M 18 N L 24 30 32 O

7. △ABD and △CBD

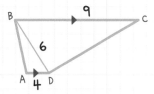

B 9 C 6 A 4 D

8. △WXZ and △VZY

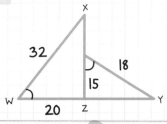

X 32 18 15 W 20 Z Y

CHECK YOUR ANSWERS

1. AA Similarity Postulate

2. SAS Similarity Theorem

3. SSS Similarity Theorem

4. AA Similarity Postulate

5. No. The corresponding side lengths are not proportional.

6. Yes, $\triangle LMO \sim \triangle ONM$ (using SSS Similarity Theorem). (The letters in the similarity statements can be rearranged, as long as the corresponding letters line up.)

7. Yes, $\triangle ABD \sim \triangle CBD$ (using SAS Similarity Theorem and Alternate Interior Angles Theorem). (The letters in the similarity statements can be rearranged, as long as the corresponding letters line up.)

8. No. The corresponding side lengths are not proportional.

Chapter 29

PROPORTIONS IN TRIANGLES

Proportions can be used to find measurements in triangles.

TRIANGLE PROPORTIONALITY THEOREM

If a line is parallel to one side of a triangle and it intersects the other two sides, then it divides the two sides proportionally.

If $\overline{BD} \parallel \overline{AE}$, then $\dfrac{v}{w} = \dfrac{z}{x}$.

The converse is also true:
If $\dfrac{v}{w} = \dfrac{z}{x}$, then $\overline{BD} \parallel \overline{AE}$.

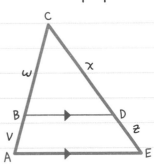

EXAMPLE: Find the value of x.

From the Triangle Proportionality
Theorem,

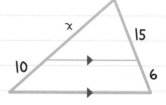

$$\frac{10}{x} = \frac{6}{15}$$

$10 \cdot 15 = x \cdot 6$

$150 = 6x$

$x = 25$

EXAMPLE: The support banisters on a stairway are
built 4 inches apart.

The length of the stair railing between the first and second
banisters (AB) is 5 inches.

AB = 5 in.

Find the length of the railing
between the other four banisters
(BD, DF, and FH).

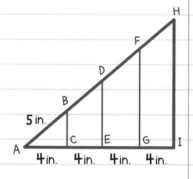

Since the banisters are parallel to each other, use the triangle proportionality theorem.

$$\frac{AC}{CE} = \frac{AB}{BD}$$

$$\frac{4}{4} = \frac{5}{BD}$$

$$4 \cdot BD = 4 \cdot 5$$

$$4BD = 20$$

$$\boxed{BD = 5}$$

Use the same proportions for DF and FH.

$$\frac{CE}{EG} = \frac{BD}{DF} \qquad \frac{EG}{GI} = \frac{DF}{FH}$$

$$\frac{4}{4} = \frac{5}{DF} \qquad \frac{4}{4} = \frac{5}{FH}$$

$$\boxed{DF = 5} \qquad \boxed{FH = 5}$$

The length of the railing between the other four banisters is 5 inches.

A **COROLLARY** is a statement that follows from a theorem or postulate and requires little or no proof.

referred to as "self-evident"

COROLLARY TO THE TRIANGLE PROPORTIONALITY THEOREM

If three or more parallel lines intersect two transversals, then they divide the transversals proportionally.

If $\overline{PX} \parallel \overline{QY} \parallel \overline{RZ}$,

then $\dfrac{PQ}{QR} = \dfrac{XY}{YZ}$.

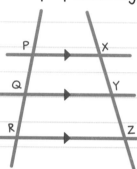

EXAMPLE: Royal Avenue, LA Avenue, and Cochran Street are parallel to one another. They are crossed by Sequoia Avenue and Sycamore Avenue.

Find the distance, x, between Royal Avenue and LA Avenue.

Using the Corollary to the Triangle Proportionality Theorem,

$$\frac{x}{1.2} = \frac{2.0}{1.6}$$

$$x \cdot 1.6 = 1.2 \cdot 2.0$$

$$1.6x = 2.4$$

$$x = 1.5$$

The distance between Royal Avenue
and LA Avenue is 1.5 miles.

ANGLE BISECTOR THEOREM

If $\overline{AD}$ is a bisector of $\angle A$, then $\frac{c}{m} = \frac{b}{n}$.

The converse of this theorem
is also true.

If $\frac{c}{m} = \frac{b}{n}$, then $\overline{AD}$ is a bisector
of $\angle A$.

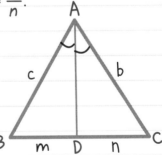

EXAMPLE: Solve for x.

By the Angle Bisector Theorem,

$$\frac{3x}{9} = \frac{2x+6}{15}$$

$3x \cdot 15 = 9 \cdot (2x + 6)$

$45x = 18x + 54$

$27x = 54$

$x = 2$

15

9

3x

2x + 6

EXAMPLE: Find the value of x.

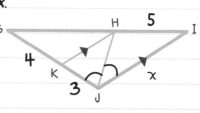

Step 1: Use the Triangle
Proportionality Theorem
to find GH.

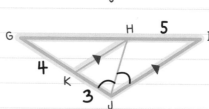

$$\frac{3}{4} = \frac{5}{GH}$$

$3 \cdot GH = 4 \cdot 5$

$3GH = 20$

$GH = \dfrac{20}{3}$

Step 2: Use the Angle Bisector Theorem
to find the value of x.

Since $GK = 4$ and $KJ = 3$,

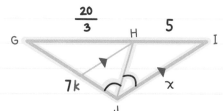

$GJ = GK + KJ = 4 + 3 = 7$

From the Angle Bisector Theorem,

$\dfrac{x}{5} = \dfrac{7}{\frac{20}{3}}$ ⟵ $\boxed{\dfrac{20}{3} = GH}$

$x \cdot \dfrac{20}{3} = 5 \cdot 7$

$\dfrac{20}{3}x = 35$

$\dfrac{20}{3}x \cdot 3 = 35 \cdot 3$

$20x = 105$

$x = \dfrac{105}{20} = \dfrac{21}{4} = 5.25$

1. Use the Triangle Proportionality Theorem to write a proportion for the triangle.

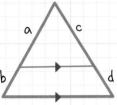

2. Mark says you can use the Triangle Proportionality Theorem to find the value of x in this triangle. Is Mark correct?

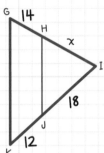

3. Solve for the value of x in the triangle to the right.

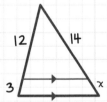

4. A skateboarding ramp has two perpendicular support beams, as shown in the diagram. Find the length of the ramp.

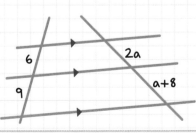

5. Find the value of a in the figure to the right.

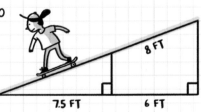

6. Find the value of w in the figure below.

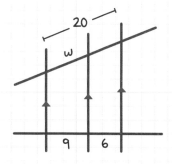

7. Find the value of y in the triangle below.

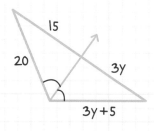

For questions 8 and 9, use the figure below.

8. Find the length of CD.

9. Find the value of x.

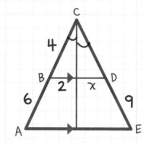

CHECK YOUR ANSWERS

1. $\dfrac{b}{a} = \dfrac{d}{c}$ (or $\dfrac{a}{b} = \dfrac{c}{d}$ or $\dfrac{a}{c} = \dfrac{b}{d}$ or $\dfrac{c}{a} = \dfrac{d}{b}$)

2. No. It is not given that $\overline{GK}$ is parallel to $\overline{HJ}$.

3. $\dfrac{3}{x} = \dfrac{12}{14}$; therefore, $x = \dfrac{7}{2}$

4. $\dfrac{6}{8} = \dfrac{7.5}{x}$; therefore, $x = 10$. The ramp is 18 feet.

5. $\dfrac{9}{a+8} = \dfrac{6}{2a}$; therefore, $a = 4$

6. (Use the ratio: $\dfrac{9}{6} = \dfrac{w}{20-w}$); $w = 12$

7. $\dfrac{3y+5}{3y} = \dfrac{20}{15}$; therefore, $y = 5$

8. $\dfrac{6}{9} = \dfrac{4}{CD}$; therefore, $CD = 6$

9. $\dfrac{4}{2} = \dfrac{6}{x}$; therefore, $x = 3$

Unit 7

Right Triangles and Trigonometry

Chapter 30

SLOPE AND LINEAR EQUATIONS

SLOPE

SLOPE (m) is ratio that describes the tilt of a line:

$$\text{slope } (m) = \frac{\text{rise}}{\text{run}}$$

↕ RISE is how much a line goes up or down.

↔ RUN is how much a line moves left or right.

> **THINK:** I **rise up** from bed.
> I **run along** a path.

EXAMPLE: A line with a slope of $\frac{3}{2}$.

RISE = 3
RUN = 2

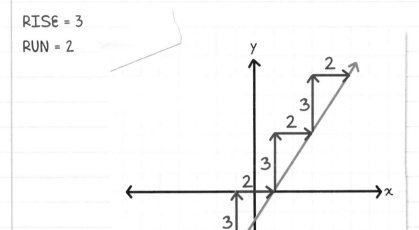

A slope (*m*) of $\frac{3}{2}$ means that every time
the line *rises* 3 units, it also *runs* 2 units.

There are four types of slope:

Positive Slope
- rises from left to right
- rise and run are positive, $\dfrac{\text{rise}}{\text{run}}$ = positive

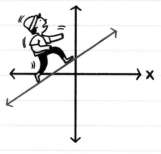

SAM GOES UP

Negative Slope
- falls from left to right
- rise is negative and run is positive, $\dfrac{\text{rise}}{\text{run}}$ = negative

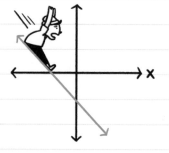

SAM GOES DOWN

Zero Slope
- is horizontal
- rise = 0, so $\dfrac{\text{rise}}{\text{run}} = \dfrac{0}{\text{run}} = 0$

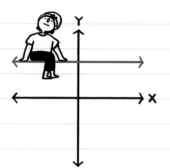

SAM GOES NOWHERE

Undefined Slope
- is vertical
- run = 0, so $\dfrac{\text{rise}}{\text{run}} = \dfrac{\text{rise}}{0}$ which is undefined.

A number divided by zero is undefined.

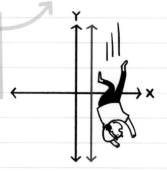

SAM IS IN TROUBLE!

5 THINGS YOU NEED TO KNOW ABOUT SLOPE:

1. Anytime you move **UP**, that is a **POSITIVE RISE**.

2. Anytime you move **DOWN**, that is a **NEGATIVE RISE**.

3. Anytime you move **RIGHT**, that is a **POSITIVE RUN**.

4. Anytime you move **LEFT**, that is a **NEGATIVE RUN**.

5. The slope is the **SAME** everywhere on a **STRAIGHT LINE**.

Finding the Slope of a Line

To find the slope of a line:

1. Pick any two points on the line.

2. Draw a right triangle that connects the two points and uses the line as the hypotenuse.

3. Count the units up or down from the line to find the **rise**.

4. Then count the units left or right to find the **run**.

EXAMPLE: Find the slope of the line.

down 3 units

$$\text{slope } (m) = \frac{\text{rise}}{\text{run}} = \frac{-3}{3} = -1$$

slope = -1   right 3 units

(A slope of $\frac{-3}{3}$ means that every time the line moves down 3 units, it also moves right 3 units.)

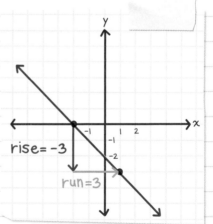

rise = -3

run = 3

Formula for slope when you know two points on a line:

$$\text{slope} = \frac{\text{change in } y}{\text{change in } x} \quad \text{or} \quad m = \frac{y_2 - y_1}{x_2 - x_1}$$

x_1 is read as "x sub 1."

subscript

Subscripts help differentiate the points. Name one point (x_1, y_1) and the other (x_2, y_2).

The order of the points being named does not matter as long as you keep the ordered pair together.

EXAMPLE: Find the slope of the line that passes through points (3, –2) and (6, –1).

Let $(x_1, y_1) = (3, -2)$ and $(x_2, y_2) = (6, -1)$.

Then, $x_1 = 3$, $y_1 = -2$, $x_2 = 6$, and $y_2 = -1$

$$\text{slope } (m) = \frac{y_2 - y_1}{x_2 - x_1} = \frac{-1 - (-2)}{6 - 3} = \frac{1}{3}$$

$$\text{slope} = \frac{1}{3}$$

Find the slope of the line on the graph.

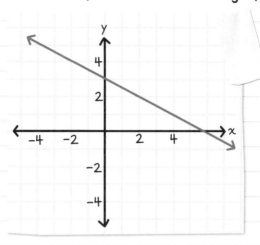

Choose any two points on the line.

For example, $(2, 2)$ and $(4, 1)$.

Let $(x_1, y_1) = (2, 2)$ and $(x_2, y_2) = (4, 1)$.

Then, $x_1 = 2$ $y_1 = 2$

       $x_2 = 4$ $y_2 = 1$

slope $(m) = \dfrac{y_2 - y_1}{x_2 - x_1} = \dfrac{1 - 2}{4 - 2} = -\dfrac{1}{2}$

slope $= -\dfrac{1}{2}$

Parallel lines have the same slope.

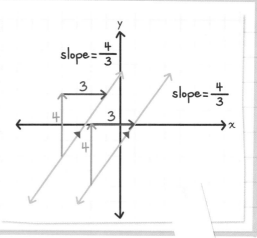

Perpendicular lines have slopes that are the NEGATIVE RECIPROCALS of each other.

$\frac{2}{1}$ and $-\frac{1}{2}$ are negative reciprocals.

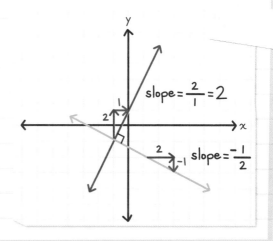

A **RECIPROCAL** is a fraction where the numerator and denominator are reversed.

$\frac{a}{b}$ and $\frac{b}{a}$ are reciprocals of each other.

$\frac{a}{b}$ and $-\frac{b}{a}$ are NEGATIVE RECIPROCALS of each other.

EXAMPLE: Determine whether the quadrilateral with vertices (0, 1), (3, 3), (-3, -5), and (0, -3) is a parallelogram.

Plot the four points on a coordinate plane. Connect the points to create a quadrilateral.

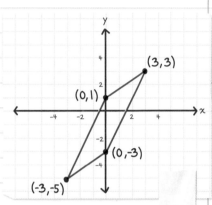

If both pairs of opposite sides are parallel, then it is a parallelogram.

The side $(x_1, y_1) = (0, 1)$ and $(x_2, y_2) = (3, 3)$ has a slope of:

$$\frac{y_2 - y_1}{x_2 - x_1} = \frac{3-1}{3-0} = \frac{2}{3}$$

The side $(x_1, y_1) = (-3, -5)$ and $(x_2, y_2) = (0, -3)$ has a slope of:

$$\frac{y_2 - y_1}{x_2 - x_1} = \frac{-3-(-5)}{0-(-3)} = \frac{-3+5}{0+3} = \frac{2}{3}$$

The two sides have the same slope, so they are parallel.

The side $(x_1, y_1) = (-3, -5)$ and $(x_2, y_2) = (0, 1)$ has a slope of:

$$\frac{y_2 - y_1}{x_2 - x_1} = \frac{1-(-5)}{0-(-3)} = \frac{1+5}{0+3} = \frac{6}{3} = 2$$

The side $(x_1, y_1) = (0, -3)$ and $(x_2, y_2) = (3, 3)$ has a slope of:

$$\frac{y_2 - y_1}{x_2 - x_1} = \frac{3 - (-3)}{3 - 0} = \frac{3 + 3}{3} = \frac{6}{3} = 2$$

The two sides have the same slope, so they are parallel.

The quadrilateral is a parallelogram.

GRAPHING LINEAR EQUATIONS

The equation of a line is a **LINEAR EQUATION**.

Linear equations can take the form:

$$y = mx + b$$

y = every y value in the line

m = slope $\left(\dfrac{\text{rise}}{\text{run}} \right)$

b = y-intercept [where the line crosses the y-axis—point $(0, b)$]

If you know both the y-intercept and the slope of a line, you can graph the line.

Linear equations can also
be written as:

$Ax + By = C$ (standard form)

A, B, and C are constants.

EXAMPLE: Graph: $y = 2x - 1$.

Format: $y = mx + b$

$m = 2$, or $\dfrac{2}{1}$ $b = -1$

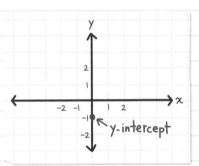

Step 1: Plot the y-intercept.

$x = 0$ and $y = -1$: $(0, -1)$

Step 2: Use slope to find
additional points.

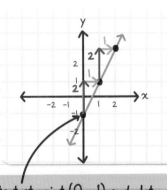

Since the slope is $\dfrac{2}{1}$, rise 2
and run 1.

Plot a few points.

Start at point $(0, -1)$ and plot
additional points using $\dfrac{\text{rise}}{\text{run}}$.

Step 3: Connect the points.

350

EXAMPLE: Graph: $x + y = 4$.

First, write the equation in the slope-intercept form $y = mx + b$.

$y = -x + 4$; $m = -\dfrac{1}{1}$; $b = 4$

> $-x$ is the same as $-1x$, so m is $-\dfrac{1}{1}$.

Step 1: Plot the y-intercept $(0, 4)$.

Step 2: Use slope $\left(-\dfrac{1}{1}\right)$ to find additional points.

$$\left(\dfrac{\text{rise}}{\text{run}} = \dfrac{-1}{1} \text{ or } \dfrac{\text{rise}}{\text{run}} = \dfrac{1}{-1}\right)$$

Step 3: Connect the points.

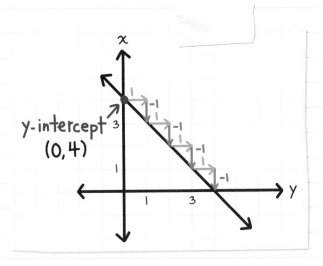

y-intercept $(0, 4)$

HORIZONTAL AND VERTICAL LINES

$x = a$ is a vertical line with x-intercept $(a, 0)$.

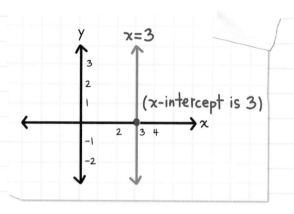

Remember: The slope of a vertical line is undefined.

$y = b$ is a horizontal line with y-intercept $(0, b)$.

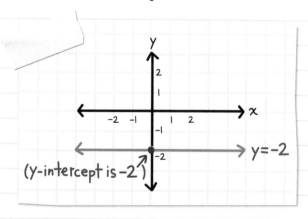

Remember: The slope of a horizontal line is zero.

CHECK YOUR KNOWLEDGE

1. What is the slope and y-intercept of $y = -\dfrac{3}{4}x - 10$?

2. Find the slope of the line that passes through $(1, -2)$ and $(5, -4)$.

3. Find the slope of the line in the graph.

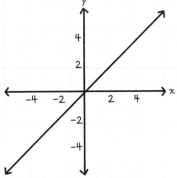

4. In parts **a** and **b**, determine if the graph shows a positive, negative, zero, or undefined slope.

a.

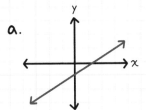

b.

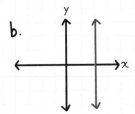

5. Line B has slope -4. What is the slope of the line that is parallel to line B?

ANSWERS

CHECK YOUR ANSWERS

1. slope $(m) = -\dfrac{3}{4}$, y-intercept = (0, −10)

2. $\dfrac{-4-(-2)}{5-1}$; therefore, slope = $-\dfrac{1}{2}$

3. slope = 1

4. **A.** Positive

    B. Undefined

5. −4

Chapter 31

THE PYTHAGOREAN THEOREM

A right triangle has two legs and a **HYPOTENUSE** —the side opposite the right angle. The legs are connected at the right angle. The lengths of the legs are a and b and c is the hypotenuse.

The **PYTHAGOREAN THEOREM** is used to find the length of a side of a right triangle.

PYTHAGOREAN THEOREM

In a right triangle, the sum of the squares of the lengths of the legs is equal to the square of the hypotenuse.

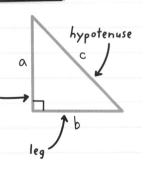

$$a^2 + b^2 = c^2$$

leg   leg   hypotenuse

EXAMPLE: Use the Pythagorean Theorem to find the value of x.

The length of the hypotenuse is 10.

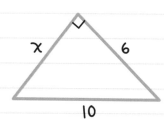

$a^2 + b^2 = c^2$

$a = x$, $b = 6$, and $c = 10$.

$x^2 + 6^2 = 10^2$

> The hypotenuse is the side opposite the right angle. It is always longer than the length of either leg.

$x^2 + 36 = 100$

$x^2 + 36 - 36 = 100 - 36$

$\sqrt{x^2} = \sqrt{64}$ (To isolate x, find the square root of both sides.)

$x = 8$

SQUARE ROOTS

The square root of a number is a number that when multiplied by itself gives the first number. It is shown by putting the number inside a radical sign, or $\sqrt{}$.

The square root of 64 is written as $\sqrt{64}$ and is read as "square root of 64."

$$\sqrt{64} = \sqrt{8 \times 8} = 8 \text{ and } \sqrt{64} = \sqrt{-8 \times -8} = -8$$

The square root of 64 is 8 and -8.

$\sqrt{64}$ is also known as a perfect square:

> the product of 2 equal integers

$$8 \times 8$$

If a number under the radical sign is NOT a perfect square it is an irrational number.

Example: $\sqrt{7}$ is irrational ←
$\quad\quad\quad$ $\sqrt{13}$ is irrational ←

A number cannot be multiplied by itself to get this number.

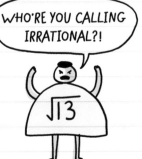

WHO'RE YOU CALLING IRRATIONAL?!

$\sqrt{13}$

EXAMPLE: Brandy takes different measurements of her door. The height is 80 inches, and the base is 36 inches. What is the diagonal height of her door?

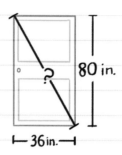

80 in.

36 in.

Let c be the height of the door,

Using the Pythagorean Theorem with a = 80, b = 36, and c = ?,

$$a^2 + b^2 = c^2$$

$$80^2 + 36^2 = c^2$$

$$6400 + 1296 = 7{,}696$$

$$c^2 = 7{,}696$$

$$\sqrt{c^2} = \sqrt{7{,}696}$$

$$c = 87.7$$

The diagonal height of the door is 87.7 in.

PYTHAGOREAN TRIPLES are three side lengths that always form a right triangle.

Here are a few commonly used triples.

$$3, 4, 5 \qquad (3^2 + 4^2 = 5^2)$$

$$5, 12, 13 \qquad (5^2 + 12^2 = 13^2)$$

$$8, 15, 17 \qquad (8^2 + 15^2 = 17^2)$$

Note: Multiples of these also form Pythagorean triples.

For example, 6, 8, 10 and 9, 12, 15.

RIGHT, ACUTE, AND OBTUSE TRIANGLE RULES

If $c^2 = a^2 + b^2$, then $\triangle ABC$ is a <u>right triangle</u>.

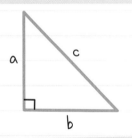

If $c^2 < a^2 + b^2$, then $\triangle ABC$ is an <u>acute triangle</u>.

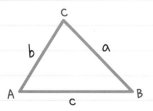

If $c^2 > a^2 + b^2$, then $\triangle ABC$ is an obtuse triangle.

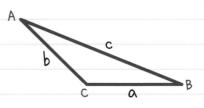

EXAMPLE: A triangle has side lengths 6, 5, and 10. Is the triangle obtuse, acute, or right?

Since 10 is the longest side length, $c = 10$.

$c^2 = 10^2 = 100$

$a^2 + b^2 = 6^2 + 5^2$

$\qquad = 36 + 25$

$\qquad = 61$

$100 > 61$

Since $c^2 > a^2 + b^2$, the triangle is an obtuse triangle.

1. Orion catches a fish 16 feet downstream on the opposite side of a river using a 34-foot-long line. How wide is the river?

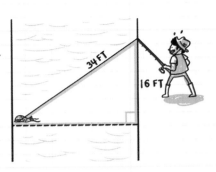

2. Daphne is trapped in a 48-foot-high castle, surrounded by a 20-foot-wide moat. Her rescuer needs a ladder to place at the edge of the moat that will reach the top of the castle. How long a ladder is needed?

In questions **3-4**, the lengths of the sides of a triangle are given. Determine if the triangle is acute, obtuse, or right.

3. 3, 4, 7

4. 12, 16, 20

CHECK YOUR ANSWERS

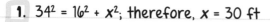

1. $34^2 = 16^2 + x^2$; therefore, $x = 30$ ft

2. $20^2 + 48^2 = x^2$; therefore, $x = 52$ ft

3. $7^2 > 4^2 + 3^2$; therefore, the triangle is obtuse

4. $20^2 = 12^2 + 16^2$; therefore, the triangle is right

Chapter 32

MIDPOINT AND DISTANCE FORMULAS

MIDPOINT FORMULA

The midpoint is the point on a line segment that is halfway between endpoints. The **MIDPOINT FORMULA** is used to find the coordinates of a line segment's midpoint on a number line or a coordinate plane.

Midpoint on a Number Line

The midpoint of $\overline{AB}$ is:

$$\text{midpoint} = \frac{a+b}{2}$$

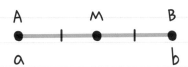

EXAMPLE: What is the midpoint of $\overline{PR}$?

Use the midpoint formula:

midpoint $= \dfrac{a+b}{2}$

endpoints of $\overline{PR}$

$a = -1$ and $b = 5$:

$= \dfrac{-1+5}{2}$

$= \dfrac{4}{2}$

$= 2$

The midpoint is 2.

Midpoint on a Coordinate Plane

The midpoint of $\overline{AB}$ is:

$$\text{midpoint} = \left(\dfrac{x_1 + x_2}{2}, \dfrac{y_1 + y_2}{2} \right)$$

(x_1, y_1) and (x_2, y_2) are the coordinates of the endpoints.

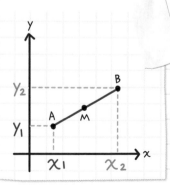

EXAMPLE: Find the midpoint of $\overline{CD}$ given C(2, -2) and D(6, 2).

Use the midpoint formula:

$$\text{midpoint} = \left(\frac{x_1 + x_2}{2}, \frac{y_1 + y_2}{2} \right)$$

$(x_1, y_1) = (2, -2)$ and $(x_2, y_2) = (6, 2)$:

$x_1 = 2, y_1 = -2, x_2 = 6, y_2 = 2$

$$= \left(\frac{2 + 6}{2}, \frac{-2 + 2}{2} \right)$$

$$= \left(\frac{8}{2}, \frac{0}{2} \right)$$

$$= (4, 0)$$

EXAMPLE: Line segment $\overline{GH}$ has endpoint G(-3, -4) and midpoint P(-1, -3). Find the coordinates of endpoint H.

Use the midpoint formula:

$G(-3, -4) = (x_1, y_1)$ and $H = (x_2, y_2)$.

$x_1 = -3, y_1 = -4$, midpoint $= (-1, -3)$

$$\text{midpoint} = \left(\frac{x_1 + x_2}{2} , \frac{y_1 + y_2}{2} \right)$$

$$(-1, -3) = \left(\frac{-3 + x_2}{2} , \frac{-4 + y_2}{2} \right)$$

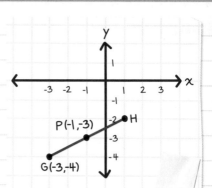

The x-coordinate is:

$$-1 = \frac{-3 + x_2}{2}$$

$$-2 = -3 + x_2$$

$$x_2 = 1$$

The y-coordinate is:

$$-3 = \frac{-4 + y_2}{2}$$

$$-6 = -4 + y_2$$

$$y_2 = -2$$

Therefore, the coordinates of H are (1, -2).

DISTANCE FORMULA

The **DISTANCE FORMULA** is used to find the distance between two points (or the length of a line segment) on a number line or coordinate plane.

Distance on a Number Line

The distance between A and B is:

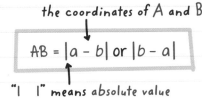

the coordinates of A and B

$$AB = |a - b| \text{ or } |b - a|$$

"| |" means absolute value

Absolute value: the distance of a number on the number line from 0 without considering which direction from 0 the number lies.

EXAMPLE: Find the value of AB. Use the Distance Formula.

$$AB = |a - b|$$

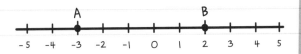

$a = -3$ and $b = 2$:

$$AB = |a - b| = |-3 - 2| = |-5| = 5$$

Distance on a Coordinate Plane

The distance between two points on a coordinate plane is the square root of the difference of the x-coordinates squared plus the difference of the y-coordinates squared.

The distance between A and B is:

$$AB = \sqrt{(x_2 - x_1)^2 + (y_2 - y_1)^2}$$

↑ ↑
the coordinates of A and B

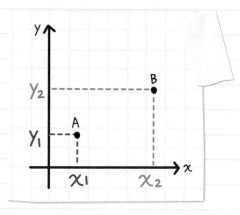

EXAMPLE: What is the distance between points S(-2, -1) and T(1, 3)?

$$AB = \sqrt{(x_2 - x_1)^2 + (y_2 - y_1)^2}$$

$(x_1, y_1) = (-2, -1)$ and $(x_2, y_2) = (1, 3)$:

$x_1 = -2$, $y_1 = -1$, $x_2 = 1$, $y_2 = 3$

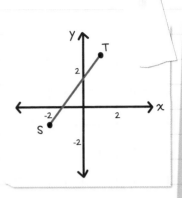

$$ST = \sqrt{(x_2 - x_1)^2 + (y_2 - y_1)^2}$$

$$= \sqrt{(1 - (-2))^2 + (3 - (-1))^2}$$

$$= \sqrt{(1 + 2)^2 + (3 + 1)^2}$$

$$= \sqrt{(3^2 + 4^2)} = \sqrt{25}$$

$$ST = 5$$

1. Find the midpoint of $\overline{AB}$ on the number line.

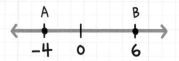

2. Complete the sentence.

Given $A(x_1, y_1)$ and $B(x_2, y_2)$, the coordinates of the midpoint M of $\overline{AB}$ are _____.

3. Find the midpoint of $\overline{CD}$ given C(2, 3) and D(4, 8).

4. Find the midpoint of $\overline{QR}$ in the graph.

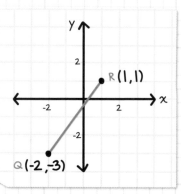

5. Line segment $\overline{EG}$ has endpoint E(-7, -5) and midpoint M(-3, -1). Find the coordinates of endpoint G.

6. Use the Distance Formula on a number line to write the formula for $\overline{RT}$.

7. What is the distance between M and N?

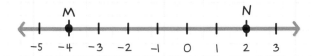

8. What is the distance between P(-5, 8) and R(0, -4)?

9. Use the Distance Formula to find the distance between Lily's house and Alex's house, located at (2, 1) and (5, 5), as shown on the map below. Each square represents one square mile.

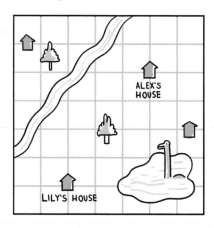

ANSWERS

CHECK YOUR ANSWERS

1. $\dfrac{-4+6}{2}$; therefore, the midpoint = 1

2. midpoint $\left(\dfrac{x_1+x_2}{2}, \dfrac{y_1+y_2}{2}\right)$

3. $\left(\dfrac{2+4}{2}, \dfrac{3+8}{2}\right) = (3, \dfrac{11}{2})$

4. $\left(\dfrac{-2+1}{2}, \dfrac{-3+1}{2}\right) = (-\dfrac{1}{2}, -1)$

5. $(-3, -1) = \left(\dfrac{-7+x}{2}, \dfrac{-5+y}{2}\right) = (1, 3)$

6. RT = $|r - t|$ or $|t - r|$

7. MN = $|-4 - 2| = 6$

8. $\sqrt{(0-(-5)^2+(-4-8)^2}$; therefore, PR = 13

9. $\sqrt{(5-2)^2+(5-1)^2}$

   The distance between Lily's house and Alex's house is 5 miles.

Chapter 33

COORDINATE TRIANGLE PROOFS

WRITING A TRIANGLE COORDINATE PROOF

A **COORDINATE PROOF** involves drawing figures on a coordinate plane. Statements about the figure can be proven using the DISTANCE and MIDPOINT FORMULAS, theorems, and postulates.

When writing a coordinate triangle proof:

1. Draw and label a coordinate graph.

2. Write the formulas that you will use to construct the coordinate proof.

3. Make a plan and write the steps you will use to show that the given information leads to what you are proving.

4. Write a final statement that states what you have proven and why it must be true.

Formulas used for coordinate proofs:

$$\text{Slope Formula: } m = \frac{y_2 - y_1}{x_2 - x_1}$$

$$\text{Distance Formula: } D = \sqrt{(x_2 - x_1)^2 + (y_2 - y_1)^2}$$

USING THE DISTANCE FORMULA

When given the coordinates of a triangle, you can prove the triangle is isosceles by using the Distance Formula to show that the graphed triangle has two congruent sides.

EXAMPLE:

Given: $\triangle GHI$ has vertices $G(1, 1)$, $H(3, 1)$, and $I(2, -1)$.

Prove: $\triangle GHI$ is isosceles.

Step 1: Plot the points on a coordinate plane and connect them. Label the points.

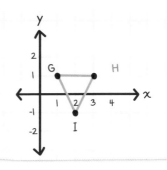

Step 2: Name the formula needed for the proof.

Distance Formula: $D = \sqrt{(x_2 - x_1)^2 + (y_2 - y_1)^2}$

Step 3: Write the steps to show the triangle has two congruent sides. — isosceles triangle

The length of $\overline{GH}$ is: $D = \sqrt{(3-1)^2 + (1-1)^2}$

$G = (x_1, y_1) = (1, 1)$
$H = (x_2, y_2) = (3, 1)$

$= \sqrt{(2^2 + 0^2)} = \sqrt{4} = 2$

The length of $\overline{HI}$ is: $D = \sqrt{(2-3)^2 + (-1-1)^2}$

$H = (x_1, y_1) = (3, 1)$
$I = (x_2, y_2) = (2, -1)$

$= \sqrt{(-1)^2 + (-2)^2} = \boxed{\sqrt{5}}$

The length of $\overline{GI}$ is: $D = \sqrt{(2-1)^2 + (-1-1)^2}$

$G = (x_1, y_1) = (1, 1)$
$I = (x_2, y_2) = (2, -1)$

$= \sqrt{1^2 + (-2)^2} = \boxed{\sqrt{5}}$

Step 4: Write a final statement.

Since $\overline{HI}$ and $\overline{GI}$ are equal in length, they are congruent.

$\triangle GHI$ is isosceles because it has two congruent sides.

EXAMPLE:

Given: $\triangle XYZ$ has vertices $X(-2, 0)$, $Y(2, 3)$, and $Z(1, -3)$.

Prove: $\triangle XYZ$ is scalene.

> A **scalene triangle** has no congruent sides.

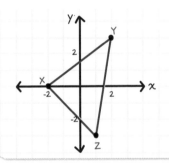

Distance Formula: $D = \sqrt{(x_2 - x_1)^2 + (y_2 - y_1)^2}$

Find the lengths:

$\overline{XY}$: $D = \sqrt{(2-(-2))^2 + (3-0)^2} = \sqrt{(2+2)^2 + 3^2} = \sqrt{4^2 + 3^2} = \sqrt{25} = \boxed{5}$

$\overline{YZ}$: $D = \sqrt{(1-2)^2 + (-3-3)^2} = \sqrt{(-1)^2 + (-6)^2} = \boxed{\sqrt{37}}$

$\overline{XZ}$: $D = \sqrt{(1-(-2))^2 + (-3-0)^2} = \sqrt{(1+2)^2 + (-3)^2} = \sqrt{3^2 + (-3)^2} = \boxed{\sqrt{18}}$

Since the three sides have different length measures, there are no congruent sides.

△XYZ is scalene because it has no congruent sides.

USING THE SLOPE FORMULA

When given the coordinates of a right triangle, you can prove the triangle has a 90° angle by using slope to show that two sides of the triangle are perpendicular.

A **reciprocal** is a fraction where numerator and denominator are reversed. If two lines have slopes that are **negative reciprocals** of each other (one is positive and the other is negative), then the lines are perpendicular.

EXAMPLE:

Given: △PQR has vertices P(-2, 3), Q(5, -1), and R(2, -3).

Prove: △PQR is a right triangle.

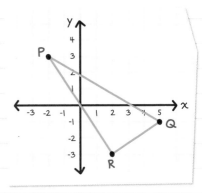

Slope Formula: $m = \dfrac{y_2 - y_1}{x_2 - x_1}$

Show ∠PRQ is a right angle by showing $\overline{PR}$ and $\overline{QR}$ are perpendicular.

The slope of $\overline{PR}$ is: $\dfrac{-3-3}{2-(-2)} = \dfrac{-6}{2+2} = \dfrac{-6}{4} = \boxed{-\dfrac{3}{2}}$

The slope of $\overline{QR}$ is: $\dfrac{-3-(-1)}{2-5} = \dfrac{-3+1}{-3} = \dfrac{-2}{-3} = \boxed{\dfrac{2}{3}}$

Since $\overline{PR}$ and $\overline{QR}$ are **negative reciprocals** of each other, they are perpendicular.

Therefore, ∠PRQ is a right angle.

△PQR is a right triangle because it contains one right angle.

USING THE PYTHAGOREAN THEOREM

Another way to prove a right triangle is to use the Pythagorean Theorem.

EXAMPLE:

Find the lengths of each side of the triangle and then show that they follow $a^2 + b^2 = c^2$.

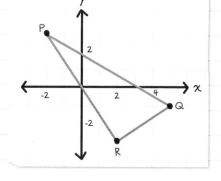

First use the Distance Formula to find the length of each side of the triangle.

$$D = \sqrt{(x_2 - x_1)^2 + (y_2 - y_1)^2}$$

$\overline{PQ}$: $D = \sqrt{(5-(-2))^2 + (-1-3)^2} = \sqrt{7^2 + (-4)^2} = \sqrt{49 + 16} = \sqrt{65}$

$\overline{QR}$: $D = \sqrt{(2-5)^2 + (-3-(-1))^2} = \sqrt{(-3)^2 + (-2)^2} = \sqrt{9 + 4} = \sqrt{13}$

$\overline{PR}$: $D = \sqrt{(2-(-2))^2 + (-3-3)^2} = \sqrt{(4)^2 + (-6)^2} = \sqrt{16 + 36} = \sqrt{52}$

Then use the Pythagorean Theorem

$$a^2 + b^2 = c^2$$

$$(\sqrt{13})^2 + (\sqrt{52})^2 = (\sqrt{65})^2$$

$$13 + 52 = 65$$

$$65 = 65$$

$\triangle$PQR is a right triangle since the length measures of its three sides follow the Pythagorean Theorem.

CHECK YOUR KNOWLEDGE

1. Given: △LMN has vertices L(-2, -1), M(0, 3), and N(1, 0).
   Prove: △LMN is isosceles.

2. Given: △STU has vertices S(1, 2), T(5, 0), and U(3, -3).
   Prove: △STU is scalene.

3. Given: △XYZ has vertices X(-2, 0), Y(-3, 3), and Z(4, 2).
   Prove: △XYZ is a right triangle.

ANSWERS 381

1.

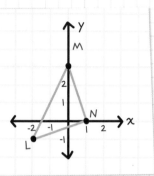

$$D = \sqrt{(x_2 - x_1)^2 + (y_2 - y_1)^2}$$

$\overline{LM}: \sqrt{(0 - (-2))^2 + (3 - (-1))^2} = \sqrt{2^2 + 4^2} = \sqrt{20}$

$\overline{MN}: \sqrt{(1 - 0)^2 + (0 - 3)^2} = \sqrt{1^2 + (-3)^2} = \sqrt{10}$

$\overline{LN}: \sqrt{(1 - (-2))^2 + (0 - (-1))^2} = \sqrt{3^2 + 1^2} = \sqrt{10}$

Since $\overline{MN}$ and $\overline{LN}$ have the same length measure, they are congruent.

$\triangle LMN$ is isosceles because it has two congruent sides.

2.

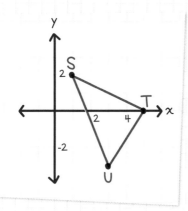

$$D = \sqrt{(x_2 - x_1)^2 + (y_2 - y_1)^2}$$

$\overline{ST}$: $\sqrt{(5-1)^2 + (0-2)^2}$ = $\sqrt{4^2 + (-2)^2}$ = $\sqrt{20}$

$\overline{TU}$: $\sqrt{(3-5)^2 + (-3-0)^2}$ = $\sqrt{(-2)^2 + (-3)^2}$ = $\sqrt{13}$

$\overline{SU}$: $\sqrt{(3-1)^2 + (-3-2)^2}$ = $\sqrt{2^2 + (-5)^2}$ = $\sqrt{29}$

Since the three sides have different length measures, there are no congruent sides.

△STU is scalene because it has no congruent sides.

3.

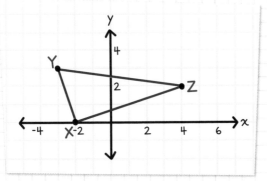

$$m = \frac{y_2 - y_1}{x_2 - x_1}$$

$\overline{XY}$: $\dfrac{3-0}{-3-(-2)} = \dfrac{3}{-1} = -3$

$\overline{XZ}$: $\dfrac{2-0}{4-(-2)} = \dfrac{2}{6} = \dfrac{1}{3}$

Since $\overline{XY}$ and $\overline{XZ}$ are negative reciprocals of each other, they are perpendicular. Therefore, $\angle YXZ$ is a right angle.

$\triangle XYZ$ is a right triangle because it contains one right angle.

Alternate method:

Distance Formula: $D = \sqrt{(x_2 - x_1)^2 + (y_2 - y_1)^2}$

$\overline{XY}$: $\sqrt{(-3 - (-2))^2 + (3 - 0)^2}$ $= \sqrt{(-1)^2 + (3)^2}$ $= \sqrt{10}$

$\overline{YZ}$: $\sqrt{(4 - (-3))^2 + (2 - 3)^2}$ $= \sqrt{(7)^2 + (-1)^2}$ $= \sqrt{50}$

$\overline{XZ}$: $\sqrt{(4 - (-2))^2 + (2 - 0)^2}$ $= \sqrt{(6)^2 + (2)^2}$ $= \sqrt{40}$

Using the Pythagorean Theorem:
$a^2 + b^2 = c^2$

$(\sqrt{10})^2 + (\sqrt{40})^2 = (\sqrt{50})^2$

$10 + 40 = 50$

$50 = 50$

$\triangle XYZ$ is a right triangle since the length measures of its three sides follow the Pythagorean Theorem.

Chapter 34

COORDINATE QUADRILATERAL PROOFS

WRITING COORDINATE QUADRILATERAL PROOFS

Statements about a quadrilateral drawn on a coordinate plane can be proven using the distance and midpoint formulas.

When writing a coordinate quadrilateral proof:

1. Draw and label a coordinate graph.

2. Write the formulas that you will use to construct the coordinate proof.

3. Make a plan and write the steps you will use to show that the given information leads to what you are proving.

4. Write a final statement that states what you have
proven and why it must be true.

Methods to prove a quadrilateral is a parallelogram:

METHOD	FORMULAS NEEDED
Show that both pairs of opposite sides are parallel.	Slope: $m = \dfrac{y_2 - y_1}{x_2 - x_1}$
Show that the quadrilateral has one pair of parallel and congruent sides.	Slope: $m = \dfrac{y_2 - y_1}{x_2 - x_1}$ Distance: $D = \sqrt{(x_2 - x_1)^2 + (y_2 - y_1)^2}$
Show that both pairs of opposite sides are congruent.	Distance: $D = \sqrt{(x_2 - x_1)^2 + (y_2 - y_1)^2}$

USING THE SLOPE FORMULA

The slope formula can be used to show that both pairs of opposite sides in a parallelogram are parallel.

EXAMPLE:

Given: Quadrilateral PQRS has vertices P(-1, 2), Q(3, 1), R(5, -3), and S(1, -2).

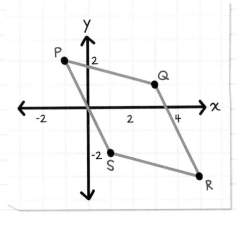

Prove: Quadrilateral PQRS is a parallelogram.

Find the slopes of each side.

If the opposite sides of quadrilateral PQRS have the same slope, then the sides are parallel.

> **Slope Formula:** $m = \dfrac{y_2 - y_1}{x_2 - x_1}$

$\overline{PQ}$ has a slope of: $\dfrac{1-2}{3-(-1)} = \dfrac{-1}{3+1} = \boxed{-\dfrac{1}{4}}$

$\overline{RS}$ has a slope of: $\dfrac{-2-(-3)}{1-5} = \dfrac{-2+3}{-4} = \boxed{-\dfrac{1}{4}}$

$\overline{PQ}$ and $\overline{RS}$ have the same slope, so they are parallel.

$\overline{PS}$ has a slope of: $\dfrac{-2-2}{1-(-1)} = \dfrac{-4}{1+1} = \dfrac{-4}{2} = -2$

$\overline{QR}$ has a slope of: $\dfrac{-3-1}{5-3} = \dfrac{-4}{2} = -2$

$\overline{PS}$ and $\overline{QR}$ have the same slope, so they are parallel.

Quadrilateral PQRS is a parallelogram since both pairs of opposite sides are parallel.

USING THE SLOPE AND DISTANCE FORMULAS

The slope and distance formulas can be used to prove a quadrilateral is a parallelogram by showing that <u>one pair of opposite sides are parallel and congruent.</u>

EXAMPLE:

Prove: Quadrilateral PQRS has one pair of opposite sides that are parallel and congruent.

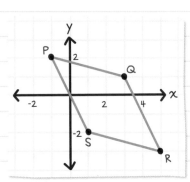

Slope Formula: $m = \dfrac{y_2 - y_1}{x_2 - x_1}$,

Distance Formula: $D = \sqrt{(x_2 - x_1)^2 + (y_2 - y_1)^2}$

$\overline{PQ}$ has a slope of: $\dfrac{1-2}{3-(-1)} = \dfrac{-1}{3+1} = \boxed{-\dfrac{1}{4}}$

$\overline{RS}$ has a slope of: $\dfrac{-2-(-3)}{1-5} = \dfrac{-2+3}{-4} = \boxed{-\dfrac{1}{4}}$

$\overline{PQ}$ and $\overline{RS}$ have the same slope, so they are parallel.

$\overline{PQ}$ has a length of: $D = \sqrt{(3-(-1))^2 + (1-2)^2} = \sqrt{4^2 + (-1)^2} = \boxed{\sqrt{17}}$

$\overline{RS}$ has a length of: $D = \sqrt{(5-1)^2 + (-3-(-2))^2} = \sqrt{4^2 + (-1)^2} = \boxed{\sqrt{17}}$

$\overline{PQ}$ and $\overline{RS}$ have the same length measures, so they are congruent.

Quadrilateral PQRS is a parallelogram since it has one pair of parallel and congruent sides.

USING THE DISTANCE FORMULA

The Distance Formula can be used to prove a quadrilateral is a parallelogram by showing <u>both pairs of opposite sides are congruent</u>.

EXAMPLE:

Prove: Quardrilateral PQRS is a parallelogram.

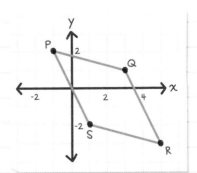

Distance Formula:
$$D = \sqrt{(x_2 - x_1)^2 + (y_2 - y_1)^2}$$

$\overline{PQ}$ has a length of: $D = \sqrt{(3-(-1))^2 + (1-2)^2} = \sqrt{4^2 + (-1)^2} = \boxed{\sqrt{17}}$

$\overline{RS}$ has a length of: $D = \sqrt{(5-1)^2 + (-3-(-2))^2} = \sqrt{4^2 + (-1)^2} = \boxed{\sqrt{17}}$

$\overline{PQ}$ and $\overline{RS}$ have the same length measure, so they are congruent.

$\overline{PS}$ has a length of: $D = \sqrt{(1-(-1))^2 + (-2-2)^2} = \sqrt{2^2 + (-4)^2} = \boxed{\sqrt{20}}$

$\overline{QR}$ has a length of: $D = \sqrt{(5-3)^2 + (-3-1)^2} = \sqrt{2^2 + (-4)^2} = \boxed{\sqrt{20}}$

$\overline{PS}$ and $\overline{QR}$ have the same length measures, so they are congruent.

Quadrilateral PQRS is a parallelogram since it has both pairs of opposite sides congruent.

EXAMPLE: A trapezoid has exactly one pair of parallel sides. Show one pair of opposite sides is parallel, and then show the other pair is not parallel.

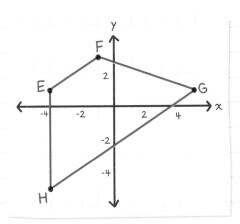

Given: Quadrilateral EFGH has vertices E(–4, 1), F(–1, 3), G(5, 1), and H(–4, –5)

Prove: Quadrilateral EFGH is a trapezoid.

Slope: $m = \dfrac{y_2 - y_1}{x_2 - x_1}$

$\overline{EF}$ has a slope of:

$\dfrac{3-1}{-1-(-4)} = \dfrac{2}{-1+4} = \boxed{\dfrac{2}{3}}$

$\overline{GH}$ has a slope of:

$\dfrac{-5-1}{-4-5} = \dfrac{-6}{-9} = \boxed{\dfrac{2}{3}}$

$\overline{EF}$ and $\overline{GH}$ have the same slope, so they are parallel.

$\overline{EH}$ has a slope of:

$$\frac{-5-1}{-4-(-4)} = \boxed{\frac{-6}{0}}$$

The slope is undefined (it is a vertical line).

$\overline{FG}$ has a slope of:

$$\frac{1-3}{5-(-1)} = \frac{-2}{5+1} = -\frac{2}{6} = \boxed{-\frac{1}{3}}$$

$\overline{EH}$ and $\overline{FG}$ have different slopes, so they are not parallel.

Quadrilateral EFGH is a trapezoid since it has exactly one pair of parallel sides.

CHECK YOUR KNOWLEDGE

For questions 1 and 2, use the slope formula.

1. Given: Quadrilateral ABCD has vertices A(2, 3), B(6, 4), C(7, 0), and D(3, −1).

    Prove: Quadrilateral ABCD is a parallelogram.

2. Given: Quadrilateral WXYZ has vertices W(1, 1), X(5, 5), Y(7, 3), and Z(3, −1).

    Prove: Quadrilateral WXYZ is a parallelogram.

For questions 3 and 4, use the slope formula.

3. Given: Quadrilateral PQRS has vertices P(0, 5), Q(4, 4), R(5, 1), and S(2, −1).

    Prove: Quadrilateral PQRS is a trapezoid.

4. Given: Quadrilateral JKLM has vertices J(−3, −3), K(−4, 1), L(2, 1), and M(1, −3).

    Prove: Quadrilateral JKLM is a trapezoid.

ANSWERS 395

1.

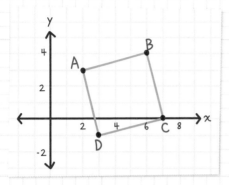

Slope Formula: $m = \dfrac{y_2 - y_1}{x_2 - x_1}$

$\overline{AB}$ has a slope of: $\dfrac{4-3}{6-2} = \dfrac{1}{4}$

$\overline{CD}$ has a slope of: $\dfrac{-1-0}{3-7} = \dfrac{-1}{-4} = \dfrac{1}{4}$

$\overline{AB}$ and $\overline{CD}$ have the same slope, so they are parallel.

$\overline{AD}$ has a slope of: $\dfrac{-1-3}{3-2} = \dfrac{-4}{1} = -4$

$\overline{BC}$ has a slope of: $\dfrac{0-4}{7-6} = \dfrac{-4}{1} = -4$

$\overline{AD}$ and $\overline{BC}$ have the same slope, so they are parallel.

Quadrilateral ABCD is a parallelogram since both pairs of opposite sides are parallel.

2.

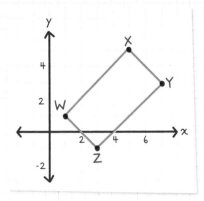

Slope Formula: $m = \dfrac{y_2 - y_1}{x_2 - x_1}$

$\overline{WX}$ has a slope of: $\dfrac{5-1}{5-1} = \dfrac{4}{4} = 1$

$\overline{YZ}$ has a slope of: $\dfrac{-1-3}{3-7} = \dfrac{-4}{-4} = 1$

$\overline{WX}$ and $\overline{YZ}$ have the same slope, so they are parallel.

$\overline{WZ}$ has a slope of: $\dfrac{-1-1}{3-1} = \dfrac{-2}{2} = -1$

$\overline{XY}$ has a slope of: $\dfrac{3-5}{7-5} = \dfrac{-2}{2} = -1$

$\overline{WZ}$ and $\overline{XY}$ have the same slope, so they are parallel.

Quadrilateral WXYZ is a parallelogram since both pairs of opposite sides are parallel.

3.

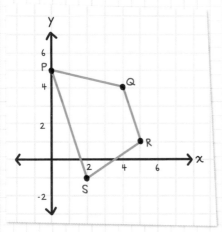

Slope Formula: $m = \dfrac{y_2 - y_1}{x_2 - x_1}$

$\overline{PS}$ has a slope of: $\dfrac{-1-5}{2-0} = \dfrac{-6}{2} = -3$

$\overline{QR}$ has a slope of: $\dfrac{1-4}{5-4} = \dfrac{-3}{1} = -3$

$\overline{PS}$ and $\overline{QR}$ have the same slope, so they are parallel.

$\overline{PQ}$ has a slope of: $\dfrac{4-5}{4-0} = \dfrac{-1}{4}$

$\overline{SR}$ has a slope of: $\dfrac{1-(-1)}{5-2} = \dfrac{1+1}{5-2} = \dfrac{2}{3}$

$\overline{PQ}$ and $\overline{SR}$ have different slopes, so they are not parallel.

Quadrilateral PQRS is a trapezoid since it has one pair of parallel sides and one pair that is not parallel.

4.

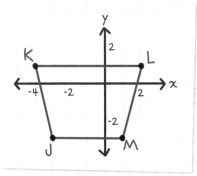

Slope Formula: $m = \dfrac{y_2 - y_1}{x_2 - x_1}$

$\overline{JM}$ has a slope of: $\dfrac{-3-(-3)}{1-(-3)} = \dfrac{-3+3}{1+3} = \dfrac{0}{4} = 0$

$\overline{KL}$ has a slope of: $\dfrac{1-1}{2-(-4)} = \dfrac{0}{6} = 0$

$\overline{JM}$ and $\overline{KL}$ have the same slope, so they are parallel.

$\overline{KJ}$ has a slope of: $\dfrac{-3-1}{-3-(-4)} = \dfrac{-4}{-3+4} = \dfrac{-4}{1} = -4$

$\overline{LM}$ has a slope of: $\dfrac{-3-1}{1-2} = \dfrac{-4}{-1} = 4$

$\overline{KJ}$ and $\overline{LM}$ have the different slopes, so they are not parallel.

Quadrilateral JKLM is a trapezoid since it has one pair of parallel sides and one pair that is not parallel.

Chapter 35

TRIGONOMETRIC RATIOS

TRIGONOMETRY is used to find measures in triangles.

> **TRIGONOMETRY**
> the study of the relationship between side lengths and angles in triangles.

Trigonometry is from the Greek
- *trigonon* = triangle
- *metron* = measure

Important right triangle terms:

HYPOTENUSE the longest side

OPPOSITE the leg that is opposite angle θ

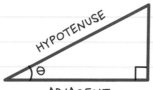

ADJACENT the leg that is next to angle θ

θ (THETA) is a Greek letter used to represent an angle.

The trigonometric functions **SINE (SIN)**, **COSINE (COS)**, and **TANGENT (TAN)** are each a ratio of sides of a right triangle. They are used to find unknown angle measures or side lengths of a right triangle.

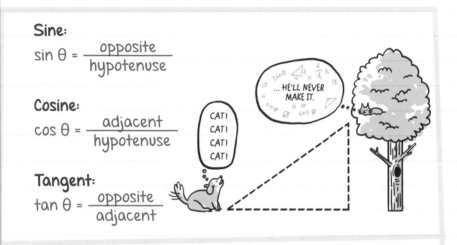

Sine:

$$\sin \theta = \frac{opposite}{hypotenuse}$$

Cosine:

$$\cos \theta = \frac{adjacent}{hypotenuse}$$

Tangent:

$$\tan \theta = \frac{opposite}{adjacent}$$

CAT!
CAT!
CAT!
CAT!

... HE'LL NEVER MAKE IT.

Remember the trigonometric functions by using:

SO̶H̶–CA̶H̶–TOA

Sin = Opposite/H̶ypotenuse
Cos = A̶djacent/H̶ypotenuse
Tan = Opposite/A̶djacent

OR

SILLY CAT!

SO̶H̶–CA̶H̶–TOA
Sam's O̶ld H̶airy Cat A̶te H̶is Tub Of A̶pplesauce.

EXAMPLE: Find sin A, cos A, tan A, sin B, cos B, and tan B.

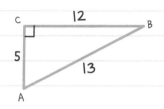

$$\sin A = \frac{\text{opposite } \angle A}{\text{hypotenuse}} = \frac{12}{13}$$

$$\cos A = \frac{\text{adjacent to } \angle A}{\text{hypotenuse}} = \frac{5}{13}$$

$$\tan A = \frac{\text{opposite } \angle A}{\text{adjacent to } \angle A} = \frac{12}{5}$$

$$\sin B = \frac{\text{opposite } \angle B}{\text{hypotenuse}} = \frac{5}{13}$$

$$\cos B = \frac{\text{adjacent to } \angle B}{\text{hypotenuse}} = \frac{12}{13}$$

$$\tan B = \frac{\text{opposite } \angle B}{\text{adjacent to } \angle B} = \frac{5}{12}$$

EXAMPLE: Find sin 22°.

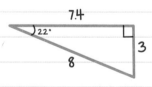

$$\sin 22° = \frac{\text{opposite}}{\text{hypotenuse}} = \frac{3}{8}$$

SPECIAL RIGHT TRIANGLES

A special right triangle is a triangle with a feature (angle or side length) measure that makes calculations easier or for which formulas exist. The two most common right triangle measurements are:

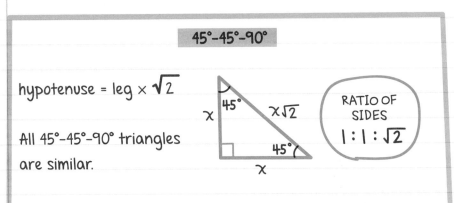

45°-45°-90°

hypotenuse = leg × $\sqrt{2}$

All 45°-45°-90° triangles are similar.

RATIO OF SIDES

$1 : 1 : \sqrt{2}$

45°-45°-90° is an isoceles right triangle.

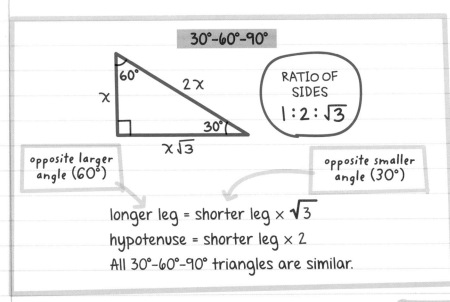

30°-60°-90°

RATIO OF SIDES

$1 : 2 : \sqrt{3}$

opposite larger angle (60°)

opposite smaller angle (30°)

longer leg = shorter leg × $\sqrt{3}$

hypotenuse = shorter leg × 2

All 30°-60°-90° triangles are similar.

EXAMPLE: Find the value of ℓ.

Given:

longer leg = ℓ

shorter leg = 5

Angles = 30°, 60°, 90°

60°

5

30°

ℓ

Using the ratio of a 30°-60°-90° triangle,

longer leg = shorter leg × $\sqrt{3}$

$\ell = 5\sqrt{3}$

> SINCE WE ARE GIVEN "LONGER LEG" AND "SHORTER LEG" VALUES, USE THIS EQUATION.

EXAMPLE: Find the value of k.

Given:

The shorter leg = k
The hypotenuse = 17
Angles = 30°, 60°, 90°

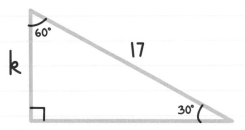

Using the ratio of a 30°-60°-90° triangle,

hypotenuse = shorter leg × 2

$17 = k \times 2$

$k = \dfrac{17}{2} = 8\dfrac{1}{2}$

SINCE WE ARE GIVEN "SHORTER LEG" AND "HYPOTENUSE" VALUES, USE THIS EQUATION.

1. Find sin θ, cos θ, and tan θ.

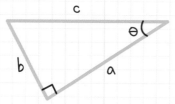

For questions 2–5, find sin A, cos A, and tan A.

2.

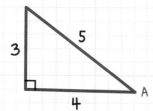

4.

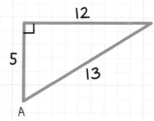

3.

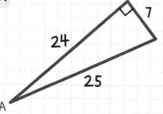

5.

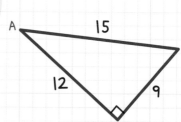

For questions 6–8, find the value of x.

6.

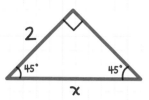

8.

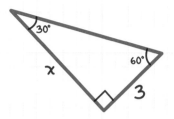

7.

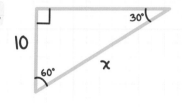

9. Find the values of a and b.

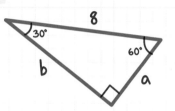

10. Caitlyn is fencing off a section of her garden. What is the length of fence needed to fence off the area shown?

ANSWERS

CHECK YOUR ANSWERS

1. $\sin \theta = \dfrac{b}{c}$, $\cos \theta = \dfrac{a}{c}$, $\tan \theta = \dfrac{b}{a}$

2. $\sin A = \dfrac{3}{5}$, $\cos A = \dfrac{4}{5}$, $\tan A = \dfrac{3}{4}$

3. $\sin A = \dfrac{7}{25}$, $\cos A = \dfrac{24}{25}$, $\tan A = \dfrac{7}{24}$

4. $\sin A = \dfrac{12}{13}$, $\cos A = \dfrac{5}{13}$, $\tan A = \dfrac{12}{5}$

5. $\sin A = \dfrac{3}{5}$, $\cos A = \dfrac{4}{5}$, $\tan A = \dfrac{3}{4}$

6. $x = 2\sqrt{2}$

7. $x = 20$

8. $x = 3\sqrt{3}$

9. $a = 4$, $b = 4\sqrt{3}$

10. 100 ft

Chapter 36

LAWS OF SINES AND COSINES

The **LAWS OF SINES AND COSINES** are used to help find a triangle's unknown angle measures and side lengths.

LAW OF SINES

The Law of Sines relates the side lengths of a non-right triangle to its angles using the sine function.

LAW OF SINES

$$\frac{\sin A}{a} = \frac{\sin B}{b} = \frac{\sin C}{c}$$

$\angle A$, $\angle B$, and $\angle C$ are opposite a, b, and c.

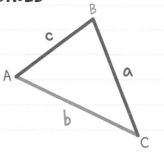

EXAMPLE: Find the value of x.

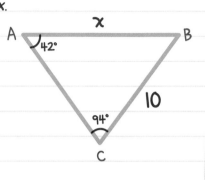

Use the Law of Sines with
$\angle A = 42°$, $a = 10$, $\angle C = 94°$,
and $c = x$:

$$\frac{\sin A}{a} = \frac{\sin C}{c}$$

$$\frac{\sin 42°}{10} \diagdown \frac{\sin 94°}{x}$$

$x \sin 42° = 10 \sin 94°$ Cross multiply.

$$\frac{x \sin 42°}{\sin 42°} = \frac{10 \sin 94°}{\sin 42°}$$ Divide both sides by sin 42°.

$x \approx 14.9$ Use a calculator. Round to
the nearest tenth.

approximately,
or about

Make sure your calculator
is in degree mode.

To find an unknown angle in a trigonometric function like ($\sin \theta = \dfrac{1}{2}$), use **INVERSE TRIGONOMETRIC FUNCTIONS**.

INVERSE TRIGONOMETRIC FUNCTIONS: These do the opposite of regular trigonometric functions. They are represented as $\sin^{-1}$, $\cos^{-1}$, $\tan^{-1}$.

The -1 is not an exponent. It just indicates "opposite of."

If $\sin \theta = \dfrac{a}{c}$, the inverse sine function is $\sin^{-1}\left(\dfrac{a}{c}\right) = \theta$

If $\cos \theta = \dfrac{b}{c}$, the inverse cosine function is $\cos^{-1}\left(\dfrac{b}{c}\right) = \theta$

If $\tan \theta = \dfrac{a}{b}$, the inverse tangent function is $\tan^{-1}\left(\dfrac{a}{b}\right) = \theta$

If you know the trigonometric ratio but not the angle, you can use the inverse function to find the angle.

So, if $\sin 30° = \dfrac{1}{2}$, then $\sin^{-1}\left(\dfrac{1}{2}\right) = 30°$.

EXAMPLE: Find the value of x.

Use the Law of Sines with $m\angle P = 49°$, $p = 11$, $m\angle R = x°$, and $r = 8$.

$$\frac{\sin P}{p} = \frac{\sin R}{r}$$

$$\frac{\sin 49°}{11} \diagup\!\!\!\!\diagdown \frac{\sin x°}{8}$$

$8 \sin 49° = 11 \sin x°$ Cross multiply.

$$\frac{8 \sin 49°}{11} = \frac{11 \sin x°}{11}$$ Divide both sides by 11.

$\frac{8}{11} \sin 49° = \sin x°$ Simplify.

$\sin x° = 0.5488 \dots$ Use a calculator.

$x = \sin^{-1}(0.5488)$ Use sine inverse ($\sin^{-1}$).

$x \approx 33.3$ Use a calculator. Round to the nearest tenth.

LAW OF COSINES

When we know the lengths of two sides of a triangle and the measure of the included angle, we can find the length of the third side using the **LAW OF COSINES**.

LAW OF COSINES

$c^2 = a^2 + b^2 - 2ab \cos C$

c (the side length)
is opposite angle C.

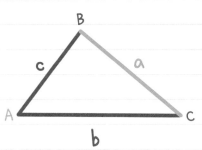

EXAMPLE: Find the value of x.

Use the Law of Cosines with
$m\angle C = 64°$, $c = x$, $a = 8$, and
$b = 5$.

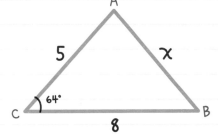

$c^2 = a^2 + b^2 - 2ab \cos C$

$x^2 = 8^2 + 5^2 - 2\,(8)(5) \cos 64°$
$x^2 = 64 + 25 - 80(0.43837) \dots$ Use a calculator.
$x^2 \approx 53.93$

$\sqrt{x^2} \approx \sqrt{53.93}$ Square root of both sides.

$x \approx 7.3$

EXAMPLE: Find the value of x.

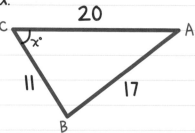

Use the Law of Cosines with
$m\angle C = x°$, $c = 17$, $a = 11$, and
$b = 20$.

$c^2 = a^2 + b^2 - 2ab \cos C$

$17^2 = 11^2 + 20^2 - 2 \times 11 \times 20 \cos x°$

$289 = 121 + 400 - 440 \cos x°$

$-232 = -440 \cos x°$

$\dfrac{232}{440} = \cos x°$

$x = \cos^{-1}\left(\dfrac{232}{440}\right)$ Use the inverse cosine function.

$x \approx 58.2$ Use a calculator. Round to
the nearest tenth.

CHECK YOUR KNOWLEDGE

For questions 1-3, use the Law of Sines to find the value of *x*. Round your answer to the nearest tenth.

1.

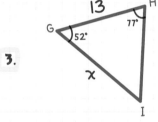

U
94°
x
T 61°
21
V

2.

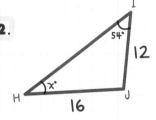

I
54°
12
H *x°*
16
J

3.

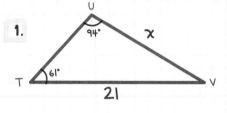

13 H
G 52° 77°
x
I

For questions 4-6, use the Law of Cosines to find the value of *x*. Round your answer to the nearest tenth.

4.

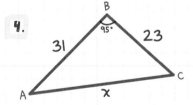

B
95°
31 23
A *x* C

5.

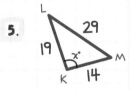

L
19 29
x°
K 14 M

6.

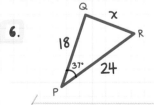

Q *x*
18 R
37° 24
P

ANSWERS

1. $\sin\dfrac{94}{21} = \sin\dfrac{61}{x}$; therefore, $x = 18.4$

2. $\sin\dfrac{54}{16} = \sin\dfrac{x}{12}$; therefore, $x = 37.4$

3. $\sin\dfrac{77}{x} = \sin\dfrac{51}{13}$; therefore, $x = 16.3$

4. $x^2 = 31^2 + 23^2 - 2(31)(23)\cos 95$; $x = 40.2$

5. $29^2 = 14^2 + 19^2 - 2(14)(19)\cos x$; $x = 122.3$

6. $x^2 = 18^2 + 24^2 - 2(18)(24)\cos 37$; $x = 14.5$

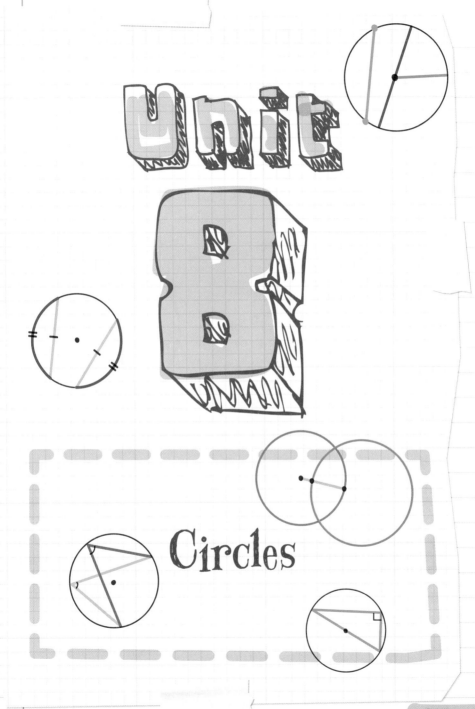

Unit

8

Circles

Chapter 37

CIRCLE FUNDAMENTALS

A **CIRCLE** (⊙) is the set of all points on a plane that are an equal distance from a point called the **CENTER**.

•P
center point

We name a circle using the center point. For example: Circle P.

PARTS OF A CIRCLE

CIRCUMFERENCE (C): The distance around the circle (the perimeter).

CHORD: A line segment whose endpoints are on the circle.

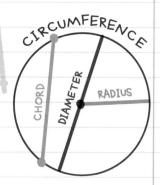
CIRCUMFERENCE
CHORD
DIAMETER
RADIUS

DIAMETER (d): A chord that passes through the center of the circle. The diameter is twice the length of the radius.

Formula: $d = 2r$

RADIUS (r): A line segment that has one endpoint on the center and the other on the circle. The radius is half the length of the diameter.

Formula: $r = \frac{1}{2}d$

> The terms **RADIUS** and **DIAMETER** describe segments of a circle as well as measures.

Pi (π): The ratio of a circle's circumference to its diameter.

Formula: $\pi = \dfrac{\text{circumference}}{\text{diameter}}$ or $\pi = \dfrac{C}{d}$

Because pi's exact value cannot be calculated, we use two approximations:

3.14 when you need a decimal

or

$\frac{22}{7}$ when you need a fraction

CIRCUMFERENCE

The circumference, C, of a circle is **π** times the diameter.

Circumference = π × diameter → C = πd

Because the diameter is twice the length of the radius, you can also find the circumference with this formula:

$$C = 2\pi r$$

EXAMPLE: Find the circumference of the circle.

C = πd

  = π(10)

  = 10π ← *Write the number before the pi symbol.*

10π is the exact answer.

Since π is approximately 3.14, 10π ≈ 10(3.14) = 31.4.

EXAMPLE: Find the circumference of ⊙O.

1. Find the diameter using the
Pythagorean Theorem.

$c^2 = a^2 + b^2$

The diameter (d) is the hypotenuse of the triangle:

$d^2 = 4^2 + 12^2$
$d^2 = 160$
$d = \sqrt{160}$
$d = \sqrt{160} = \sqrt{16 \times 10} = \sqrt{16} \times \sqrt{10} = 4\sqrt{10}$

2. Use the information to find the circumference.

$C = \pi d$
$ = \pi(4\sqrt{10})$
$ = 4\pi\sqrt{10} \approx 4(3.14)(\sqrt{10}) \approx 39.7$

We can use what we know about the circumference of a
circle to find the measures of other parts of the circle.

EXAMPLE: Find the radius and diameter of a circle with circumference 16π.

C = 2πr   Diameter = 2r
16π = 2πr

$r = \dfrac{16\pi}{2\pi}$ d = 2 (8)
                            d = 16

r = 8

CONCENTRIC CIRCLES are circles with the same center.

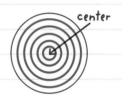

center

EXAMPLE: Dani and Niki are running on a circular track. Dani runs in the inside lane, 64 meters from the center, while Niki runs in the outside lane, 74 meters from the center. They each run one complete lap. How much farther did Niki run than Dani? Round to the nearest tenth.

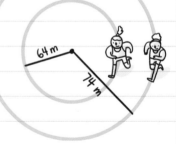

64 m

74 m

Find the distance each girl ran (the circumference of their track) and subtract.

Step 1: Find the distance Dani ran.

Dani's distance is the circumference
of a circle with radius 64 m.

$C = 2\pi r$
  $= 2\pi(64)$
  $= 128\pi \ (\approx 402.1 \text{ m})$

Step 2: Find the distance Niki ran.

Niki's distance is the circumference of a circle with
radius 74 m.

$C = 2\pi r$
  $= 2\pi(74)$
  $= 148\pi \ (\approx 464.9 \text{ m})$

Step 3: Subtract.

$148\pi - 128\pi = 20\pi \approx 62.8$

Niki ran approximately 62.8 m more than Dani.

EXAMPLE: The circumference of ⊙I is 42π, FG = 4, and HI = 6. Find the circumference of ⊙F.

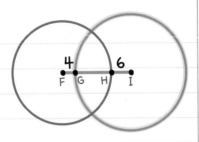

To find the circumference of ⊙F, we need to know FH, which means we need to first find GH.

We can find GH using ⊙I (since we know its circumference).

Step 1: Find GI, using ⊙I.

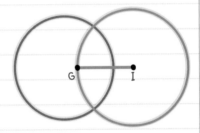

$C = 2\pi r$

$C = 42\pi$

$42\pi = 2\pi \times GI$ ⟵ radius of ⊙I

$\dfrac{42\pi}{2\pi} = \dfrac{2\pi \times GI}{2\pi}$ Divide both sides by 2π. (The π's will cancel out.)

$GI = 21$

Step 2: Find GH.

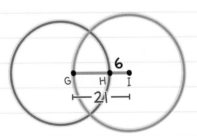

$GI = GH + HI$

$21 = GH + 6$

$GH = 15$

Step 3: Find the circumference of ⊙F.

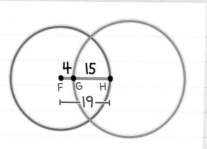

The radius of ⊙F is:

FG + ~~GH~~ = 4 + 15 = 19

The circumference of ⊙F is:

$C = 2\pi r$

$= 2\pi(19)$

$= 38\pi$

1. Name the center, a radius, a diameter, and a chord in ⊙C.

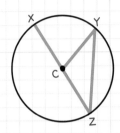

2. Find the radius and diameter of a circle with circumference 51π.

3. Find the circumference of the circle.

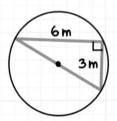

4. A hamster wheel has a 5-inch diameter. How many inches does the hamster travel per revolution (one complete turn)? Round to the nearest tenth.

5. The circumference of the larger circle in the concentric circles is 52π. Find the circumference of the smaller circle.

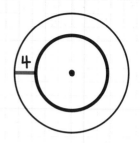

6. Outdoors, Keisha's pupil has a circumference of 3π mm. She walks indoors, and the radius of her pupil widens by 2 mm. What is the new circumference of her pupil?

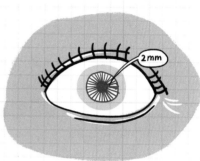

Use the image below for questions 7 and 8.

The circumference of ⊙P is 16π and PQ = 6.

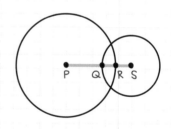

7. Find QR.

8. Find the circumference of ⊙S if RS = 3.

ANSWERS

CHECK YOUR ANSWERS

1. Center: C; radius: $\overline{CX}$, $\overline{CY}$, or $\overline{CZ}$; diameter: $\overline{XZ}$; chord: $\overline{YZ}$ or $\overline{XZ}$

2. $r = \dfrac{51}{2}$, $d = 51$

3. $d^2 = 6^2 + 3^2$, so $d = \sqrt{45} = 3\sqrt{5}$

$C = \pi d = 3\pi\sqrt{5}$ m ≈ 21.1 m

4. $C = \pi d = 5\pi \approx 15.7$ in.

5. Larger circle:
$C = 2\pi r$
$52\pi = 2\pi r$
$r = \dfrac{52\pi}{2\pi} = 26$

Smaller circle:
$r = 26 - 4 = 22$
$C = 2\pi r = 2\pi(22) = 44\pi \approx 138.2$

6. Outdoors:

$C = 2\pi r$

$3\pi = 2\pi r$

$r = \dfrac{3\pi}{2\pi} = 1.5$

Indoors:

$r = 1.5 + 2 = 3.5$

$C = 2\pi r = 2\pi(3.5) = 7\pi$ mm ≈ 22.0 mm

7. $C = 2\pi r$

$16\pi = 2\pi \times PR$

$PR = \dfrac{16\pi}{2\pi} = 8$

$QR = PR - PQ = 8 - 6 = 2$

8. $QS = QR + RS = 2 + 3 = 5$

$C = 2\pi \times QS = 2\pi(5) = 10\pi \approx 31.4$

Chapter 38

CENTRAL ANGLES AND ARCS

A **CENTRAL ANGLE** is an angle that has its vertex on the center of a circle. The segments forming the central angle are radii of the circle.

An **ARC** is a part of the circumference. We name an arc by its two endpoints under a ⌒ symbol: $\overset{\frown}{AB}$

A **SECTOR** is a "slice" of the circle.

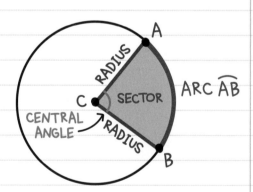

The MEASURE OF AN ARC is equal to the measure of its central angle.

m∠POQ = 62°, so m $\overarc{PQ}$ = 62°

m $\overarc{PQ}$ is read as "the measure of arc $\overarc{PQ}$."

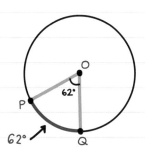

In an entire circle, the measure of the central angle is 360° and the measure of the arc is 360°.

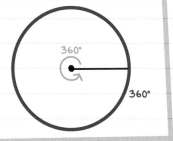

An arc that is 180° is a SEMICIRCLE.

half a circle

m $\overarc{ADB}$ = 180°

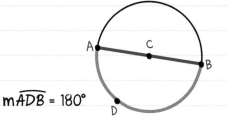

MINOR ARC: smaller than a semicircle (less than 180°)

MAJOR ARC: larger than a semicircle (greater than 180°)

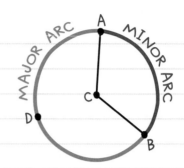

The minor arc is $\overset{\frown}{AB}$ and the major arc is $\overset{\frown}{ADB}$.

Always use three letters to name a major arc.

Since the measure of a circle is 360°:

Central angles equal 360°.

$x° + y° + z° = 360°$

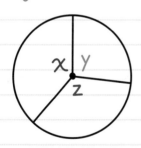

A minor arc and major arc of the same circle add to 360°.

$m\overset{\frown}{AB} + m\overset{\frown}{ADB} = 360°$

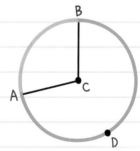

EXAMPLE: Find m$\widehat{XZY}$.

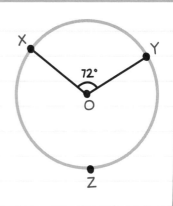

Since the measure of an arc
is equal to the measure of its
central angle,

m$\widehat{XY}$ = m$\angle$XOY = 72°

The minor arc and major arc add to 360°, so:

m$\widehat{XY}$ + m$\widehat{XZY}$ = 360°

72° + m$\widehat{XZY}$ = 360°

m$\widehat{XZY}$ = 288°

ADJACENT ARCS are next to each other. They share
one endpoint.

ARC ADDITION POSTULATE

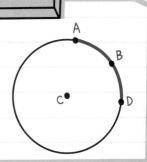

The sum of two adjacent arcs equals
the total arc.

m$\widehat{AD}$ = m$\widehat{AB}$ + m$\widehat{BD}$

EXAMPLE: KN is a diameter of ⊙P. Find $\overset{\frown}{LN}$.

Since $\overset{\frown}{KLN}$ is a semicircle, $m\overset{\frown}{KLN} = 180°$.

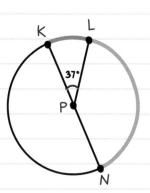

From the Arc Addition Postulate,

$m\overset{\frown}{KL} + m\overset{\frown}{LN} = 180°$

$m\angle KPL + m\overset{\frown}{LN} = 180°$

$37° + m\overset{\frown}{LN} = 180°$

$m\overset{\frown}{LN} = 143°$

ARC LENGTH

ARC LENGTH is the length of an arc (the distance from endpoint to endpoint).

Two arcs can have the same measure but different lengths.

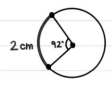

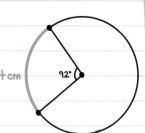

Two arcs can have the same length but different measures.

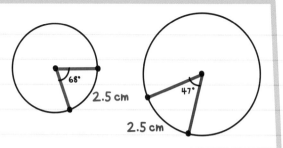

2.5 cm

2.5 cm

Arc measure is equal to the measure of the central angle.

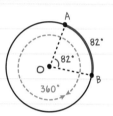

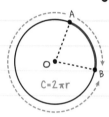

Arc length is a fraction of the circumference.

$C = 2\pi r$

CONGRUENT ARCS are arcs that have the same measure and are in the same circle or congruent circles.

Two circles are congruent if they have the same radius.

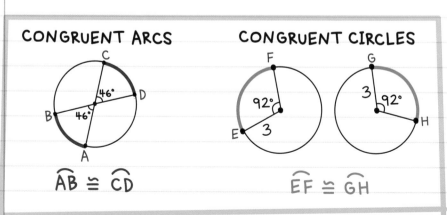

CONGRUENT ARCS

$\overarc{AB} \cong \overarc{CD}$

CONGRUENT CIRCLES

$\overarc{EF} \cong \overarc{GH}$

ARC LENGTH FORMULA

To calculate the ARC LENGTH (ℓ) of a sector
with central angle $x°$, use this formula:

$$\ell = \frac{x}{360} \times 2\pi r$$

Calculate the formula by writing a proportion that compares
a portion of the circle (a sector) to the whole circle.

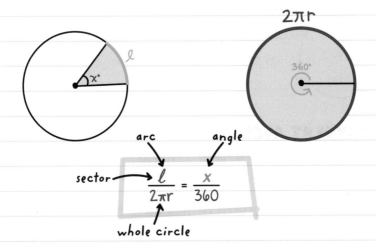

2πr

360°

arc   angle

sector $\longrightarrow$ $\dfrac{\ell}{2\pi r} = \dfrac{x}{360}$

whole circle

The measure of an arc length is equal to the measure of the
central angle divided by 360 and multiplied by $2\pi r$:

$$\text{measure of the arc length} = \frac{\text{measure of the central angle}}{360} \times 2\pi r$$

$$\ell = \frac{x}{360} \times 2\pi r$$

EXAMPLE: Alexandra swings on a tree swing with a rope length of 5 feet.

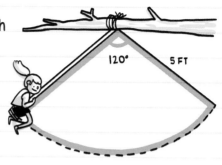

120°   5 FT

If she swings through an angle of 120°, what is the distance she swings?

The length she swings is the arc length of a sector with central angle 120°.

$$\ell = \frac{x}{360} \times 2\pi r$$

Use the arc length formula with $x = 120$ and $r = 5$.

$$= \frac{120}{360} \times 2\pi(5)$$

Alexandra swings 10.5 feet.

$$= \frac{10\pi}{3} \approx 10.5 \text{ ft}$$

1. Name the major arc and minor arc of ⊙Q.

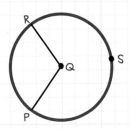

3. Find m$\overarc{KLM}$.

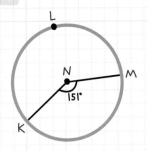

2. Find the measure of ∠x.

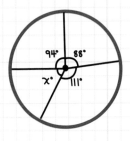

4. $\overline{AD}$ is a diameter of ⊙C. Find m$\overarc{BD}$.

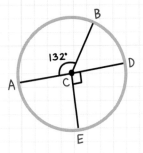

5. For parts A and B, tell whether each statement is true or false.

A. $\overline{AB} \cong \overline{CD}$

B. $\overline{CD} \cong \overline{DE}$

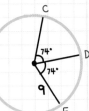

6. Find the length of $\overset{\frown}{VW}$. Round your answer to the nearest tenth.

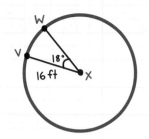

7. Find the length of $\overset{\frown}{LMN}$.

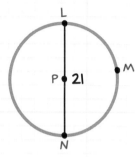

8. Find the length of $\overset{\frown}{LG}$.

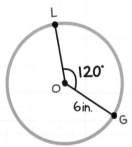

9. Javier has a circular garden with a radius of 9 feet. He is placing a stone border around a quarter of the circumference (an arc of 90°). How many feet of stone will he need?

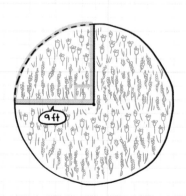

ANSWERS

CHECK YOUR ANSWERS

1. Major arc $\overset{\frown}{PSR}$ (or $\overset{\frown}{RSP}$), minor arc $\overset{\frown}{PR}$ (or $\overset{\frown}{RP}$)

2. $x = 67°$

3. $m\overset{\frown}{KM} + m\overset{\frown}{KLM} = 360°$
$151° + m\overset{\frown}{KLM} = 360°$
$m\overset{\frown}{KLM} = 209°$

4. $m\overset{\frown}{BD} = 48°$

5. A. False. The arcs must have the same measure AND be in either the same circle or congruent circles.

B. True. The arcs have the same measure and are in the same circle.

6. Length of $\overset{\frown}{VW} = \dfrac{18}{360} \times 2\pi(16)$

$= \dfrac{8\pi}{5} \text{ ft} \approx 5.0 \text{ ft}$

7. Length of $\overparen{LMN} = \dfrac{180}{360} \times 2\pi(10.5)$

$$= \dfrac{21\pi}{2} \approx 33.0$$

8. Length of $\overparen{LG} = \dfrac{120}{360} \times 2\pi(6)$

$$= 4\pi \approx 12.6 \text{ in.}$$

9. Length of stone border $= \dfrac{90}{360} \times 2\pi(9)$

$$= \dfrac{9\pi}{2} \approx 14.1 \text{ ft}$$

Chapter 39

RADIANS

THE RADIAN

Another way to measure angles is using **RADIANS** (rad).

One **radian** is the measure of a central angle that has an arc length that is equal to the radius.

IT'S JUST ANOTHER UNIT FOR ANGLE MEASURE. LIKE MEASURING LENGTH IN FEET INSTEAD OF METERS.

arc length = radius (r)

$m\angle\theta = 1$ radian

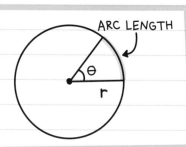

ARC LENGTH

Since C = 2πr, we know that there are 2π radii in the circumference of a circle.

> In a full circle, there are **2π** radians.
>
> 2π radians = 360°
>
> π radians = 180°
>
> 1 radian = $\frac{180°}{π}$ ≈ 57.3°

Common Radian Measures

$\frac{π}{6}$ rad = 30°

$\frac{π}{4}$ rad = 45°

$\frac{π}{3}$ rad = 60°

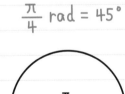
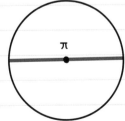
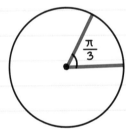
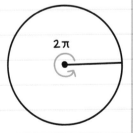

$\frac{π}{2}$ rad = 90°

π rad = 180°

2π rad = 360°

CONVERTING DEGREES AND RADIANS

To convert radians to degrees, multiply by $\frac{180°}{\pi}$.

To convert degrees to radians, multiply by $\frac{\pi}{180°}$.

EXAMPLE: Convert 30° to radians.

Multiply 30° by $\frac{\pi}{180°}$.

$30° \times \frac{\pi}{180°}$

$\frac{30\pi}{180°} = \frac{1\pi}{6} = \frac{\pi}{6}$

EXAMPLE: Convert $\frac{3\pi}{2}$ to degrees.

Multiply $\frac{3\pi}{2}$ by $\frac{180°}{\pi}$.

$$\frac{3\overset{1}{\cancel{\pi}}}{\underset{1}{2}} \times \frac{\overset{90}{\cancel{180°}}}{\underset{1}{\cancel{\pi}}} = 3 \cdot 90° = 270°$$

CHECK YOUR KNOWLEDGE

For questions 1–5, convert the following measures to radians.

1. 180°

2. 330°

3. 75°

4. 45°

5. 110°

For questions 6–10, convert the following measures to degrees.

6. $\frac{5\pi}{6}$ rad

7. $\frac{\pi}{6}$ rad

8. $\frac{3\pi}{2}$ rad

9. $\frac{4\pi}{3}$ rad

10. $\frac{\pi}{12}$ rad

ANSWERS 445

CHECK YOUR ANSWERS

1. π

2. $\dfrac{11\pi}{6}$

3. $\dfrac{5\pi}{12}$

4. $\dfrac{\pi}{4}$

5. $\dfrac{11\pi}{18}$

6. $150°$

7. $30°$

8. $270°$

9. $240°$

10. $15°$

Chapter 40

ARCS AND CHORDS

A **CHORD** divides a circle into major and minor arcs (unless the chord is a diameter).

The minor arc is called the
ARC OF THE CHORD.

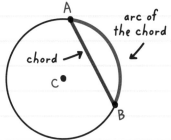

Chord $\overline{AB}$ has arc $\overparen{AB}$.

THEOREMS ABOUT CHORDS

> In a circle or in congruent circles, congruent chords have congruent arcs.

If $\overline{PQ} \cong \overline{RS}$, then $\overparen{PQ} \cong \overparen{RS}$.

The converse is also true:
If $\overparen{PQ} \cong \overparen{RS}$, then $\overline{PQ} \cong \overline{RS}$.

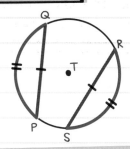

In a circle or in congruent circles, congruent chords are equidistant from the center.

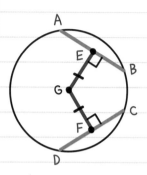

If $\overline{AB} \cong \overline{CD}$, then $EG = FG$.

The converse is also true:
If $EG = FG$, then $\overline{AB} \cong \overline{CD}$.

If a diameter is perpendicular to a chord, then it bisects the chord and its arc.

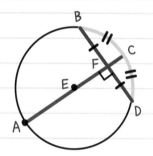

If $\overline{AC} \perp \overline{BD}$, then $\overline{BF} \cong \overline{FD}$ and $\overarc{BC} \cong \overarc{CD}$.

The perpendicular bisector of a chord is a diameter.

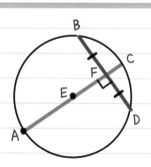

If $\overline{AC}$ is a perpendicular bisector of $\overline{BD}$, then $\overline{AC}$ is a diameter of $\odot E$.

EXAMPLE: In $\odot$T, m$\widehat{QR}$ = 177° and m$\widehat{SP}$ = 33°.

Find m$\widehat{PQ}$ and m$\widehat{RS}$.

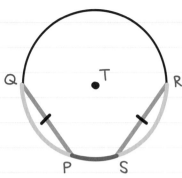

Since congruent chords ($\overline{PQ}$ and $\overline{RS}$) have congruent arcs:

$\widehat{RS} \cong \widehat{PQ}$ and m$\widehat{RS}$ = m$\widehat{PQ}$

The arcs in a circle add to 360°, so

m$\widehat{PQ}$ + m$\widehat{QR}$ + m$\widehat{RS}$ + m$\widehat{SP}$ = 360°

m$\widehat{PQ}$ + 177° + m$\widehat{PQ}$ + 33° = 360°   Since m$\widehat{RS}$ = m$\widehat{PQ}$ and m$\widehat{SP}$ = 33°

m$\widehat{PQ}$ + m$\widehat{PQ}$ = 360° − 177° − 33°

2 × m$\widehat{PQ}$ = 150°

m$\widehat{PQ}$ = 75°

m$\widehat{RS}$ = m$\widehat{PQ}$ = 75°

EXAMPLE: Find the length of $\overline{ST}$ and $\overline{UV}$ in ⊙W.

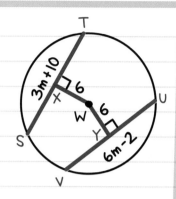

Since $\overline{ST}$ and $\overline{UV}$ are equidistant to W, they are congruent and have equal measure:

ST = UV

3m + 10 = 6m – 2

12 = 3m

m = 4

Therefore, ST = 3m + 10 = 3(4) + 10 = 22

UV = 6m – 2 = 6(4) – 2 = 22

Since ST = UV, we know our calculations are correct.

EXAMPLE: Find the value of x.

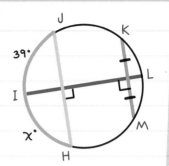

We know $\overline{IL}$ is a diameter of the circle since it is a perpendicular bisector of $\overline{KM}$.

Since diameter $\overline{IL}$ is perpendicular to $\overline{JH}$, it bisects arc $\overarc{HJ}$:

$\overarc{IH} \cong \overarc{IJ}$

$m\overarc{IH} = m\overarc{IJ}$

$x = 39°$

EXAMPLE: Find the value of x in $\odot F$.

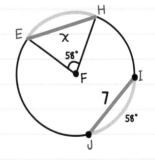

Since we know $m\overarc{EH} = m\angle EFH$, then $m\overarc{EH} = 58°$, which means $\overarc{EH}$ and $\overarc{IJ}$ are congruent.

Since congruent arcs have congruent chords,

$\overline{EH} \cong \overline{IJ}$

$EH = IJ$

$x = 7$

1. Find the value of x.

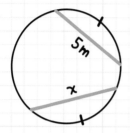

5m

x

2. Find m∠BEC.

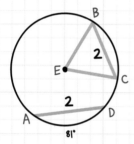

B

2

E

2

C

A

D

81°

3. Find the value of x.

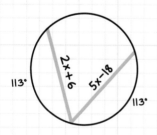

113°

2x+6

5x-18

113°

4. Find m $\widehat{WX}$ and m $\widehat{YZ}$.

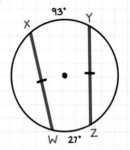

93°

X   Y

W   27°   Z

5. Find c if $\overline{WX} \cong \overline{YZ}$.

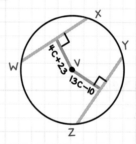

X

4c+23

W   V   Y

13c-10

Z

6. The length of $\overline{GJ}$ is 7. Find the length of $\overline{HI}$.

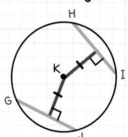

H

K   I

G

J

7. Find the value of x.

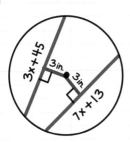

9. Find m∠AEC.

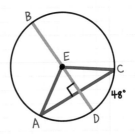

8. Find the lengths of $\overline{NR}$ and $\overline{RP}$ if NP = 31.

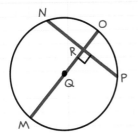

10. Find the values of x and y so that $\overline{FH}$ is a diameter of ⊙J.

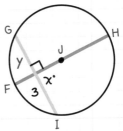

CHECK YOUR ANSWERS

1. $x = 5m$

2. $m\angle BEC = 81°$

3. $2x + 6 = 5x - 18$; therefore, $x = 8$

4. $m\overarc{WX} = 120°$, $m\overarc{YZ} = 120°$

5. $4c + 23 = 13c - 10$; therefore, $c = \dfrac{11}{3}$

6. $\overline{HI} = 7$

7. $3x + 45 = 7x + 13$; therefore, $x = 8$

8. $\overline{NR} = \dfrac{31}{2}$, $\overline{RP} = \dfrac{31}{2}$

9. $m\angle AEC = 96°$

10. $x = 90°$, $y = 3$

Chapter 41

INSCRIBED ANGLES

An **INSCRIBED ANGLE** is formed by two intersecting chords with a vertex on the circle.

The **INTERCEPTED ARC** is the part of the circle that is in the interior of the inscribed angle.

> The measure of an inscribed angle is half the measure of its intercepted arc.
>
> $$m\angle A = \frac{1}{2}\, m\widehat{BC}$$

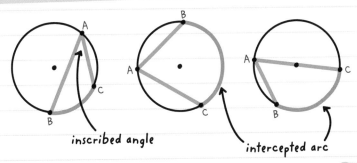

inscribed angle

intercepted arc

If two inscribed angles have the same intercepted arc, then those angles are congruent.

$m\angle A = \frac{1}{2}m\angle \overset{\frown}{BC}$

$m\angle D = \frac{1}{2}m\angle \overset{\frown}{BC}$

$m\angle A = m\angle D$

$\angle A \cong \angle D$

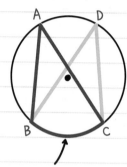

same intercepted arc

An angle inscribed in a semicircle is a right angle.

$m\angle B = \frac{1}{2}m\overset{\frown}{ADC}$

$= \frac{1}{2}(180°)$

$= 90°$

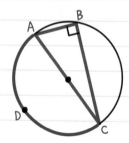

EXAMPLE: Find m∠QPR, with P the center of the circle.

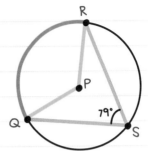

$m\angle S = \frac{1}{2} m\overset{\frown}{QR}$

$79° = \frac{1}{2} m\overset{\frown}{QR}$

$m\overset{\frown}{QR} = 158°$

Since the measure of arc $\overset{\frown}{QR}$ is equal to the measure of its central angle ∠QPR:

$m\angle QPR = 158°$

EXAMPLE: Find the values of x, m∠NKM, and m∠NLM.

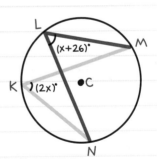

Since ∠K and ∠L are inscribed angles with the same intercepted arc $\overset{\frown}{NM}$:

$\angle K \cong \angle L$

$m\angle K = m\angle L$

$2x = x + 26$

$x = 26°$

$m\angle K = (2x)° = (2 \times 26)° = \boxed{52°}$

$m\angle L = (x + 26)° = (26 + 26)° = \boxed{52°}$

Since $m\angle K = m\angle L$, we know our calculations are correct.

An **INSCRIBED SHAPE** is inside another shape, just touching the sides.

The triangle is inscribed in the circle.

The vertices are on the circle.

If a quadrilateral is inscribed in a circle, then its opposite angles are supplementary.

$\angle A$ and $\angle C$ are supplementary.

$\angle B$ and $\angle D$ are supplementary.

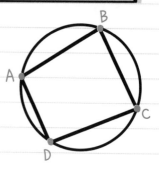

EXAMPLE: A necklace charm has a shape of a quadrilateral inscribed in a circle. Find m∠U and m∠W.

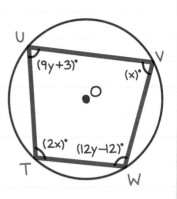

Since the quadrilateral is inscribed in a circle, we know opposite angles are supplementary:

m∠U + m∠W = 180°

(9y + 3) + (12y − 12) = 180
21y − 9 = 180
21y = 189
y = 9

m∠U = (9y + 3)° = (9 × 9 + 3)° = ⟨84°⟩

Since 84° + 96° = 180° we know our calculations are correct.

m∠W = (12y − 12)° = (12 × 9 − 12)° = ⟨96°⟩

1. m∠ABC = 105°.
Find m$\overgroup{CDA}$.

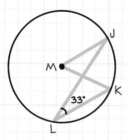

2. Find m∠JMK.

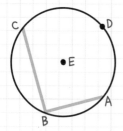

3. Find m∠2.

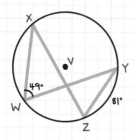

4. Find the value of x, m∠B, and m∠C.

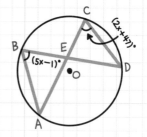

5. Find m∠A.

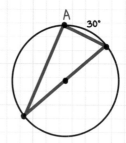

6. Find the value of x.

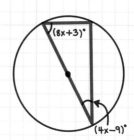

7. Find m∠A, m∠B, and m∠C.

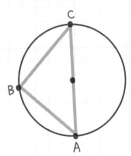

9. Find the value of x.

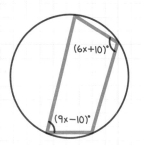

8. Find m∠G and m∠H.

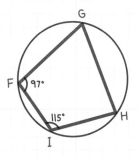

10. Find m∠E and m∠G.

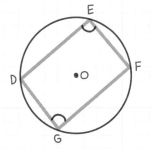

CHECK YOUR ANSWERS

1. m$\overarc{CDA}$ = 210°

2. m∠JMK = 66°

3. m∠2 = 49°

4. $5x - 1 = 2x + 47$; therefore, $x = 16$, m∠B = 79°, m∠C = 79°

5. m∠A = 90°

6. $(8x + 3) + (4x - 9) = 90$; therefore, $x = 8$

7. m∠A = 45°, m∠B = 90°, m∠C = 45°

8. m∠G = 65°, m∠H = 83°

9. $(9x - 10) + (6x + 10) = 180$; therefore, $x = 12$

10. m∠E = 90°, m∠G = 90°

Chapter 42

TANGENTS

A **TANGENT** is a line, segment, or ray that intersects a circle in exactly one point (called the POINT OF TANGENCY).

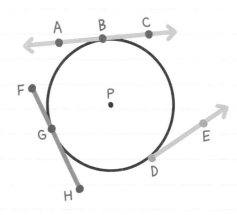

$\overleftrightarrow{AC}$, $\overrightarrow{DE}$, and $\overline{FH}$ are tangent to ⊙P.

B, D, and G are the **points of tangency**.

Two circles have a COMMON TANGENT if a line is tangent to both circles.

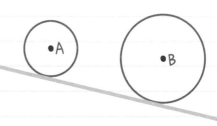

Line ℓ is a common tangent of ⊙A and ⊙B.

Circles can have more than one common tangent.

⊙A and ⊙B have four common tangent lines.

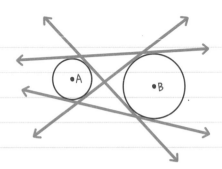

A line is tangent to a circle if and only if it is perpendicular to the radius drawn to the point of tangency.

$\overleftrightarrow{AC}$ is tangent to ⊙O if and only if (iff) $\overline{OB} \perp \overleftrightarrow{AC}$.

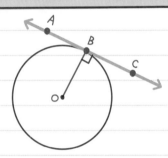

Tangent segments from the same point outside a circle are congruent.

If $\overline{AB}$ and $\overline{AC}$ are tangent to ⊙O at points B and C, then $\overline{AB} \cong \overline{AC}$.

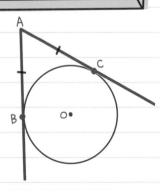

EXAMPLE: Determine if $\overline{QR}$ is a tangent to $\odot$S.

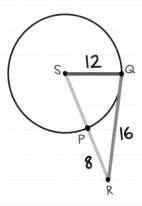

If $\overline{SQ} \perp \overline{QR}$, then $\overline{QR}$ is a tangent. We can use the Pythagorean Theorem to check if $\triangle SQR$ is a right triangle.

1. Find the length of $\overline{SR}$:

SP = 12, since it is a radius of the circle.

SR = SP + PR

SR = 12 + 8 = 20

> All radii of a circle are congruent.
>
> SQ = 12, so SP = 12

2. Check if $\triangle SQR$ is a right triangle:

$a^2 + b^2 = c^2$

$SQ^2 + QR^2 = SR^2$

$12^2 + 16^2 = 20^2$

144 + 256 = 400

400 = 400 ✔

Since SQ² + QR² = SR², △SQR is a right triangle and
$\overline{SQ} \perp \overline{QR}$.

Therefore, $\overleftrightarrow{QR}$ is a tangent to ⊙S.

EXAMPLE: Find the value of x
given that $\overline{PQ}$ and $\overline{QR}$ are tangent
to circle O and m∠Q = 115°.

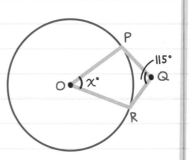

Since $\overline{PQ}$ and $\overline{QR}$ are tangent to
circle O, $\overline{OP} \perp \overline{PQ}$ and $\overline{OR} \perp \overline{RQ}$.

Therefore, m∠P = 90° and m∠R = 90°.

Since the sum of the measures of a quadrilateral equals 360°,

m∠O + m∠P + m∠Q + m∠R = 360°

x + 90 + 115 + 90 = 360
x + 295 = 360
x = 65

EXAMPLE: $\overline{FG}$ and $\overline{FH}$ are tangent to $\odot I$.

Find the value of x.

Since $\overline{FG}$ and $\overline{FH}$ are tangent to $\odot I$, they are congruent.

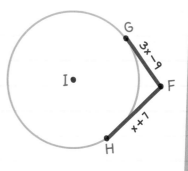

$FG = FH$

$3x - 9 = x + 7$

$2x = 16$

$x = 8$

For questions 1 and 2, state whether the pairs of circles have a common tangent line. If so, state how many common tangents they have.

1.

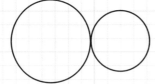

2.

For questions 3 and 4, determine whether $\overline{AB}$ is tangent to ⊙P.

3.

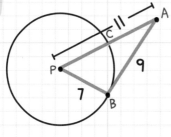

4.

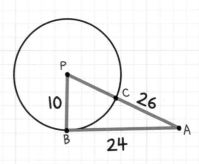

For questions **5-10**, find the value of x. Assume segments that appear tangent are tangent.

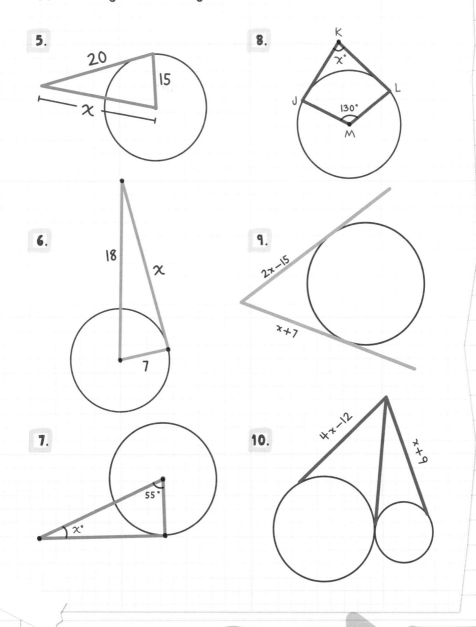

5.

20

15

x

8.

K

x°

J

130°

M

L

6.

18

x

7

9.

2x−15

x+7

7.

55°

x°

10.

4x−12

x+9

ANSWERS 469

CHECK YOUR ANSWERS

1. Yes, 3

2. No

3. No, $7^2 + 9^2 \neq 11^2$

4. Yes, $10^2 + 24^2 = 26^2$

5. $20^2 + 15^2 = x^2$; therefore, $x = 25$

6. $x^2 + 7^2 = 18^2$; therefore, $x = 16.6$, approximately

7. $x + 55 + 90 = 180$; therefore, $x = 35$

8. $x + 90 + 130 + 90 = 360$; therefore, $x = 50$

9. $2x - 15 = x + 7$; therefore, $x = 22$

10. $4x - 12 = x + 9$; therefore, $x = 7$

Chapter 43

SECANTS

A **SECANT** is a line that intersects a circle at two points.

> Line ℓ is a secant of $\odot$P.

When two secants intersect **inside a circle:**

The measure of the angle that is formed is equal to one-half the sum of the intercepted arcs.

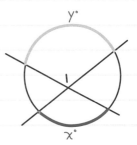

$$1 = \frac{1}{2}(x° + y°)$$

When two secants intersect **outside a circle**:

The measure of the angle that is formed is equal to one-half the difference of the far arc less the near arc.

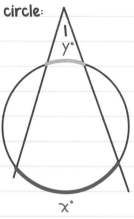

$$\frac{1}{2}(x° - y°)$$

ALSO TRUE FOR:

A SECANT OR TANGENT   TWO TANGENTS

EXAMPLE: Find the value of x.

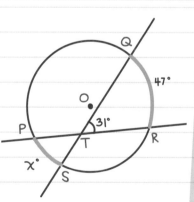

$$m\angle QTR = \frac{1}{2}(m\overset{\frown}{PS} + m\overset{\frown}{QR})$$

$$31 = \frac{1}{2}(x + 47)$$

intersection inside circle

$$62 = x + 47$$

$$x = 15°$$

EXAMPLE: Find m∠A.

First, find m$\overgroup{BCD}$:

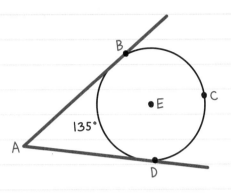

m$\overgroup{BCD}$ + m$\overgroup{BD}$ = 360° (from the Arc Addition Postulate)

m$\overgroup{BCD}$ + 135° = 360°

m$\overgroup{BCD}$ = 225°

Then find m∠A:

$$m\angle A = \frac{1}{2}(m\overgroup{BCD} - m\overgroup{BD})$$

intersection outside circle

$$= \frac{1}{2}(225° - 135°)$$

$$= \frac{1}{2}(90°) = 45°$$

When secants and tangents intersect, their segment lengths have special properties.

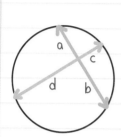

secants intersecting within a circle

$a \times b = c \times d$

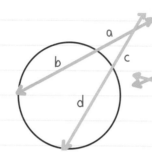

secants intersecting outside a circle

$a \times (a + b) = c \times (c + d)$

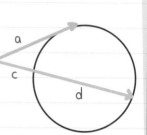

tangent and secant intersecting

$a^2 = c \times (c + d)$

EXAMPLE: Find the value of x.

Use $a \times (a + b) = c \times (c + d)$

$5(5 + x) = 4(4 + 12)$

$25 + 5x = 16 + 48$

$5x = 39$

$x = \dfrac{39}{5}$

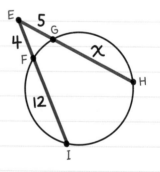

CHECK YOUR KNOWLEDGE

For questions 1–6, find the value of x. Assume that segments that appear tangent are tangent.

1.

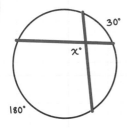

30°
x°
180°

4.

x°
22°
61°

2.

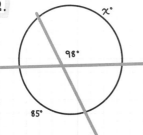

x°
98°
85°

5.

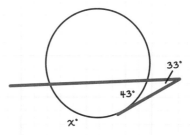

33°
43°
x°

3.

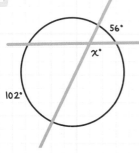

56°
x°
102°

6.

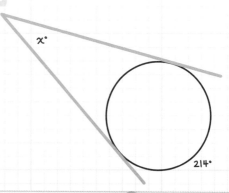

x°
214°

ANSWERS

CHECK YOUR ANSWERS

1. $x = \frac{1}{2}(30 + 180)$; therefore, $x = 105°$

2. $98 = \frac{1}{2}(x + 85)$; therefore, $x = 111°$

3. $180 - x = \frac{1}{2}(56 + 102)$; therefore, $x = 101°$

4. $x = \frac{1}{2}(61 - 22)$; therefore, $x = \frac{39}{2} = 19.5°$

5. $33 = \frac{1}{2}(x - 43)$; therefore, $x = 109°$

6. $x = \frac{1}{2}(214 - 146)$; therefore, $x = 34°$

Chapter 44

EQUATIONS OF CIRCLES

A circle can be graphed on a coordinate plane, using the coordinates of its center and radius.

WRITING AN EQUATION OF A CIRCLE WITH CENTER (0, 0)

The equation of a circle with its center at the origin and radius r is:

$$x^2 + y^2 = r^2$$

Center: (0, 0)

Radius: 2

Equation: $x^2 + y^2 = 4$ ← 2^2

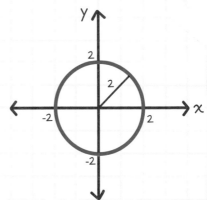

This equation can be reached using the Pythagorean Theorem.

For any point (x, y) on the circle,

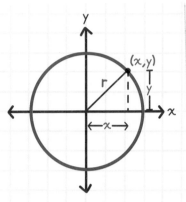

$x^2 + y^2 = r^2$ (Pythagorean Theorem)

The circle is the shape formed by all (x, y) points where $x^2 + y^2 = r^2$ is true.

WRITING AN EQUATION OF A CIRCLE WITH CENTER (h, k)

If a circle's center is not at the origin, use the standard form equation:

$$(x - h)^2 + (y - k)^2 = r^2$$

↑
Pythagorean Theorem

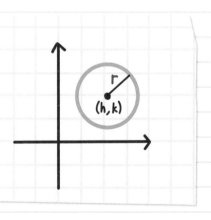

The center is (h, k) and the radius is r.

EXAMPLE: Find the equation of the circle.

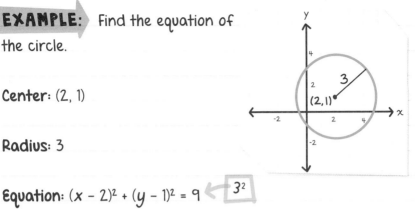

Center: (2, 1)

Radius: 3

Equation: $(x - 2)^2 + (y - 1)^2 = 9$ ← 3^2

The equation for a circle with center (h, k) and radius r can be taken from the Pythagorean Theorem:

Draw a right triangle using a radius of the circle as the hypotenuse.

The length of the horizonal leg of the triangle is: $x - h$.

The length of the vertical leg of the triangle is: $y - k$.

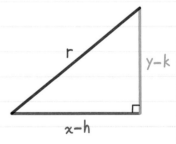

Using the Pythagorean Theorem,

$(x - h)^2 + (y - k)^2 = r^2$

EXAMPLE: Find the equation of the circle with center (−1, 2) and radius 4.

Draw a right triangle using a radius of the circle as the hypotenuse. Label the endpoint of the radius (x, y).

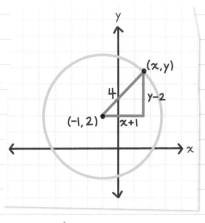

The length of the horizontal leg of the triangle is:
$x − (−1) = x + 1$

The length of the vertical leg of the triangle is: $y − 2$.

Using the Pythagorean Theorem,

$(x − (−1))^2 + (y − 2)^2 = 4^2$

$(x + 1)^2 + (y − 2)^2 = 16$ Simplify.

To graph the circle above:

Step 1: Graph the center point (−1, 2).

Step 2: Graph four points using the radius.

The radius is 4, so count 4 units up from the center.
Plot point (−1, 6).

Repeat counting
4 units down (−1, −2),
right (3, 2), and left
(−5, 2) from the center.

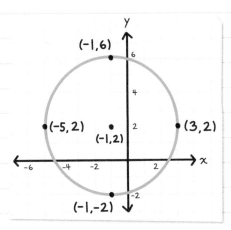

Step 3: Use a compass to
connect the points.

You can also plot the center and one
additional point 4 units away from
the center. Then use your compass to
draw a perfect circle.

CENTER

CONVERTING TO STANDARD FORM

Equations of circles are not always in standard form.

We use the process of COMPLETING THE SQUARE to rewrite
equations in standard form. Then we can find the center
and radius more easily.

Completing the square is an algebraic process where a quadratic equation is rewritten as the sum or difference of a perfect square and a constant.

Completing the square for $x^2 + 6x + 4 = 0$

$x^2 + 6x + 4 = 0$

Step 1: Add/subtract so x-terms are on the left and constants (numbers without the x) on the right.

$x^2 + 6x = -4$

Step 2: Divide the number in front of x (x-coefficient) by 2 and square it. Add that number to both sides.

$x^2 + 6x + \boxed{9} = -4 + \boxed{9}$

$$\left(\frac{6}{2}\right)^2 \qquad \left(\frac{6}{2}\right)^2$$

Step 3: Simplify and write as a square (factor it).

$(x + 3)^2 = 5$

$$\frac{6}{2}$$

EXAMPLE: Write the following equation in standard form.

$x^2 + y^2 - 8x + 4y - 16 = 0$

Since this equation has both x's and y's, we will complete the square for each variable.

Step 1: Get constants on the right.

$x^2 + y^2 - 8x + 4y = 16$

Group x-terms and y-terms together.

$x^2 - 8x \qquad + y^2 + 4y = 16$

Step 2: Divide the number in front of x by 2 and square it. Add it to both sides.

$x^2 - 8x + \boxed{16} + y^2 + 4y = 16 + \boxed{16}$

$\left(\dfrac{-8}{2}\right)^2$

Divide the number in front of y by 2 and square it. Add it to both sides.

$$x^2 - 8x + 16 + y^2 + 4y + \boxed{4} = 16 + 16 + \boxed{4}$$

$$\left(\frac{4}{2}\right)^2$$

Step 3: Simplify and write as squares.

$$(x - 4)^2 + (y + 2)^2 = 36$$

$$\frac{-8}{2} \qquad \frac{4}{2}$$

The center is (4, –2).

The radius is 6.

For questions 1 and 2, find the center and radius of the given circle. Then draw the graph.

1. $x^2 + (y - 3)^2 = 9$

2. $(x + 2)^2 + (y + 1)^2 = 1$

For questions **3–5**, write the equation of a circle with the given information or graph.

3. Center at the origin, radius 9

4. Center (–5, 8), radius 6

5.

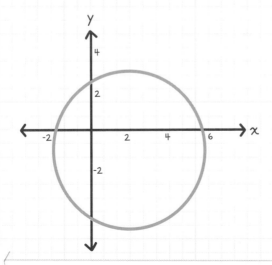

For questions 6 and 7, complete the square in the equation.

6. $x^2 + 8x + 5 = 0$

7. $x^2 - 14x - 8 = 3$

For questions 8 and 9, write the equation of the circle in standard form. Then find the center and radius and draw the graph.

8. $x^2 - 2x + y^2 + 2y - 14 = 0$

9. $x^2 + y^2 - 6x - 4y + 9 = 0$

CHECK YOUR ANSWERS

1. Center (0, 3), radius 3

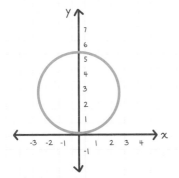

2. Center (–2, –1), radius 1

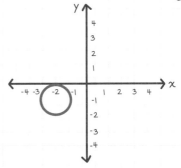

3. $x^2 + y^2 = 81$

4. $(x + 5)^2 + (y - 8)^2 = 36$

5. $(x - 2)^2 + (y + 1)^2 = 16$

6. $(x + 4)^2 = 11$

7. $(x - 7)^2 = 60$

8. $(x - 1)^2 + (y + 1)^2 = 16$,
center $(1, -1)$, radius 4

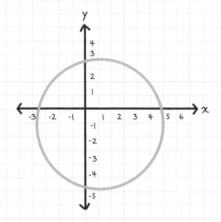

9. $(x - 3)^2 + (y - 2)^2 = 4$,
center $(3, 2)$, radius 2

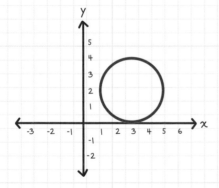

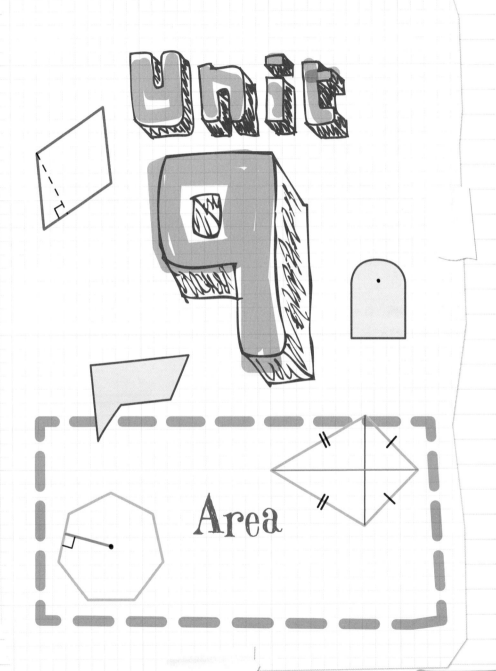

Unit

9

Area

Chapter 45

AREAS OF PARALLELOGRAMS AND TRIANGLES

AREA OF PARALLELOGRAMS

AREA (A) is the amount of space inside a two-dimensional object. Area is written in "units squared" or units^2.

AREA OF A FIGURE is the number of equal-sized squares that the figure encloses.

6 ft

3 ft

An area of 18 square feet means that 18 squares, each with an area of 1 foot^2 can fit inside.

The area of a parallelogram is the length of the base times the height. (This formula applies to rectangles, rhombuses, and squares, too.)

A = base × height
or
A = bh

The formula for the area of a parallelogram is the same as the formula for the area of a rectangle because it is made up of the same parts. If we translate the shaded triangle in the parallelogram to the right, the parallelogram becomes a rectangle.

The base of the parallelogram is the length of the rectangle, and the height of the parallelogram is the width of the rectangle. The rectangle's area is:

$$A = lw = bh$$

Find the height of a parallelogram by drawing a perpendicular line from the line that contains the base to the line that contains the opposite side. This can be inside or outside the parallelogram.

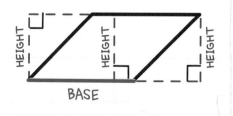

EXAMPLE: Find the area of the parallelogram.

Since a perpendicular line is drawn from $\overline{AE}$ to $\overline{BD}$, use $\overline{AE}$ as the base and $\overline{EC}$ as the height.

A = bh

= 14 × 7 = 98

A = 98 ft²

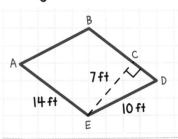

EXAMPLE: Find the value of h in the parallelogram.

The area of this parallelogram can be expressed by:

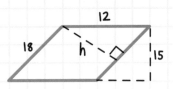

Using base = 12 and height = 15 OR
Using base = 18 and height = h

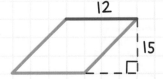
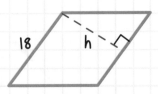

Since the area is same no matter what method we use:

Area = Area

bh = bh

12 × 15 = 18h

h = 10

AREA OF TRIANGLES

In order to calculate the area of a triangle, multiply $\frac{1}{2}$ by the length of the base times the height.

$A = \frac{1}{2} \cdot \text{base} \cdot \text{height}$

$A = \frac{1}{2} \cdot bh$ $A = \frac{bh}{2}$ $\begin{array}{l} b = base \\ h = height \end{array}$

The height is the length of the perpendicular line drawn from a vertex to the base. This can be inside or outside the triangle.

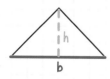
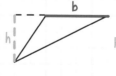

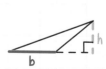

If you cut a rectangle in half diagonally, the area formed by the remaining triangle is only half as large as the area of the original rectangle—that's why the formula for the area of a triangle is:

$$A = \frac{bh}{2} \text{ OR } \frac{1}{2}bh$$

h

b

EXAMPLE: Find the area of the triangle.

$A = \dfrac{bh}{2}$

$A = \dfrac{(18)(20)}{2} = 180$

$A = 180 \text{ mm}^2$

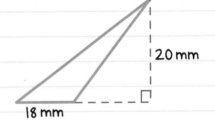

20 mm

18 mm

EXAMPLE: Find the area of the triangle.

Use AC = 17 for the base and BD for the height.

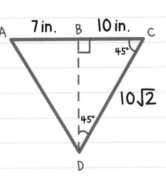

A   7 in.   B   10 in.   C

45°

$10\sqrt{2}$

45°

D

We can find the length BD by using special right triangle 45°-45°-90°:

B ── 10 in. ── C

The legs are congruent, so:

BD = BC

BD = 10 in.

Now we have all the information we need to find the area,

$$A = \frac{bh}{2}$$

$$A = \frac{(17)(10)}{2} = 85$$

$$A = 85 \text{ in.}^2$$

CHECK YOUR KNOWLEDGE

In questions 1 and 2, find the area of the parallelograms.

1.

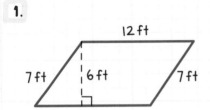

12 ft

7 ft 6 ft 7 ft

2.

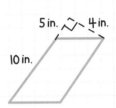

5 in. 4 in.

10 in.

3. Ray puts force on a rectangular frame to attempt to move it, but instead he distorts the shape into a parallelogram. What is the area of the parallelogram?

$7\sqrt{2}$ ft

12 ft

INITIAL FRAME

45°

DISTORTED FRAME

Hint: The side lengths do not change but the height does. Use special right triangle 45°-45°-90° to find the height of the parallelogram.

In questions 4 and 5, find h in the parallelogram.

4.

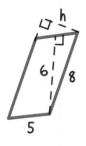

5.

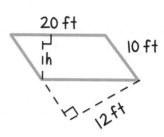

In questions 6-8, find the area of the triangles.

6.

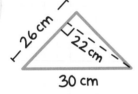

7.

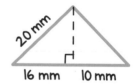

8.

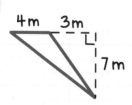

CHECK YOUR ANSWERS

1. (Use the formula A = bh = (12)(6).); 72 ft²

2. (Use the formula A = bh = (10)(4).); 40 in.²

3. (Use the formula A = bh = (12)(7).); 84 ft²

4. (Use the formula A = bh = 5(6) = 30. Then substitute 30 back into the equation to find the value of h. 30 = 8h.); $\frac{15}{4}$

5. (Use the formula A = bh = 12(10) = 120. Then substitute 120 into the equation to find the value of h. 120 = 20h.); 6 ft²

6. (Use the formula A = $\frac{1}{2}$ bh = $\frac{1}{2}$ (22)(26).); 286 cm²

7. (First find the height of the triangle 16² + h² = 20², so h = 12. Then use the formula A = $\frac{1}{2}$ bh = $\frac{1}{2}$ (16 + 10)(12).); 156 mm²

8. (Use the formula A = $\frac{1}{2}$ bh = $\frac{1}{2}$ (4)(7).); 14 m²

Chapter 46

AREAS OF OTHER POLYGONS

AREAS OF TRAPEZOIDS

In order to calculate the area of a trapezoid, use the formula:

$$A = \frac{1}{2}h(b_1 + b_2)$$

h = height (the distance between the two bases)

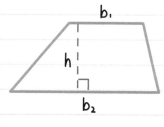

b_1 and b_2 are the lengths of the two bases (the parallel sides) in any order

EXAMPLE: Find the area of the trapezoid.

$A = \dfrac{1}{2}h(b_1 + b_2)$

$\quad = \dfrac{1}{2}(11)(21 + 14) = 192.5$

$A = 192.5$ in.^{2}

EXAMPLE: Find the area of the trapezoid.

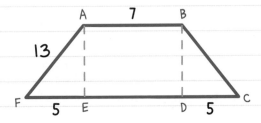

Step 1: Find the height, AE.

Use $\triangle$AEF and the Pythagorean Theorem to find height AE.

$a^2 + b^2 = c^2$

> Or use Pythagorean triples.

$FE^2 + AE^2 = AF^2$

$5^2 + h^2 = 13^2$

$h^2 = 144$

$h = 12$

Step 2: Find the length of the bases.

$\overline{AB}$ is one base, so $\overline{AB} = b_1 = 7$.

$\overline{FC}$ is the other base, but we need to find ED in order to know the length of $\overline{FC}$.

ABDE is a rectangle, therefore, AB = ED.

Opposite sides of a rectangle are equal in length.

$\overline{FC}$ = FE + ED + DC
$\overline{FC}$ = 5 + 7 + 5
   = 17
$b_2 = 17$

Step 3: Find the area.

$A = \frac{1}{2} h (b_1 + b_2)$

$= \frac{1}{2} (12)(7 + 17)$

$= \frac{1}{2} (12)(24)$

$= 144$

The area is 144.

501

AREAS OF RHOMBUSES AND KITES

To find the area of a rhombus or kite, use this formula:

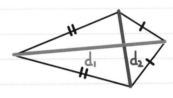

$$A = \frac{1}{2} d_1 d_2$$

d_1 and d_2 are the lengths of the two diagonals (in any order)

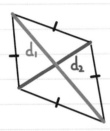

EXAMPLE: Find the area of the rhombus.

$A = \frac{1}{2} d_1 d_2$

$= \frac{1}{2}(6 + 6)(4 + 4)$

$= \frac{1}{2}(12)(8)$

$= 48$

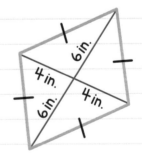

The area of the rhombus is 48 in.²

EXAMPLE: A large kite is being decorated with roses for a float in a parade. If 30 roses per square foot are used to decorate the float, how many roses are needed for the kite?

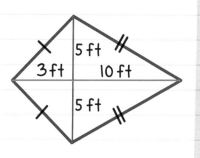

5 ft

3 ft | 10 ft

5 ft

First, find the area of the kite.

$$A = \frac{1}{2}d_1d_2$$

$$= \frac{1}{2}(13)(10)$$

$$= \frac{1}{2}(130)$$

$$= 65$$

Area of kite = 65 ft²

Now we can find the number of roses needed.

$$65 \text{ ft}^2 \left(\frac{30 \text{ roses}}{\text{ft}^2}\right) = 1950 \text{ roses}$$

1,950 roses are needed to decorate the kite.

AREAS OF REGULAR POLYGONS

Use this formula to find the area of a regular polygon:

$$A = \frac{1}{2} aP$$

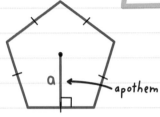

a = length of the **APOTHEM**, the perpendicular distance from the center to a side

A regular polygon has side lengths that are all congruent.

P = perimeter, the sum of the lengths of all the sides

EXAMPLE: Find the area of the regular heptagon.

A regular heptagon has 7 congruent sides.

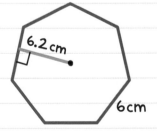

Since the heptagon has 7 sides that are all 6 cm, the perimeter is:

P = 7(6 cm) = 42 cm

or 6 + 6 + 6 + 6 + 6 + 6 + 6 = 42

Apothem = 6.2 cm

$A = \dfrac{1}{2}aP$

$= \dfrac{1}{2}(6.2)(42) = 130.2$

$A = 130.2 \text{ cm}^2$

If the apothem is not known, try using trigonometry to find it.

EXAMPLE: A board game is in the shape of a regular hexagon. What is the area of the board if the length of each side is 10 inches?

10 in.

A regular hexagon can be divided into 6 congruent triangles. The central angle of each is 60°.

$360° \div 6 = 60°$

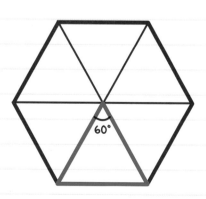

60°

The apothem divides this equilateral triangle into two 30°-60°-90° triangles.

Not every polygon will divide to this triangle. This is specifically for regular hexagons.

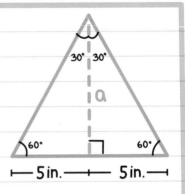

We use special right triangle 30°-60°-90° to find the apothem.

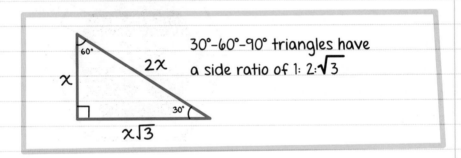

30°-60°-90° triangles have a side ratio of 1: 2:$\sqrt{3}$

longer leg = shorter leg × $\sqrt{3}$

$a = 5 \times \sqrt{3}$ in.

The apothem is: $a = 5\sqrt{3}$ in.

The perimeter of the hexagon is:

$P = 6(10 \text{ in.}) = 60 \text{ in.}$

Now we have all the information we need to find the area:

$A = \dfrac{1}{2}aP$

$\quad = \dfrac{1}{2}(5\sqrt{3} \text{ in.})(60 \text{ in.})$

$\quad = 150\sqrt{3} \text{ in.}^2 \approx 259.8 \text{ in.}^2$

CHECK YOUR KNOWLEDGE

1. Find the area of the trapezoid. (Hint: Use the Pythagorean Theorem to find the height.)

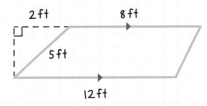

2 ft   8 ft

5 ft

12 ft

2. Jessica is painting the wall of her room, which is in the shape of the isosceles trapezoid shown below. She bought one gallon of paint, which covers 400 feet². Jessica plans to paint two coats on her wall. Does she have enough paint?

10 ft

15 ft   9 ft   15 ft

4 ft

3. Find the area of the rhombus.

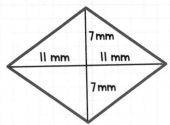

7 mm

11 mm   11 mm

7 mm

4. Find the area of the kite.

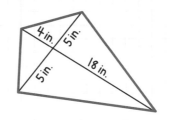

5. A baker is baking a giant cookie in the shape of a rhombus. What is the area of the cookie if the length of one side is 21 inches and the length of one diagonal is 34 inches? Round to the nearest square inch.

21 in.

34 in.

For questions 6 and 7, find the area of the regular polygons.

6.

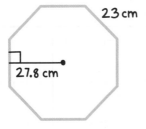

23 cm

27.8 cm

7.

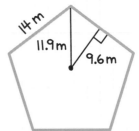

14 m

11.9 m

9.6 m

8. Mishal is paving her regular hexagon-shaped patio shown below. The stone she is using is $3.15 per square foot. How much will she spend on the stone to repave her patio? Round to the nearest cent.

12 FT

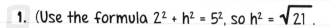

CHECK YOUR ANSWERS

1. (Use the formula $2^2 + h^2 = 5^2$, so $h^2 = \sqrt{21}$.

    Then use $A = \frac{1}{2}h(b_1 + b_2) = \frac{1}{2}\sqrt{21}\,(8 + 12)$.)

    $10\sqrt{21}$ ft² ≈ 45.8 ft²

2. Yes (The area of the wall is 126 ft².)

3. (Use the formula $A = \frac{1}{2}d_1d_2 = \frac{1}{2}(7 + 7)(11 + 11)$.); 154 mm²

4. (Use the formula $A = \frac{1}{2}d_1d_2 = \frac{1}{2}(5 + 5)(4 + 18)$.); 110 in.²

5. (Use the Pythagorean Theorem. $21^2 = x^2 + 17^2$; $x = \sqrt{152}$.

    Then $A = \frac{1}{2}d_1d_2 = \frac{1}{2}(34)(2\sqrt{152})$.); 419.2 in.²

6. (Use the formula $A = \frac{1}{2}aP = \frac{1}{2}(27.8)(8)(23)$.); 2,557.6 cm²

7. (Use the formula $A = \frac{1}{2}aP = \frac{1}{2}(9.6)(5)(14)$.); 336 m²

8. $A = \frac{1}{2}aP = \frac{1}{2}(6\sqrt{3})(72) ≈ 374.12$

    Total cost = total area × cost per square foot
    = 374.12 × \$3.15 = \$1,178.48

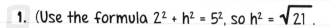

Chapter 47

AREAS OF CIRCLES AND SECTORS

AREA OF A CIRCLE

To find the formula for the area of a circle, divide the circle into triangles.

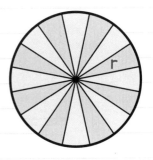

The triangles from the circle can be rearranged to form a rectangle.

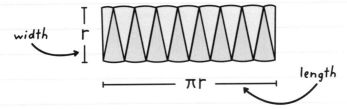

The width of the rectangle is the radius of the circle. The length of the rectangle is half of the circumference.

The area is:

A = length × width

   = πr × r

   = πr²

Formula for area of a circle.

Area = π • radius²   OR

A = πr² ← answer is in units squared

r

Memory Tip:
Think
Area = **π**r²

"Pies Are Squared"

EXAMPLE: Find the area of the circle.

A = πr²

A = π • 2² = 4π

2 cm

A = 4π cm² ≈ 12.6 cm²

EXAMPLE: Find the area of a circle with a circumference of 10π meters.

Use the circumference to find the radius:

$C = 2\pi r$
$10\pi = 2\pi r$
$r = 5$

Now find the area:

$A = \pi r^2$
$\quad = \pi \times 5^2 = 25\pi$
$A = 25\pi \text{ m}^2 \approx 78.5 \text{ m}^2$

EXAMPLE: Find the radius of a circle with an area of 144π inches².

$A = \pi r^2$
$144\pi = \pi r^2$
$144 = r^2$
$r = 12$

The radius is 12 in.

Area of a Sector

The area of a **sector** (slice) can be found using a PROPORTION that compares the sector to the whole circle.

Formula for area of a sector:

$$A = \frac{\theta}{360°} \times \pi r^2$$

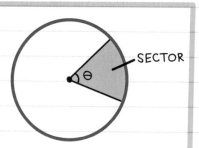

SECTOR

θ = measure of the sector's angle

To find the area of this sector:

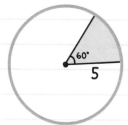

$$\frac{\text{Area of the sector}}{\pi(5)^2} = \frac{60°}{360°}$$

measure of sector's angle

Area of circle →

$$\frac{\text{Area of the sector}}{\pi r^2} = \frac{\theta}{360°}$$

measure of circle

$$\pi(5)^2 \times \frac{\text{Area of the sector}}{\pi(5)^2} = \frac{60°}{360°} \times \pi(5)^2 \quad \text{Multiply both sides by } \pi(5)^2.$$

$$\text{Area of the sector} = \frac{60°}{360°} \times \pi(5)^2 \qquad \text{Simplify.}$$

$$= \frac{25\pi}{6} \approx 13.1$$

EXAMPLE: Find the area of the shaded sector.

$$A = \frac{\theta}{360°} \times \pi r^2$$

$$= \frac{175°}{360°} \times \pi(12)^2 = 70\pi$$

$$A = 70\pi \ ft^2 \approx 219.8 \ ft^2$$

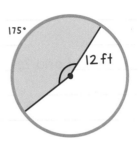

175°

12 ft

THE MEASURE OF A CENTRAL ANGLE EQUALS THE MEASURE OF ITS INTERCEPTED ARC.

EXAMPLE: A dartboard with radius 8.8 inches has one sector with an angle of 18°. Find the area of the sector.

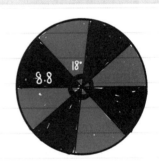

18°

8.8

$$A = \frac{\theta}{360°} \times \pi r^2$$

$$A = \frac{18°}{360°} \times \pi(8.8)^2$$

$$A \approx 12.2 \ in.^2$$

For questions 1 and 2, find the area of the circle.

1.

15 m

2.

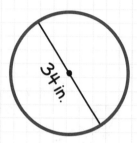

34 in.

3. Find the radius of a circle with area 121π ft².

4. Find the diameter of a circle with area 81π cm².

5. Find the area of a circle with circumference 28π mm².
   Round to the nearest tenth.

For questions 6 and 7, find the area of the shaded portion
of the circle. Round to the nearest tenth.

6.

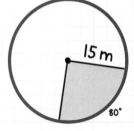

15 m

80°

7.

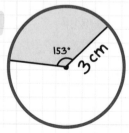

153°

3 cm

For questions 8 and 9, find the area of the shaded portion of the circle. Round to the nearest tenth.

8.

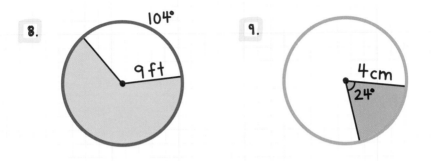

9.

10. A pizza has a diameter of 16 inches. James eats one 45°-angle slice. What is the area of the remaining pizza? Round to the nearest tenth.

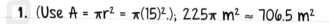

CHECK YOUR ANSWERS

1. (Use $A = \pi r^2 = \pi(15)^2$.); 225π m$^2 \approx 706.5$ m^2

2. (Use $A = \pi r^2 = \pi(17)^2$.); 289π in.$^2 \approx 907.9$ in.^{2}

3. 11 ft

4. 18 cm

5. (First use the radius: $C = 2\pi r$, $28\pi = 2\pi r$, $r = 14$.
Then use $A = \pi r^2 = \pi(14)^2$.); 615.4 mm^2

6. (Use $A = \dfrac{\theta}{360°} \times \pi r^2 = \dfrac{80}{360} \times \pi(15)^2$.); 157.1 m^2

7. (Use $A = \dfrac{\theta}{360°} \times \pi r^2 = \dfrac{153}{360} \times \pi(3)^2$.); 12.0 cm^2

8. (Use $A = \dfrac{\theta}{360°} \times \pi r^2 = \dfrac{360-104}{360} \times \pi(9)^2$.); 181.0 ft^2

9. (Use $A = \dfrac{\theta}{360°} \times \pi r^2 = \dfrac{24}{360} \times \pi(4)^2$.); 3.4 cm^2

10. (Use $A = \dfrac{\theta}{360°} \times \pi r^2 = \dfrac{360-45}{360} \times \pi(8)^2$.); 175.9 in.^{2}

Chapter 48

AREAS OF COMPOSITE FIGURES

A **COMPOSITE FIGURE** is a shape made up of two or more basic geometric shapes.

Examples:

To find the area of a composite figure:

Step 1: Break the composite figure into its basic shapes.

Step 2: Find the area of each shape.

Step 3: Add all the areas together (and subtract any missing parts if necessary) to find the area of the entire composite figure.

Formulas needed to calculate the areas of composite figures:

SHAPE	FORMULA	FIGURE
Rectangle	$A = \ell w$ ℓ = length, w = width	
Parallelogram	$A = bh$ b = base, h = height	
Triangle	$A = \dfrac{bh}{2}$ b = base, h = height	
Trapezoid	$A = \dfrac{1}{2} h (b_1 + b_2)$ h = height, b_1 and b_2 are the bases	

SHAPE	FORMULA	FIGURE
Rhombus	$A = \frac{1}{2} d_1 d_2$ d_1 and d_2 are the diagonals	
Kite	$A = \frac{1}{2} d_1 d_2$ d_1 and d_2 are the diagonals	
Regular Polygon	$A = \frac{1}{2} aP$ a = apothem P = perimeter	
Circle	$A = \pi r^2$ r = radius	
Sector	$A = \frac{\theta}{360°} \cdot \pi r^2$ θ is the angle of the sector r = radius	

EXAMPLE: Find the area of the composite figure.

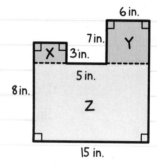

Step 1: Break the composite figure into three rectangles.

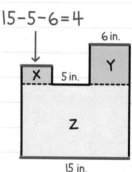

Since the area of a rectangle is length × width, we need to find the missing length of the green rectangle . . .

$$15 - 5 - 6 = 4$$

. . . and width of the blue rectangle.

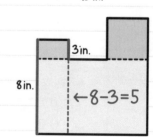

$$\leftarrow 8 - 3 = 5$$

Step 2: Calculate the area of each figure.

Total area = lw + lw + lw

= (4)(3) + (6)(7) + (15)(5)

= 12 + 42 + 75 = 129

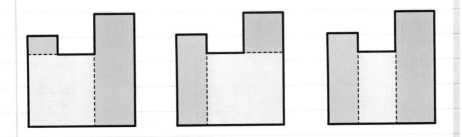

4 in.
3 in.

6 in.
7 in.

5 in.

15 in.

The area of the figure is 129 in.²

Note: The figure could have been divided other ways.

Choose the way that requires the fewest
or easiest calculations.

EXAMPLE: Find the area of the composite figure.

1. Break the figure into a rectangle and a triangle.

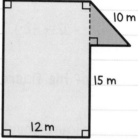

10 m

23 m

15 m

12 m

2. Find the base and height of the triangle:

h = 23 – 15 = 8

The triangle is a right triangle, so we use the Pythagorean Theorem to find the base:

$8^2 + b^2 = 10^2$

$b^2 = 36$

$b = 6$

23 m

12 m

8 m   10 m

6 m

3. Calculate the area of each shape and add the areas together.

Total Area = area of rectangle + area of triangle

$$= lw + \frac{bh}{2}$$

$$= (12)(23) + \frac{(6)(8)}{2}$$

$$= 276 + 24 = 300$$

The area of the figure is 300 m².

We can also find areas of composite figures by subtracting the areas of the shapes.

EXAMPLE: Find the area of the circle.

The diameter of the circle is the width of the rectangle, 10 feet.

Therefore, the radius is 5 feet.

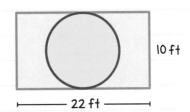

10 ft

22 ft

The area of the circle is:

$A = \pi r^2$

$A = \pi(5)^2$

$A = 25\pi \ ft^2 \approx 78.5 \ ft^2$

EXAMPLE: Find the area of the shaded figure.

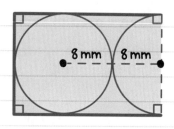

1. Remove the circle and the semicircle from the rectangle.

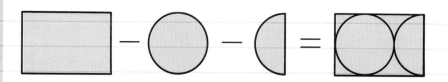

2. Find the length and width of the rectangle using the radii of the circle and semicircle.

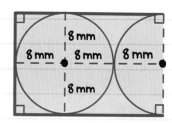

The length of = diameter of + radius of
the rectangle   the circle   the circle

l = 8 + 8 + 8 = 24

The width of the rectangle = the diameter of the circle

w = 8 + 8 = 16

3. Subtract the area of the circle and $\frac{1}{2}$ the area of the circle from the area of the rectangle.

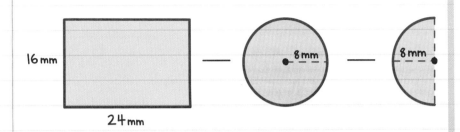

16 mm

24 mm

8 mm

8 mm

Total Area =

= Area of rectangle – Area of circle – Area of semicircle

$$= \quad lw \quad - \quad \pi r^2 \quad - \quad \frac{1}{2}\pi r^2$$

$$= \quad (24)(16) \quad - \quad \pi(8)^2 \quad - \quad \frac{1}{2}\pi(8)^2$$

= 384 – 64π – 32π = 384 – 96π ≈ 82.4

half of the area of a circle

The area of the figure is 82.4 mm².

CHECK YOUR KNOWLEDGE

For questions 1–8, find the area of the shaded figures. Assume all angles that appear to be right are right. Round to the nearest tenth when necessary.

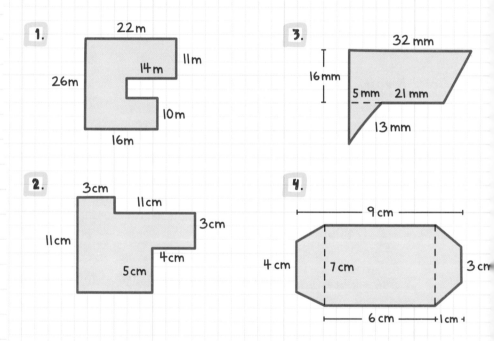

1.
22 m
14 m
11 m
26 m
10 m
16 m

2.
3 cm
11 cm
3 cm
11 cm
4 cm
5 cm

3.
32 mm
16 mm
5 mm   21 mm
13 mm

4.
9 cm
4 cm   7 cm   3 cm
6 cm   1 cm

5.

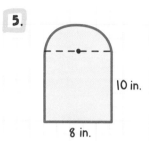

10 in.

8 in.

7.

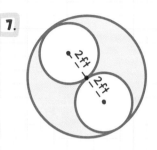

2 ft

2 ft

6.

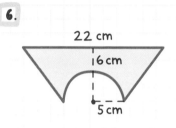

22 cm

6 cm

5 cm

8.

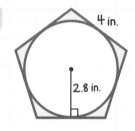

4 in.

2.8 in.

CHECK YOUR ANSWERS

1. 442 m²

3. 494 mm²

2. 101 cm²

4. 58 cm²

5. 105.1 in.²

6. Total Area = Area of trapezoid − Area of semicircle

$$= \frac{1}{2}h(b_1 + b_2) - \frac{1}{2}\pi r^2$$

$$= \frac{1}{2}(11)(22 + 10) - \frac{1}{2}\pi(5)^2 = 136.7 \text{ cm}^2$$

7. Total Area = Area of large circle − 2 × Area of the small circle

$$= \pi r^2 - 2\pi r^2$$
$$= \pi(4)^2 - 2\pi(2)^2 = 25.1 \text{ ft}^2$$

8. Total Area = Area of the pentagon − Area of the circle

$$= \frac{1}{2}aP - \pi r^2$$

$$= \frac{1}{2}(2.8)(20) - \pi(2.8)^2 = 3.4 \text{ in.}^2$$

Unit 10

Surface Area and Volume

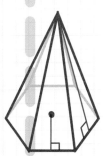

Chapter 49

SURFACE AREAS OF PRISMS AND CYLINDERS

THREE-DIMENSIONAL (3-D) figures are shapes that have length, width, and height. They are also called SPACE FIGURES or SOLIDS.

SURFACE AREA is the area of a shape's surfaces.

A **POLYHEDRON** is a 3-D figure made up of polygons. The polygons' flat surfaces are called FACES. The line segments where the faces meet are called EDGES. The VERTICES (plural of VERTEX) are the points where three or more edges meet (the corners).

> *Poly* is Greek for "many."
> *Hedron* is Greek for "base."

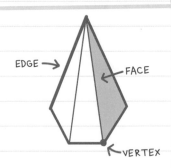

EDGE →

← FACE

← VERTEX

PRISMS

PRISMS are a type of polyhedron made up of two polygon faces that are parallel and congruent, called the BASES. The remaining faces are called the LATERAL FACES, which are parallelograms.

Prisms are categorized by the type of bases they have.

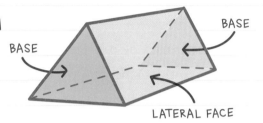

BASE

BASE

LATERAL FACE

A RECTANGULAR PRISM has all right angles, the bases are parallel rectangles, and the lateral faces are parallelograms.

A TRIANGULAR PRISM has bases that are parallel triangles and lateral faces that are parallelograms.

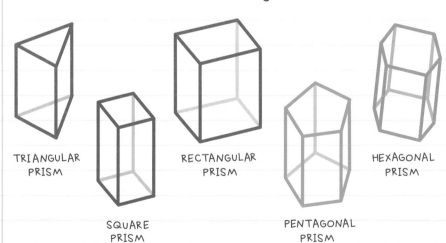

TRIANGULAR
PRISM

SQUARE
PRISM

RECTANGULAR
PRISM

PENTAGONAL
PRISM

HEXAGONAL
PRISM

The **SURFACE AREA (SA)** of a polyhedron is the sum of the area of its faces. We can calculate the surface area of a polyhedron by adding together the area of the bases and the lateral faces.

The **LATERAL AREA (LA)** is the total area of the lateral faces.

The surface area of a prism can be calculated by unfolding the prism and looking at the **NET**, the two-dimensional representation of the prism's faces.

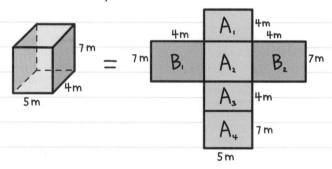

We can find the total surface area by adding the area of each face.

Surface Area = $B_1 + B_2 + A_1 + A_2 + A_3 + A_4$ lateral faces

bases

$$= (4 \times 7) + (4 \times 7) + (5 \times 4) + (5 \times 7) + (5 \times 4) + (5 \times 7)$$
$$= 28 + 28 + 20 + 35 + 20 + 35$$
$$= 166$$

Surface Area = 166 m²

Another way to solve:

Add the area of the two bases (pink rectangles) and the area of the lateral faces—the lateral area (the green rectangle).

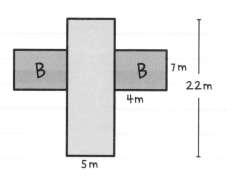

Area of Base = lw

= 4 × 7 = 28

Lateral Area = lw

= (5)(4 + 7 + 4 + 7)

= 5 × 22

= 110

> The length of the lateral area is equal in measure to the perimeter of the base (P).

Surface Area = 2 × Area of the base + Lateral Area

= 2(28) + 110

= 56 + 110

= 166

Surface Area = 166 m²

Lateral Area of a Prism	Surface Area of a Prism
LA = Ph	**SA = 2B + Ph**

B = area of base
P = perimeter of base
h = height of prism

Find the surface area
of the rectangular prism.

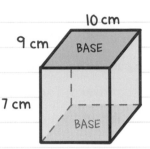

9 cm

10 cm

BASE

7 cm

BASE

You can look at the net to see the
surface area more clearly.

$\ell = 10$ cm

BASE

$w = 9$ cm

$w = 9$ cm | $\ell = 10$ cm | $w = 9$ cm | $\ell = 10$ cm

$h = 7$ cm

BASE

To use SA = 2B + Ph, first find the value for B, the area of
the rectangular base:

B = lw (length × width)

= 10 × 9 = 90

Then find the value of P, the perimeter of the base:

P = 9 + 10 + 9 + 10 = 38

Now we have all the information to find the surface area:

One Way

$SA = 2B + Ph$

$= 2(90) + (38)(7)$

$= 180 + 266 = 446$

$SA = 446 \text{ cm}^2$

The answer is given in units squared.

Another Way

Since we know $B = lw$ we can use $SA = 2lw + Ph$:

$SA = 2(lw) + Ph$

$= 2(10)(9) + [9 + 10 + 9 + 10](7)$

$= 180 + 266 = 446$

$SA = 446 \text{ cm}^2$

EXAMPLE: Find the surface area of the triangular prism.

The prism's bases are triangles, so in order to find the area of the base ($B = \frac{1}{2}$ bh), we first need to find the length of the triangle's base (b = l + l).

Using the Pythagorean Theorem (or Pythagorean triples),

$3^2 + \ell^2 = 5^2$

$9 + \ell^2 = 25$

$\ell^2 = 16$

$\ell = 4$

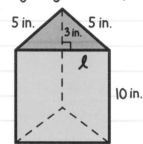

5 in.   5 in.

3 in.

ℓ

10 in.

The length of the base of the triangle is b = l + l = 4 + 4 = 8.

Now we have all the information we need to find the surface area.

SA = 2B + Ph

    $= 2 \times \frac{1}{2}$ bh + Ph

    $= 2 \times \frac{1}{2}$ (8)(3) + (5 + 5 + 8)(10)

    = 24 + 180 = 204

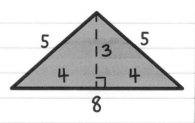

5   3   5

4   4

8

SA = 204 in.²

CYLINDERS

To find the surface area of a cylinder, open the cylinder and flatten it out. Look at the net.

When you unfold a cylinder, the lateral area is shaped like a rectangle. The bases are shaped like circles.

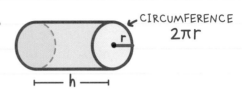

Add the area of the two circle bases and the rectangle (lateral area) to get the total surface area.

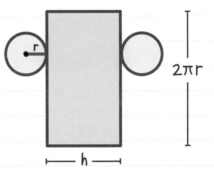

The length of the rectangle is the same as the circumference of the circle—it wraps completely around the circle.

Surface Area = Area of two circles + Area of the rectangle

= 2 × Area of base + Lateral Area

= 2 × πr^2 + 2πr × h

= 2πr^2 + 2πrh

LATERAL AREA OF A CYLINDER	SURFACE AREA OF A CYLINDER
$LA = 2\pi rh$	$SA = 2\pi r^2 + 2\pi rh$

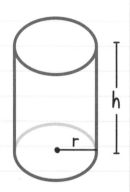

r = radius of the base
h = height of the cylinder

EXAMPLE: Find the surface area of the cylinder.

The diameter of the base is
15 feet, which means the radius
is 7.5 feet.

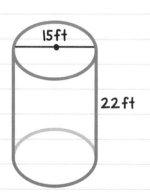

15ft

22 ft

$SA = 2\pi r^2 + 2\pi rh$

$= 2\pi(7.5)^2 + 2\pi(7.5)(22)$

$= 112.5\pi + 330\pi = 442.5\pi \approx 1{,}390$

The surface area is about 1,390 ft².

EXAMPLE: A company is making labels for cans of pineapple chunks. The radius of each can is 2 inches and the height is 6 inches. What is the surface area of each label?

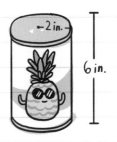

We don't need to find the total surface area of the can, because the label only covers the lateral area.

The net of the can is:

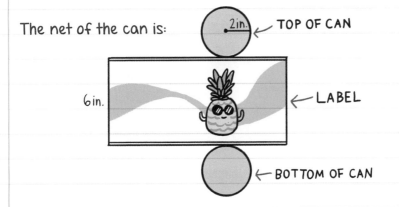

The surface area of each label is just the lateral area of the can.

LA = 2πrh

   = 2π(2)(6)

   = 24π ≈ 75.4

The surface area of each label is approximately 75.4 in.².

For questions 1-4, find the surface area of each prism. Round the answer to the nearest tenth, if necessary.

1.

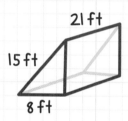

10 m

5 m   8 m

2.

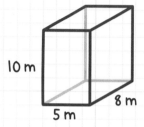

21 ft

15 ft

8 ft

3.

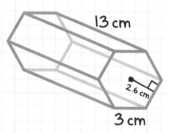

13 cm

2.6 cm

3 cm

4.

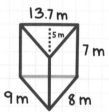

13.7 m

5 m

7 m

9 m   8 m

5. David is wrapping a present in a rectangular prism-shaped box that is 13 inches high. The top and bottom of the box measure 9 inches long by 11 inches wide. What is the minimum amount of wrapping paper David will need to wrap the present?

13 in.

9 in.

11 in.

For questions 6-8, find the surface area of each cylinder.
Round the answer to the nearest tenth.

6.

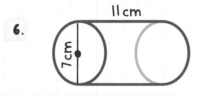

7.

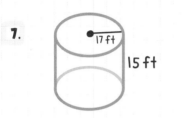

8.

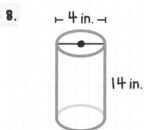

9. Trevor and Manuel each have cylindrical cans of soup.
   Trevor's can has a diameter of 3.2 inches and a height
   of 3.8 inches. Manuel's can has a diameter of 2.9 inches
   and a height of 4.3 inches. Whose can has the larger
   surface area?

1. $2(5)(10) + 2(5)(8) + 2(10)(8)$; 340 m²

2. $2(\frac{1}{2})(8)(12.7) + 8(21) + 15(21) + 12.7(21)$ (Use the Pythagorean Theorem to find the height of the triangle); 851 ft²

3. $2(\frac{1}{2})(2.6)(6)(3) + 6(13)(3)$; 280.8 cm²

4. $7(8) + 9(7) + 13.7(7) + 2(\frac{1}{2})(13.7)(5)$; 283.4 m²

5. $2(11)(9) + 2(9)(13) + 2(13)(11)$; 718 in.²

6. $2\pi(3.5^2) + 11(2\pi(3.5))$; 318.7 cm²

7. $2\pi(17^2) + 15(2\pi(17))$; 3,416.3 ft²

8. $2\pi(2^2) + 14(2\pi(2))$; 201.1 in.²

9. Trevor's can has the larger surface area. (Trevor's can: SA ≈ 54.3 in.², Manuel's can: SA ≈ 52.4 in.².)

Chapter 50

SURFACE AREAS OF PYRAMIDS AND CONES

PYRAMIDS

A **PYRAMID** is a polyhedron in which the base is a polygon and the lateral faces are triangles. The faces meet at one point called the VERTEX or APEX.

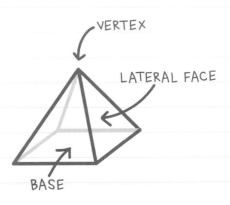

VERTEX

LATERAL FACE

BASE

A **REGULAR PYRAMID** has congruent lateral faces and a regular polygon for its base.

> All the sides in **a regular polygon** are congruent.

The SLANT HEIGHT (l) of a regular pyramid is the height of a triangular lateral face.

The HEIGHT OF THE PYRAMID (h) is the length of the perpendicular line drawn from the vertex to the base.

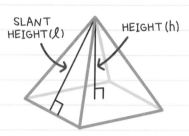

Pyramids are named by the shape of their base.

TRIANGULAR
PYRAMID

SQUARE
PYRAMID

PENTAGONAL
PYRAMID

HEXAGONAL
PYRAMID

Surface Area of Pyramids

To calculate the surface area of a pyramid, add the area of all the faces. To calculate the surface area of a regular pyramid, use the following formulas:

LATERAL AREA OF A REGULAR PYRAMID	SURFACE AREA OF A REGULAR PYRAMID
$LA = \frac{1}{2}P\ell$	$SA = B + \frac{1}{2}P\ell$

P = perimeter of base
ℓ = slant height
B = area of base

For example, when using the formula $SA = B + \frac{1}{2}P\ell$

$SA = 81 + \frac{1}{2}(9 + 9 + 9 + 9)(10)$

$= 81 + \frac{1}{2}(36)(10)$

$= 81 + \frac{1}{2}(360)$

$= 81 + 180$

$= 261$ in.²

$\ell = 10$ in.

B

9 in.

$B = 81$ in.²

Find the surface area of the triangular pyramid using the lateral area.

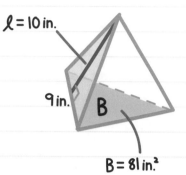

$\ell = 10$ in.

9 in.

B

$B = 81$ in.^{2}

$LA = \dfrac{1}{2} P\ell$

$\quad = \dfrac{1}{2}(9 + 9 + 9)(10)$

$\quad = 135$

$LA = 135$ in.^{2}

$SA = B + \dfrac{1}{2} P\ell$

$\quad = 81 + \dfrac{1}{2}(9 + 9 + 9)(10)$

$\quad = 81 + 135 = 216$

$SA = 216$ in.^{2}

EXAMPLE: Find the surface area of the regular pentagonal pyramid.

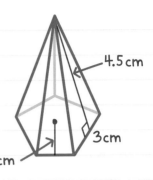

If we use SA = B + $\frac{1}{2}$ Pℓ, first we must find P, the perimeter of the base, and then B, the area of the base.

The perimeter of the pentagonal base with 5 equal sides of length 3 cm is:

P = 5 × 3 = 15

Since the base is a regular pentagon, its area is:

B = $\frac{1}{2}$ aP

The area of the base is:

A = $\frac{1}{2}$ × apothem × perimeter or

A = $\frac{1}{2}$ aP

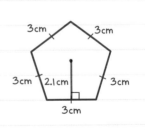

One Way

$$B = \frac{1}{2}(2.1)(15) = 15.75$$

$$SA = B + \frac{1}{2}P\ell$$

$$= 15.75 + \frac{1}{2}(15)(4.5)$$

$$= 49.5$$

$$SA = 49.5 \text{ cm}^2$$

Another Way

Since we know $B = \frac{1}{2}aP$, we can use the formula:

$$SA = \frac{1}{2}aP + \frac{1}{2}P\ell$$

$$= \frac{1}{2}(2.1)(5 \times 3) + \frac{1}{2}(5 \times 3)(4.5)$$

$$= 49.5$$

$$SA = 49.5 \text{ cm}^2$$

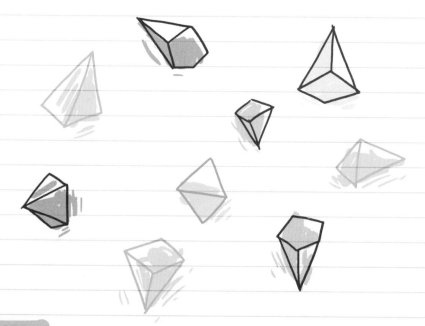

CONES

A **CONE** is a solid with a circular base and one vertex.

A cone is not a polyhedron; a polyhedron has no curved surfaces.

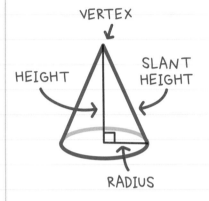

VERTEX

HEIGHT

SLANT HEIGHT

RADIUS

Use the following formulas to calculate the surface area of a cone:

LATERAL AREA OF A CONE
$LA = \pi r l$

SURFACE AREA OF A CONE
$SA = \pi r^2 + \pi r l$

l = slant height
r = radius of base

POLYHEDRONS

SORRY, YOU'RE NOT ON THE LIST.

EXAMPLE: Find the surface area of the cone.

First find the radius of the cone using the Pythagorean Theorem.

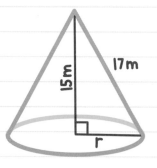

$r^2 + 15^2 = 17^2$

$r^2 = 64$

$r = 8$

Then, find the surface area.

$SA = \pi r^2 + \pi r\ell$

$\quad = \pi(8)^2 + \pi(8)(17)$

$\quad = 200\pi \approx 628.3$

The surface area of the cone is 200π m² or about 628.3 m².

EXAMPLE: Indira is making decorative paper snow cone cups for a party. The radius of the cone's opening (the base) is 1.3 inches and the height is 4 inches. What is the lateral area of the cups?

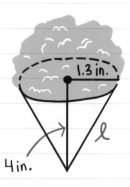

Step 1: Find the slant height using the Pythagorean Theorem:

$1.3^2 + 4^2 = \ell^2$

$17.7 = \ell^2$

$\ell = 4.2$ in.

Step 2: Find the surface area.

We need to find only the lateral area since there is no actual base on the cup.

$LA = \pi r \ell$

$\quad = \pi(1.3)(4.2)$

$\quad = 17.2$ in.^{2}

CHECK YOUR KNOWLEDGE

1. Find the lateral area of the regular pyramid.

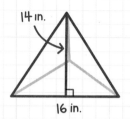

14 in.

16 in.

For questions 2-5, find the surface area of each regular pyramid. Round the answer to the nearest tenth, if necessary.

2.

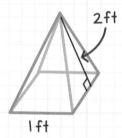

2 ft

1 ft

4.

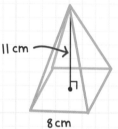

11 cm

8 cm

3.

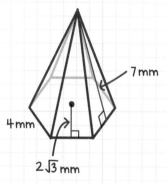

7 mm

4 mm

$2\sqrt{3}$ mm

5.

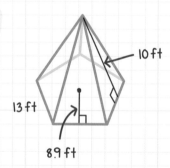

10 ft

13 ft

8.9 ft

6. Find the lateral area of the cone. Round the answer to the nearest tenth.

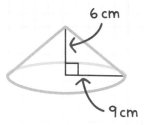

6 cm

9 cm

For questions 7 and 8, find the surface area of each cone. Leave your answer in terms of π.

7.

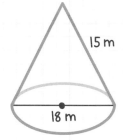

15 m

18 m

8.

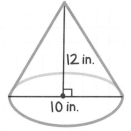

12 in.

10 in.

9. Javier is painting his square pyramid-shaped fort that has a height of 10 feet and a base with side lengths of 9 feet. He has a half gallon of paint, which will cover 200 square feet. Does he have enough paint to cover the fort?

10. Dani is making artificial cone-shaped decorative pine trees covered in netting. The netting costs $0.65 per square foot. How much will Dani spend on netting for four trees that are 4 feet high with a base radius of 1.8 feet? Round to the nearest cent.

ANSWERS

CHECK YOUR ANSWERS

1. $\frac{1}{2}(3)(16)(14)$; 336 in.²

2. $1 + \frac{1}{2}(4)(2)$; 5 ft²

3. $(2\sqrt{3})(24) + \frac{1}{2}(24)(7)$; 165.6 mm²

4. $64 + \frac{1}{2}(32)(11.7)$ (slant height can be found by using the Pythagorean Theorem: $11^2 + 4^2 = \ell^2$, $\ell = 11.7$); 251.3 cm²

5. $\frac{1}{2}(8.9)(65) + \frac{1}{2}(65)(10)$; 614.3 ft²

6. $\pi(9)(10.8)$ (Use the Pythagorean Theorem to find ℓ. $6^2 + 9^2 = \ell^2$); 305.2 cm²

7. $\pi(9^2) + \pi(9)(15)$; 216π m²

8. $\pi(5^2) + \pi(5)(13)$ (Use the Pythagorean Theorem to find ℓ. $12^2 + 5^2 = \ell^2$); 90π in.²

9. $\frac{1}{2}(36)(11.0)$ (Use the Pythagorean Theorem to find ℓ.

   $10^2 + 4.5^2 = \ell^2$); yes, the lateral area of the fort is 198 ft².

10. $\pi(1.8^2) + \pi(1.8)(4.4) = $ SA; multiply by 4; multiply by 0.65 to get the cost. (Use the Pythagorean Theorem to find ℓ); $91.96

Chapter 51

VOLUMES OF PRISMS AND CYLINDERS

The **VOLUME** (V) of a 3-D figure refers to the amount of space that the solid encloses. Volume is expressed in CUBIC UNITS—the number of cubes that have an edge length of 1 unit that fit inside the solid.

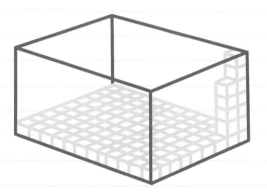

| CUBIC UNIT

PRISMS

To **find the volume** of most prisms, use the formula:

> Volume = Area of the base × Height of the Prism
>
> or V = Bh

Use a capital B to show that it's the area of the base.

The answer is given in units³.

The exponent "3" means "cubic"—how many cubes fit inside.

Rectangular Prisms

To find the VOLUME OF A RECTANGULAR PRISM, use the formula:

V = Bh   **B** = area of the base

h = height

or

V = lwh   **l** = length

w = width

h = height

EXAMPLE: The base of a rectangular prism has 16 cubic units. There are 6 layers of 16 units. Find the volume.

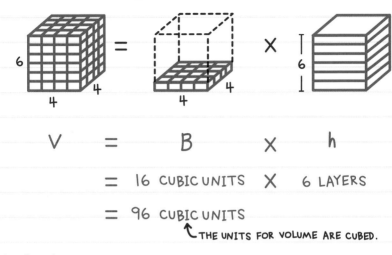

$$V \quad = \quad B \quad \times \quad h$$

$$= \quad 16 \text{ CUBIC UNITS} \quad \times \quad 6 \text{ LAYERS}$$

$$= \quad 96 \text{ CUBIC UNITS}$$

↳THE UNITS FOR VOLUME ARE CUBED.

$V = B \times h$

$\quad = 16 \times 6$

$\quad = 96$ cubic units

We can also use V = length × width × height or V = lwh to find the volume of the rectangular prism.

$V = l \times w \times h$

$\quad = 4 \times 4 \times 6$

$\quad = 96$ cubic units

EXAMPLE: Find the volume of the prism.

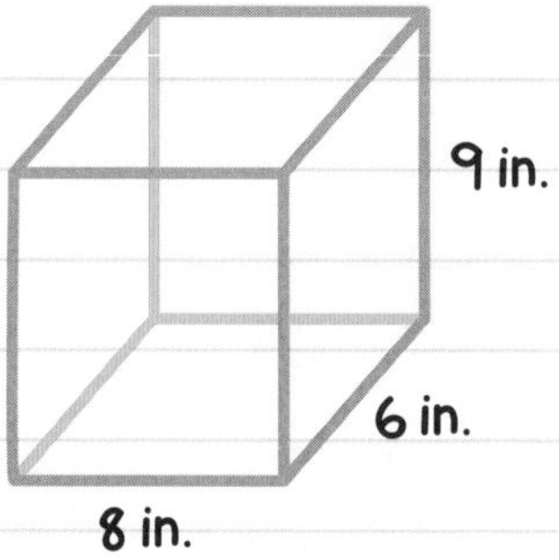

9 in.

6 in.

8 in.

One Way

B = lw

= (8)(6)

= 48

V = Bh

= (48)(9)

= 432

The volume is 432 in.³.

Another Way

V = lwh

= (8)(6)(9)

= 432

The volume is 432 in.³.

Triangular Prisms

To find the VOLUME OF A TRIANGULAR PRISM, use

$$V = Bh \quad \text{or}$$
$$V = \frac{1}{2} \times \text{base} \times \text{height} \times \text{length} \ (V = \frac{1}{2}bhl)$$

height of triangle   length of prism

EXAMPLE: Find the volume of the triangular pyramid.

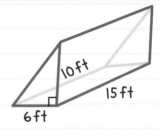

10 ft

15 ft

6 ft

One Way

$B = \frac{1}{2}bh$

$= \frac{1}{2}(6)(10)$

$= 30$

$V = Bh$

$= (30)(15)$

$= 450$

The volume is 450 ft³.

Another Way

$V = \frac{1}{2}bhl$

$= \frac{1}{2}(6)(10)(15)$

$= 450$

The volume is 450 ft³.

EXAMPLE: Find the volume of
the triangular prism.

Multiply the area of the base
$(B = \frac{1}{2} \times 7 \times 4)$ by the height of
the prism $(h = 8)$.

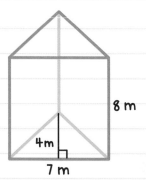

8 m

4 m

7 m

$V = Bh$

$= (\frac{1}{2} \times 7 \times 4)(8)$

$= 112$

> This example uses h
> for the height of the
> triangle and l for the
> height of the prism.

The volume is 112 m³.

Volume of a Cylinder

The formula for the volume of a cylinder is the area of the
base times the height:

$$V = Bh$$

Since the base is a circle, use the formula for the area of
a circle $(A = \pi r^2)$ to find the area of the base.

$$V = \pi \times radius^2 \times height \ (\pi r^2 h)$$

area of base

$V = Bh$ B = area of the base

    $= \pi r^2 h$ r = radius of the base

                h = height

EXAMPLE: Find the volume of the cylinder.

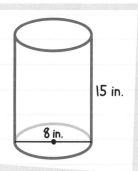

$V = \pi r^2 h$

    $= \pi(4)^2(15)$

    $= 240\pi$ in.³ $\approx$ 754.0 in.³

15 in.

8 in.

Oblique Prisms and Cylinders

An OBLIQUE PRISM or CYLINDER does not have right angles between the sides and the base.

The volume of an oblique prism is taken from the volume of a regular (right angle) prism.

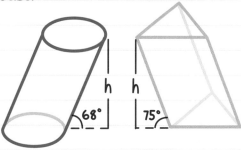

h   h

68°   75°

OBLIQUE

means slanted, not parallel or perpendicular

A stack of papers is like a rectangular prism with volume
$V = Bh$.

Imagine the same stack slanted a bit.

The height of the papers didn't change. Neither did the
volume of the papers. Only the orientation changed.

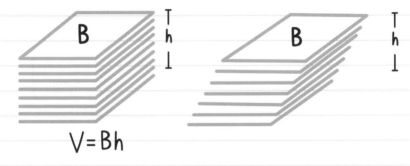

$V = Bh$

So, the volume of an oblique prism is the same as
a right prism with the same base and height, $V = Bh$.

CAVALIERI'S PRINCIPLE
Bonaventura Francesco Cavalieri
(1598–1647; an Italian mathematician)

If two solids have the same height and the same
cross-sectional area at every level (like the area of one
sheet of paper), then they have equal volume.

Cavalieri's Principle can also be used to show that the volume of an oblique cylinder is the same as the volume of a right cylinder, $V = \pi r^2 h$.

EXAMPLE: Find the volume of the cylinder.

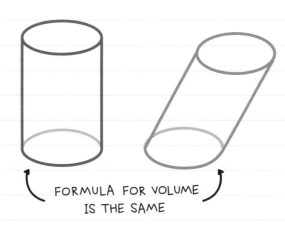

7cm

4cm

$V = \pi r^2 h$

$\quad = \pi(4)^2(7) = 112\pi$

$V = 112\pi$ in.³

FORMULA FOR VOLUME
IS THE SAME

CHECK YOUR KNOWLEDGE

For questions 1–8, find the volume of the prism or cylinder.

1.

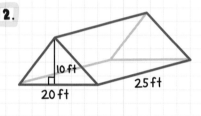

9 ft
5 ft
14 ft

5.

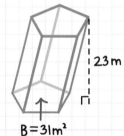

7 mm
3 mm

2.

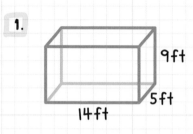

10 ft
20 ft
25 ft

6.

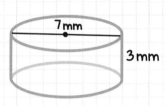

23 m
B = 31 m²

3.

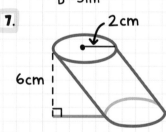

4 m
1 m
4 m

7.

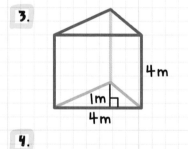

2 cm
6 cm

4.

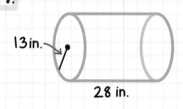

13 in.
28 in.

8.

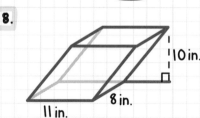

10 in.
8 in.
11 in.

9. The Leaning Tower of Pisa is 56 meters high, with a radius of 7.7 meters. What is the volume of the tower? Round to the nearest cubic meter.

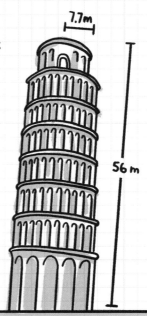

7.7m

56 m

10. A fruit juice company's cans have the dimensions shown. What is the volume of one can? Round to the nearest tenth.

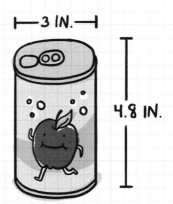

⊢— 3 IN. —⊣

4.8 IN.

CHECK YOUR ANSWERS

1. 14(5)(9); 630 ft³

2. $\frac{1}{2}$ (20)(10)(25); 2,500 ft³

3. $\frac{1}{2}$ (4)(1)(4); 8 m³

4. π(13²)(28); 4732π in.³ ≈ 14,858.1 in.³

5. π(3.5²)(3); 36.75π mm³ ≈ 115.4 mm³

6. 31(23); 713 m³

7. π(2²)(6); 24π cm³ ≈ 75.4 cm³

8. 11(8)(10); 880 in.³

9. π(7.7²)(56); 10,426 m³

10. π(1.5²)(4.8); 33.9 in.³

Chapter 52

VOLUMES OF PYRAMIDS AND CONES

VOLUME OF A PYRAMID

To calculate the volume of a pyramid, multiply one-third by the area of the base of the pyramid times the height.

The formula for the volume of a pyramid is:

$$V = \frac{1}{3} \times \text{area of base} \times \text{height}$$

or

$$V = \frac{1}{3}Bh$$

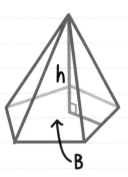

EXAMPLE: Find the volume of the pyramid.

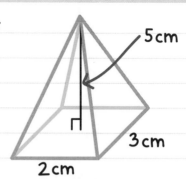

5cm

3cm

2cm

One Way

First, find the value for B, the area of the base.

B = lw (length × width)

$= 2 \times 3$

$= 6 \text{ cm}^2$

$V = \frac{1}{3}Bh$

$= \frac{1}{3}(6)(5) = 10$

$V = 10 \text{ cm}^3$

Another Way

B = lw, we can use $V = \frac{1}{3}lwh$

$V = \frac{1}{3}lwh$

$= \frac{1}{3}(2)(3)(5)$

$V = 10 \text{ cm}^3$

Find the height of
the regular pentagonal prism with
volume 453.6 in.^{3}.

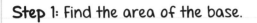

Step 1: Find the area of the base.

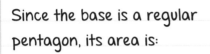

Since the base is a regular
pentagon, its area is:

$B = \dfrac{1}{2}aP$

$\quad = \dfrac{1}{2}(4.8)(35)$

$\quad = 84$

Step 2: Find the height.

$V = \dfrac{1}{3}Bh$

$453.6 = \dfrac{1}{3}(84)h$

$h = 16.2$

The height is 16.2 in.

VOLUME OF A CONE

To calculate the volume of a cone, use the formula:

Volume = $\frac{1}{3}$ area of the base × height:

$$V = \frac{1}{3} \text{ base} \times \text{height}$$

or

$$V = \frac{1}{3} Bh$$

Since the base of a cone is a circle with area πr^2, this formula becomes:

Volume = $\frac{1}{3} \times \pi \times \text{radius}^2 \times \text{height}$:

$$V = \frac{1}{3} \pi r^2 h$$

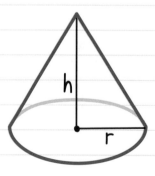

EXAMPLE: Find the volume of the cone.

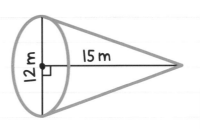

Since the radius is half the length of the diameter, r = 6.

$V = \dfrac{1}{3}\pi r^2 h$

$\quad = \dfrac{1}{3}\pi(6)^2(15)$

$\quad = 180\pi \approx 565.5$

The volume of the cone is 180π m³ or about 565.5 m³.

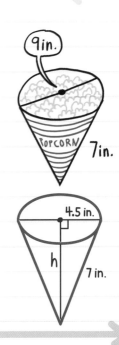

EXAMPLE: June has a cone-shaped container that is filled to the top with popcorn. Find the volume of the cone.

Before we can use $V = \dfrac{1}{3}\pi r^2 h$, we need to find the height of the container, h, using the Pythagorean Theorem.

$h^2 + 4.5^2 = 7^2$

$h^2 = 28.75$

$h \approx 5.36$ in.

Now we have all the information we need
to find the volume.

$$V = \frac{1}{3}\pi r^2 h$$

$$= \frac{1}{3}\pi(4.5)^2(5.36)$$

$$\approx 113.7$$

The volume of the cone is about 113.7 in.³.

Volume of a Frustum

The **FRUSTUM** is the part of a pyramid or cone that is left
when its top is cut off by a plane parallel to its base.

Find the volume of a frustum by subtracting the volume
of the missing portion of the solid from the volume of
the entire solid.

FRUSTUM

EXAMPLE: Find the volume of the frustum.

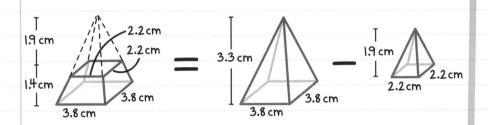

Volume of = Volume of − Volume of
frustum = entire prism − missing portion

$$= \frac{1}{3}Bh - \frac{1}{3}Bh$$

formula for
volume of a pyramid

$$= \frac{1}{3}lwh - \frac{1}{3}lwh$$

$$= \frac{1}{3}(3.8 \times 3.8)(3.3) - \frac{1}{3}(2.2 \times 2.2)(1.9)$$

$$= 15.884 - 3.065$$

$$= 12.82$$

The volume of the frustum is 12.82 cm³.

For questions 1 and 2, find the volume of each regular pyramid. Round to the nearest tenth if necessary.

1.

10 cm

12 cm

2.

7 mm

a = 3.6 mm

3 mm

For questions 3 and 4, find the volume of the pyramids. Round to the nearest tenth if necessary.

3.

26 in.

17 in.

23 in.

4.

16 ft

9 ft

14 ft

For questions 5–7, find the volume of the cone. Round to the nearest tenth if necessary.

5.

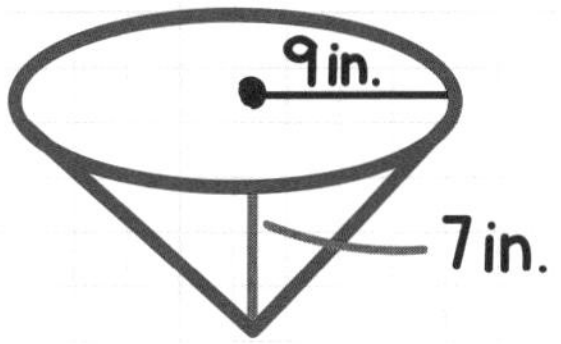

9 in.
7 in.

7.

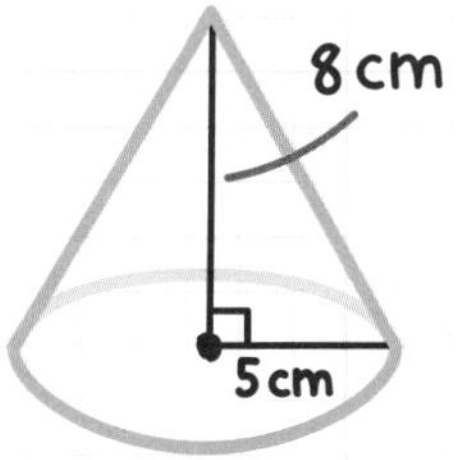

8 cm
5 cm

6.

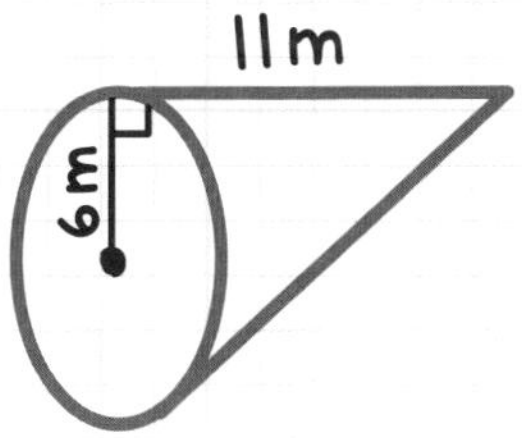

11 m
6 m

8. Find the volume of the frustum.

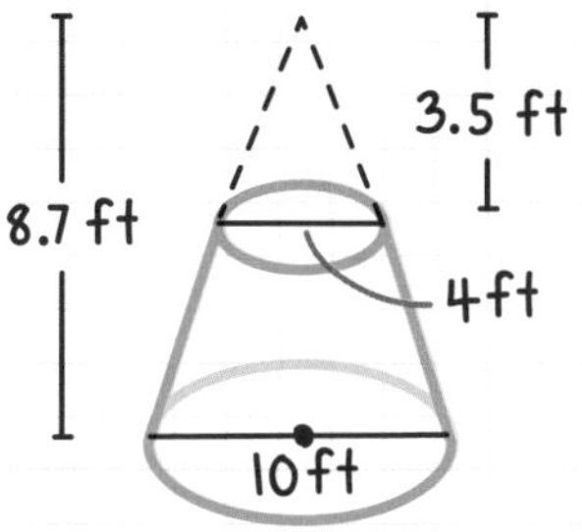

8.7 ft
3.5 ft
4 ft
10 ft

9. Find the height of a pyramid with volume 72 in.³ and base area 36 in.².

10. Find the radius of a cone with volume 147 m³ and height 9 m. Round to the nearest tenth.

1. $\frac{1}{3}$ (12)(12)(8); 384 cm³

2. $\frac{1}{3}$ ($\frac{1}{2}$)(3.6)(24)(7); 100.8 mm³

3. $\frac{1}{3}$ (23)(17)(26); 3,388.7 in.³

4. $\frac{1}{3}$ ($\frac{1}{2}$)(14)(9)(16); 336 ft³

5. $\frac{1}{3}$ π(9²)(7); 593.5 in.³

6. $\frac{1}{3}$ π(6²)(11); 414.5 m³

7. $\frac{1}{3}$ π(5²)(8); 209.3 cm³

8. $\frac{1}{3}$ π(5²)(8.7) − $\frac{1}{3}$ π(2²)(3.5); 213.1 ft³

9. $72 = \frac{1}{3}$ (36)h; 6 in.

10. $147 = \frac{1}{3}$ πr²(9); 3.9 m

Chapter 53

SURFACE AREA AND VOLUME OF SPHERES

A **SPHERE** is a set of points in a space that are equidistant from a center point, like a ball.

an equal distance

A radius of a sphere is a line segment from the center to a point on the sphere.

Every line from the center of a sphere to the edge is a radius.

A diameter of a sphere is a line segment that passes through the center with both ends on the sphere.

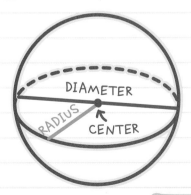

DIAMETER

RADIUS

CENTER

A **HEMISPHERE** is half a sphere.

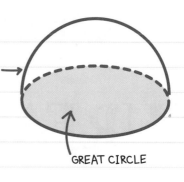

hemisphere →

The circle that divides a sphere into two hemispheres is called the **GREAT CIRCLE**.

GREAT CIRCLE

SURFACE AREA OF A SPHERE

To calculate the surface area of a sphere, use the formula:

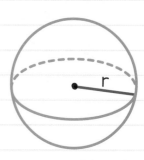

$SA = 4\pi r^2$ r = radius of the sphere

EXAMPLE: Find the surface area of the sphere.

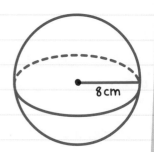

8 cm

$SA = 4\pi r^2$

$= 4\pi(8)^2$

$= 256\pi \approx 804.2$

$SA = 256\pi$ cm² or about 804.2 cm²

EXAMPLE: Find the surface area of a sphere that has a great circle with circumference 65π in.

Before we can use $SA = 4\pi r^2$, we must find the radius. We will find it using the great circle, since it has the same radius as the sphere.

Since the circumference of the great circle is 65π in.,

$C = 2\pi r$

$65\pi = 2\pi r$

radius of great circle = radius of sphere

$r = 32.5$ in.

$SA = 4\pi r^2$

$\quad = 4\pi(32.5)^2$

$\quad = 4225\pi$

The surface area is 4225π in.^{2}.

The SURFACE AREA OF A HEMISPHERE is half the surface area of a sphere plus the area of the great circle.

SA OF HEMISPHERE $=$ ½ SA OF SPHERE $\left(\frac{1}{2} \cdot 4\pi r^2\right)$ $+$ AREA OF GREAT CIRCLE (πr^2)

$$SA = \frac{1}{2} (4\pi r^2) + \pi r^2$$

EXAMPLE: Hiro baked cookies in the shape of hemispheres. Each cookie has a radius of 3 cm. Hiro is going to completely coat each with chocolate. He has enough chocolate to cover a surface area of 2,000 cm². How many cookies can Hiro coat?

$$\text{NUMBER OF COOKIES} = \frac{2,000 \text{ CM}^2}{\substack{\text{SURFACE AREA} \\ \text{OF ONE COOKIE}}}$$

The surface area of each cookie is:

$$SA = \frac{1}{2}(4\pi r^2) + \pi r^2$$

$$= \frac{1}{2}[4\pi(3)^2] + \pi(3)^2$$

$$= 27\pi \text{ cm}^2$$

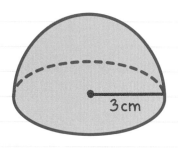

3 cm

The number of cookies Hiro can coat is:

$$\frac{\text{Total SA}}{\text{SA per cookie}} = \frac{2,000}{27\pi} \approx 23.6$$

Hiro can coat 23 cookies with chocolate.

VOLUME OF A SPHERE

To calculate the volume of a sphere,
use the formula:

$$V = \frac{4}{3}\pi r^3$$ r = radius of the sphere

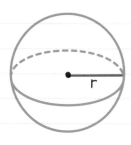

r

TO SOLVE, ALL YOU
NEED TO KNOW IS THE
RADIUS OF THE SPHERE.

EXAMPLE: Find the volume of the sphere.

The radius is half the diameter, so r = 6 ft.

$$V = \frac{4}{3}\pi r^3$$

$$= \frac{4}{3}\pi(6 \text{ ft})^3$$

$$= 288\pi \text{ ft}^3$$

EXAMPLE: Find the volume of a ball that has a surface area of 100π inches^2.

First find the radius of the ball using the surface area:

$$SA = 4\pi r$$

$$100\pi = 4\pi r^2$$

$$r^2 = \frac{100\pi}{4\pi}$$

$$r^2 = 25$$

$$r = 5 \qquad \text{The radius is 5 inches.}$$

Then find the volume:

$$V = \frac{4}{3}\pi r^3$$

$$= \frac{4}{3}\pi (5)^3$$

$$= \frac{500}{3}\pi \approx 523.6$$

The volume of the ball is approximately 523.6 in.³.

The **volume of a hemisphere** is one-half the volume of a sphere. The formula is:

$$V = \frac{1}{2} \times \frac{4}{3}\pi r^3$$

**HALF THE SHAPE;
HALF THE FORMULA!**

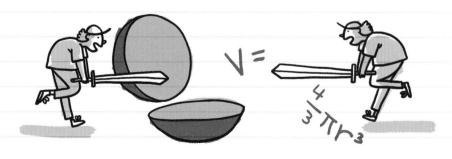

CHECK YOUR KNOWLEDGE

For questions 1–3, find the surface area of each sphere or hemisphere. Leave answers in terms of pi.

1.

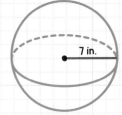

7 in.

2.

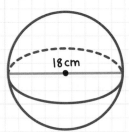

18 cm

3.

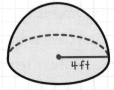

4 ft

4. Find the surface area of a sphere if the circumference of the great circle is 20 meters. Round to the nearest tenth.

5. Find the surface area of a hemisphere if the area of the great circle is π ft². Leave your answer in terms of pi.

6. Find the volume of a sphere if the surface area is 31π m. Round to the nearest tenth.

For questions 7-9, find the volume of each sphere or hemisphere. Leave answers in terms of pi.

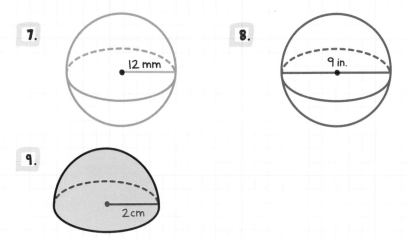

7.

12 mm

8.

9 in.

9.

2 cm

10. Find the volume of a hemisphere if the circumference of the great circle is 45 feet. Round to the nearest tenth.

11. Steel weighs .2904 pounds per inches³. How much does a steel ball with a diameter of 6 inches weigh? Round to the nearest tenth.

12. Nicole is exercising with a piece of equipment that is hollow and in the shape of a hemisphere. The base of the ball has an area of 169π in.². What is the volume of the air inside the ball to the nearest tenth?

ANSWERS ➤

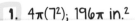

1. $4\pi(7^2)$; 196π in.^{2}

2. $4\pi(9^2)$; 324π cm^2

3. $\frac{1}{2}(4)\pi(4^2) + \pi(4^2)$; 48π ft^2

4. $4\pi(3.2^2)$; 127.3 m^2

5. $\frac{1}{2}(4)\pi(1^2) + \pi(1^2)$; 3π ft^2

6. $\frac{4}{3}\pi(2.8^3)$; 91.9 m^3

7. $\frac{4}{3}\pi(12^3)$; $2{,}304\pi$ mm^3

8. $(\frac{4}{3}\pi(4.5^3))$; $\frac{243}{2}\pi = 121.5\pi$ in.^{3}

9. $\frac{1}{2}(\frac{4}{3}\pi(2^3))$; $\frac{16}{3}\pi$ cm^3

10. $\frac{1}{2}(\frac{4}{3}\pi(7.2^3))$; 781.3 ft^3

11. $0.2904(\frac{4}{3}\pi(3^3))$; 32.8 lbs

12. Area of the base $= \pi r^2$; $169\pi = \pi r^2$; $r^2 = 169$; $r = 13$
$V = \frac{1}{2} \times \frac{4}{3}\pi r^3 = \frac{1}{2} \times \frac{4}{3}\pi(13^3) = 4{,}599.1$ in.^{3}

Chapter 54

VOLUMES OF COMPOSITE FIGURES

A **3-D COMPOSITE FIGURE** is a shape made up of two or more basic geometric solids.

We can split a composite figure into its basic geometric solids to make calculations.

> **P** = perimeter of the base
> **B** = area of the base
> **r** = radius of the base
> **h** = height
> **ℓ** = slant height

Formulas used to calculate volume in composite 3-D figures:

SOLID	LATERAL AREA	SURFACE AREA	VOLUME
Cone	$\pi r \ell$	$B + \pi r \ell$ or $\pi r^2 + \pi r \ell$	$\frac{1}{3} Bh$ or $\frac{1}{3} \pi r^2 h$

SOLID	LATERAL AREA	SURFACE AREA	VOLUME
Cylinder	$2\pi rh$	$2B + 2\pi rh$ or $2\pi r^2 + 2\pi rh$	Bh or $\pi r^2 h$
Hemisphere		$\frac{1}{2}(4\pi r^2) + \pi r^2$	$\frac{1}{2}\left(\frac{4}{3}\pi r^3\right)$
Prism	Ph	$2B + Ph$	Bh
Pyramid	$\frac{1}{2}Pl$	$B + \frac{1}{2}Pl$	$\frac{1}{3}Bh$
Sphere		$4\pi r^2$	$\frac{4}{3}\pi r^3$

SURFACE AREA OF COMPOSITE FIGURES

The surface area of a composite figure is the area that covers the entire outside of the solid. To find the surface area, add up the areas of the faces, including any curved surfaces (only the parts on the outside).

EXAMPLE: Find the surface area of the composite figure.

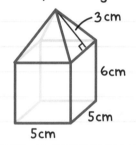

The parts on the surface are the lateral area of the pyramid, the lateral area of the prism, and the bottom of the composite figure, which is the base of the prism.

Do not include the top base of the prism (which is also the base of the pyramid) because it is not on the surface.

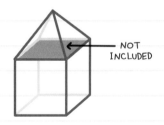

NOT INCLUDED

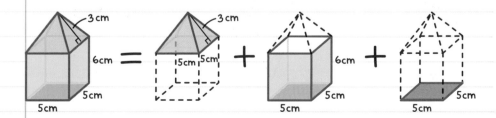

$$\text{Total surface area} = \text{Lateral area of the pyramid} + \text{Lateral area of the prism} + \text{Area of one of the prism's bases}$$

$$= \frac{1}{2}P\ell + Ph + lw$$

$$= \frac{1}{2}(5 + 5 + 5 + 5)(3) + (5 + 5 + 5 + 5)(6) + 5 \times 5$$

$$= 30 + 120 + 25$$

$$= 175$$

The surface area of the composite figure is 175 cm².

EXAMPLE: Find the surface area of the ice cream cone and the ice cream.

Separate the solid into the cone and the hemisphere.

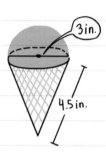

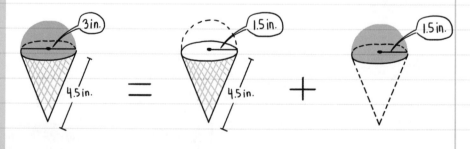

$$\begin{aligned}\text{Total} \atop \text{surface area} &= \text{Lateral area} \atop \text{of the cone} + \frac{1}{2}\text{Surface area of a sphere}\end{aligned}$$

$$= \pi r \ell + \frac{1}{2}(4\pi r^2)$$

$$= \pi(1.5)(4.5) + \frac{1}{2}\left[4\pi(1.5)^2\right]$$

$$\approx 35.3$$

The surface area of the cone and ice cream is approximately 35.3 in.^{2}.

Note: For the hemisphere, use half the surface area of a sphere because the surface area of a hemisphere adds the area of the great circle, which is not on the surface, and so not part of the surface area.

not included

VOLUME OF COMPOSITE FIGURES

To find the volume of a composite figure, separate the shape into its basic solids. Then we find the volume of each solid, using the volume formulas. Finally, add all the volumes together.

EXAMPLE: Find the volume of the composite figure.

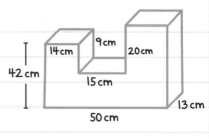

Separate the solid into three prisms.

Since the volume of each prism is V = lwh, find the missing length, width, and height of each solid.

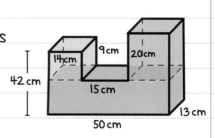

Use the horizontal lengths to find the length of the red prism:

l = 50 – 14 – 15 = 21

Use the total height to find the height of the green prism:

h = 42 – 9 = 33

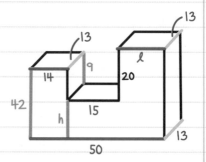

The width is the same throughout the solid, so the width of every prism is:

w = 13

Now, we have all the information we need to find the volume.

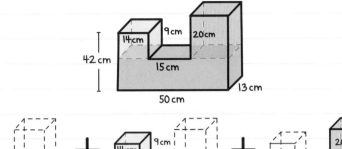

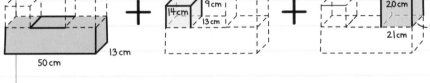

Total Volume = Volume of green prism + Volume of blue prism + Volume of red prism

= lwh + lwh + lwh

= (50)(13)(33) + (14)(13)(9) + (21)(13)(20)

= 28,548

The volume is 28,548 cm³.

EXAMPLE: Find the volume of the solid.

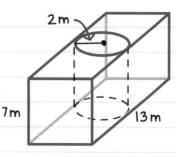

If we subtract the volume of the cylinder from the volume of the rectangular prism, we end up with the volume of the remaining solid.

The length of the prism is the diameter of the cylinder,

l = 2 m + 2 m = 4 m

Total volume = Volume of the prism - Volume of the cylinder

= lwh - πr²h

= (4)(13)(7) - π(2)²(7)

= 364 - 28π

≈ 276.0

The volume is approximately 276.0 m³.

CHECK YOUR KNOWLEDGE

For questions 1 and 2, find the surface area of each composite figure. Round to the nearest tenth if necessary.

1.

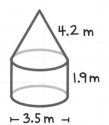

4.2 m

1.9 m

⊢ 3.5 m ⊣

2.

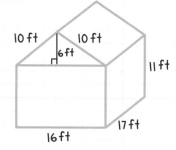

10 ft   10 ft

6 ft

11 ft

17 ft

16 ft

For questions 3–6, find the volume of the composite figures. Round to the nearest tenth if necessary.

3.

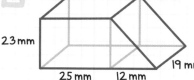

23 mm

25 mm   12 mm   19 mm

5.

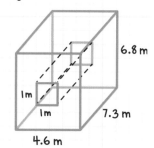

6.8 m

1 m

1 m   7.3 m

4.6 m

4.

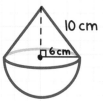

10 cm

6 cm

6.

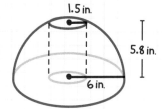

1.5 in.

5.8 in.

6 in.

ANSWERS

CHECK YOUR ANSWERS

1. $2\pi(1.75)(1.9) + \pi(1.75^2) + \pi(1.75)(4.2)$; 53.6 m²

2. $2(\frac{1}{2})(16)(6) + 2(10)(17) + 2(17)(11) + 2(16)(11) + 16(17)$; 1,434 ft²

3. $23(25)(19) + \frac{1}{2}(12)(23)(19)$; 13,547 mm³

4. $\frac{1}{2}(\frac{4}{3})\pi(6^3) + \frac{1}{3}\pi(6^2)(8)$; 754.0 cm³

5. $4.6(7.3)(6.8) - 1(1)(7.3)$; 221.0 m³

6. $\frac{1}{2}(\frac{4}{3})\pi(6^3) - \pi(1.5^2)(5.8)$; 411.2 in.³

Chapter 55

SOLIDS OF REVOLUTION

A **SOLID OF REVOLUTION** is the solid formed when a two-dimensional object is rotated about a line, called the AXIS.

Examples of a solid of revolution:

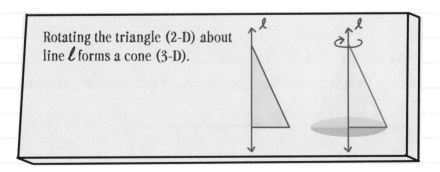

Rotating the triangle (2-D) about line l forms a cone (3-D).

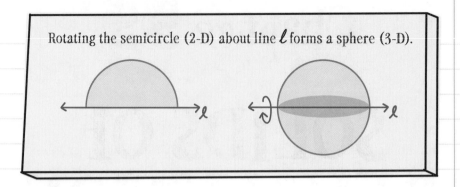

Rotating the semicircle (2-D) about line ℓ forms a sphere (3-D).

EXAMPLE: Find the volume of the solid formed when the triangle is rotated about line ℓ.

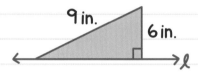

9 in.

6 in.

The solid formed is a cone. The hypotenuse of the triangle becomes the slant height of the cone, so ℓ = 9 in. The 6-in. leg of the triangle becomes the radius of the base of the cone, so r = 6 in.

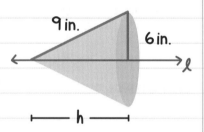

9 in.

6 in.

├── h ──┤

To use the formula for the volume of a cone, $V = \frac{1}{3}\pi r^2 h$, first find the height of the cone, using the Pythagorean Theorem.

$h^2 + r^2 = \ell^2$

$h^2 + 6^2 = 9^2$

$h^2 + 36 = 81$

$h^2 = 45$

$h = \sqrt{45} = \sqrt{9} \cdot \sqrt{5} = 3\sqrt{5}$

Then insert the solution into the formula:

$$V = \frac{1}{3}\pi r^2 h$$

$$= \frac{1}{3}\pi(6)^2(3\sqrt{5})$$

$$= 36\sqrt{5}\,\pi$$

The volume of the cone is $36\sqrt{5}\,\pi$ in.^{3}.

EXAMPLE: Find the volume of the solid formed when the rectangle is rotated about line ℓ.

The solid formed is a cylinder.
The 10-cm side of the rectangle becomes the height of the cylinder.
The 4-cm side of the rectangle becomes the radius of the base of the cylinder.

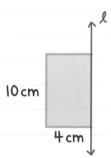

The volume is:

$$V = \pi r^2 h$$

$$= \pi(4)^2(10)$$

$$= 160\pi$$

The volume of the cylinder is 160π cm^3.

EXAMPLE: Find the surface area of the solid formed when the semicircle is rotated about line ℓ.

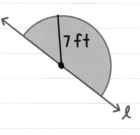

The solid formed is a sphere with a radius of 7 feet.

The surface area is:

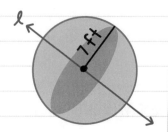

$$SA = 4\pi r^2$$
$$= 4\pi(7)^2$$
$$= 196\pi$$

The surface area is 196π ft².

SOLIDS OF REVOLUTION ON A COORDINATE PLANE

A two-dimensional figure rotated around the x- or y-axis (or another line in the plane) also forms a three-dimensional object.

> Rotating a figure around the y-axis rotates the figure horizontally (left and right). Rotating a figure around the x-axis rotates the figure vertically (up and down).

EXAMPLE: Find the surface area of the triangle rotated about the y-axis.

The solid formed is a cone with a height of 3 units and base radius of 4 units.

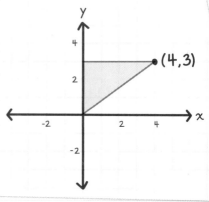

In order to use the surface area formula for a cone, SA = $\pi r^2 + \pi r \ell$, we must find ℓ, the slant height.

Since the hypotenuse of the triangle becomes the slant height, we can use Pythagorean triples 3, 4, 5 (or the Pythagorean Theorem) to find slant height, $\ell = 5$.

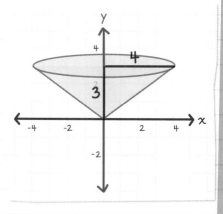

The surface area:

SA = $\pi r^2 + \pi r \ell$

   = $\pi(4)^2 + \pi(4)(5)$

   = 36π

The surface area of the cone is 36π units^2.

EXAMPLE: Find the volume of the solid formed by rotating the shaded figure around the x-axis.

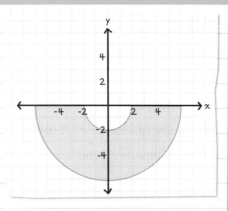

The solid formed by each semicircle is a sphere. The portion between the spheres (the shaded part) is the volume we need to find.

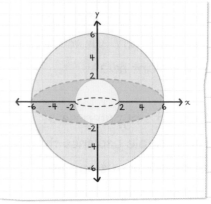

Volume of shaded portion = Volume of larger sphere – Volume of the smaller sphere.

$$= \frac{4}{3}\pi r^3 - \frac{4}{3}\pi r^3$$

$$= \frac{4}{3}\pi(6)^3 - \frac{4}{3}\pi(2)^3$$

$$= 277.3\pi$$

The volume of the shaded portion is 277.3π units³.

CHECK YOUR KNOWLEDGE

For questions 1–3, name the solid formed when the shaded figure is rotated about line ℓ.

1.

2.

3.

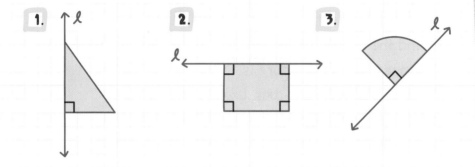

For questions 4 and 5, find the volume of the solid formed when the shaded figure is rotated about line ℓ. Round answer to the nearest tenth.

4.

5.

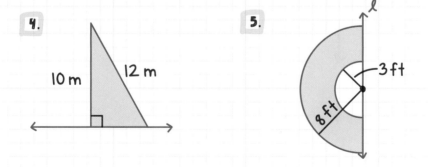

6. Find the surface area of the solid formed when the rectangle is rotated about line ℓ. Leave answer in terms of pi.

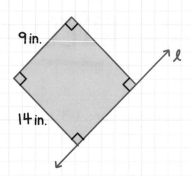

9 in.

14 in.

7. Find the volume of the solid formed when the figure is rotated about the x-axis. Leave answer in terms of pi.

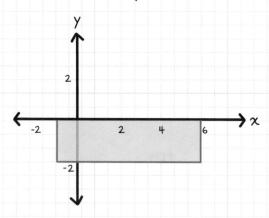

For questions 8 and 9, find the volume of the solid formed when the shaded figure is rotated about the y-axis. Leave answers in terms of pi.

8.

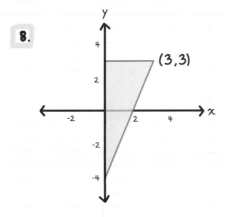

(3,3)

9.

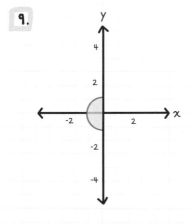

1. Cone

2. Cylinder

3. Hemisphere

4. $\frac{1}{3}\pi(10^2)\sqrt{44}$; 694.6 m³

5. $\frac{4}{3}\pi(8^3) - \frac{4}{3}\pi(3^3)$; 2,031.6 ft³

6. $2\pi(14^2) + 2\pi(14)(9)$; 644π in.²

7. $\pi(2^2)(7)$; 28π units³

8. $\frac{1}{3}\pi(3^2)(7)$; 21π units³

9. $\frac{4}{3}\pi(1^3)$; $\frac{4}{3}\pi$ units³

✦INDEX✦

609